Level H Science

NEW! Measuring Up Express™

for the

New York State Test

Quick and easy test preparation that mirrors the New York State Test

Peoples Education®
Your partner in student success®

(800) 822-1080 ● PeoplesEducation.com

Executive Vice President, Chief Creative Officer: Diane Miller

Editorial Development: Publisher's Partnership

Managing Editor: Kerri Gero

Copy Editor: Katy Leclercq

Vice President of Marketing: Victoria Ameer Kiely

Senior Marketing Manager: Christine Grasso

Production Director: Jason Grasso

Production Manager: Jennifer Bridges Brewer

Assistant Production Managers: Steven Genzano, Jennifer Tully

Director of Permissions: Kristine Liebman

Cover Design: Joe Guerrero, Chris Kennedy, Todd Kochakji

New York Advisory Panel:

Karlene Adam-Comrier, Assistant Principal Jean Nuzzi IS109, Queens, New York

Michael Chan, Director of Science, Rochester City School District

Dawn Ferro, Science Coordinator, Deer Park, New York

Robert Hansen, Teacher, Kingston City School District

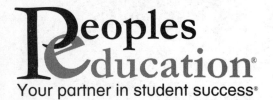

Peoples Education®
Your partner in student success®

Copyright © 2010
Peoples Education, Inc.
299 Market Street
Saddle Brook, New Jersey 07663

ISBN 978-1-4138-7369-6

Printed in the United States of America.

10   9   8   7   6   5   4   3   2   1

Contents

*Measuring Up® **Personal Prescriptive Path® (P3)®**
Go to the separate Measuring Up® worktext for instructional lessons on the skills
with which you need help! Ask your teacher for lesson assignments.

Formative Assessments (Teacher Edition)
Your teacher may choose to assign Formative Assessments
periodically to check your understanding of what you just learned.

*Your Personal Prescriptive Path® – P3®–
for instructional help.

Go to Measuring Up®
worktext lesson . . .

Chapter 1: Scientific Inquiry

NYS Learning Standard	Major Understandings	Lesson	Page		
1	S2.1a, S2.2a, S2.3a	1	1	**Lab Safety**	3
1	M1.1a, S1.1a, S1.1b, S1.1c, S1.2a	2	4	**Scientific Processes**	1
1, 7	S2.1b, S2.1c, S2.1d, S2.2b, S2.2c, S2.2d, S2.2e, S2.3b, S2.3c, IPS 1.3, IPS 1.4, IPS 2.1	3	7	**Designing and Performing Experiments**	2
1, 6, 7	M3.1a, S3.1a, S3.1b, S3.2h, ICT 5.2, IPS 2.1	4	10	**Displaying Data**	4
1, 7	M1.1b, M1.1c, M2.1a, M2.1b, S1.3, S3.2a, S3.2b, S3.2c, S3.2h, IPS 1.3, IPS 2.1	5	14	**Analyzing and Interpreting Data**	4
1	S1.4, S3.2d, S3.2e, S3.2f, S3.2g, S3.3	6	17	**Evaluating Scientific Conclusions**	1
1, 6	S1.2b, IS 1.5, ICT 2.1, ICT 2.2, ICT 2.3	7	20	**Making Scientific Models**	5
1, 6	M1.1a, M1.1b, M2.1a, S1.2a, S2.1c, S2.2b, S2.2c, S2.2d, S3.2h, ICT 5.2		23	**Practice for H.O.T.S.**	

Chapter 1: Scientific Inquiry (continued)

Formative Assessment 1

Chapter 2: Organisms in the Environment

Formative Assessment 2

Chapter 3: Human Body Systems

Formative Assessment 3

Chapter 4: Earth in Space

Chapter 4: Earth in Space (continued)

Formative Assessment 4

Chapter 5: Matter and Energy

Chapter 5: Matter and Energy (continued)

NYS Learning Standard	Major Understandings	Lesson	Page	For instructional help, go to Measuring Up® worktext lesson...	
4	PS 3.3d, PS 4.3a, PS 4.5a, PS 4.5b	50	164	**Energy and Chemical Reactions**	**46, 52**
4	PS 4.4a, PS 4.4b, PS 4.4c	51	167	**Electromagnetic and Sound Waves**	**50, 51**
4	PS 4.4d, PS 4.4e, PS 4.4f, PS 4.4g	52	171	**Electrical Energy and Magnetism**	**51**
4	PS 3.1a, PS 3.1c, PS 3.1e, PS 3.1f, PS 3.1g, PS 3.1h, PS 4.1d, PS 4.1e, PS 4.2c, PS 4.4b, PS 4.5a		174	**Practice for H.O.T.S.**	
1, 4	M1.1a, S1.2a, S1.3, S2.1a, S2.1b, S2.1d, S2.2d, S2.3b, S2.3c, PS 3.2c, PS 3.2e		175	**Higher-Order Performance Task: Conservation of Mass in Chemical Reaction**	

Formative Assessment 5

Chapter 6: Forces and Motion

NYS Learning Standard	Major Understandings	Lesson	Page	For instructional help, go to Measuring Up® worktext lesson...	
4	PS 5.1a, PS 5.1b	53	177	**The Motion of Objects**	**53**
4	PS 5.1c, PS 5.1d, PS 5.1e, PS 5.2d	54	180	**Forces and Motion**	**53**
4	PS 5.2a, PS 5.2b	55	183	**Universal Forces**	**54**
4	PS 5.2c, PS 5.2e, PS 5.2f, PS 5.2g	56	186	**Simple and Complex Machines**	**57**
4	PS 5.1b, PS 5.1c, PS 5.1d, PS 5.2a, PS 5.2f, PS 5.2g		189	**Practice for H.O.T.S.**	
1, 4	M1.1a, S1.2a, S1.3, S2.1a, S2.1b, S2.1d, S2.2d, S2.3b, S2.3c, PS 5.2c, PS 5.2d, PS 5.2e, PS 5.2f, PS 5.2g		190	**Higher-Order Performance Task: Work, Friction, Inclined Plane**	

Formative Assessment 6

Student Resources

Measuring Up Express™ **Supplements**

NYS Success Diagnostic Practice Tests

Your teacher may choose to administer Diagnostic Practice Tests (DPTs) that mimic the length and format of the Grade 8 Intermediate-Level Science Test to diagnose your New York State Learning Standards knowledge and direct you to help in this worktext and the Measuring Up® worktext. These tests may be administered three times throughout the school year as a pretest, retest, and dress rehearsal right before the New York State Test.

Measuring Up e-Path® **online formative assessments**

Your teacher may choose to give Measuring Up e-Path® online formative and summative assessments that assess your New York State Learning Standards knowledge and identify areas where you need extra support in this worktext and in the Measuring Up® worktext.

Correlation to the New York State Learning Standards and Major Understandings

This worktext is customized to the tested *New York State Learning Standards for Science* and will help you prepare for the *Grade 8 New York State Intermediate-Level Test*.

New York State Learning Standards and Major Understandings		Measuring Up Express™ Lessons
STANDARD 1—Analysis, Inquiry, and Design **Students will use mathematical analysis, scientific inquiry, and engineering design, as appropriate, to pose questions, seek answers, and develop solutions.**		
Mathematical Analysis		
M1.1	Extend mathematical notation and symbolism to include variables and algebraic expressions in order to describe and compare quantities and express mathematical relationships.	
M1.1a	Identify independent and dependent variables.	2, Ch. 1 H.O.T.S., PT 1, PT 2, PT 5, PT 6
M1.1b	Identify relationships among variables including: direct, indirect, cyclic, constant; identify non related material.	5, Ch. 1 H.O.T.S.
M1.1c	Apply mathematical equations to describe relationships among variables in the natural world.	5
M2.1	Use inductive reasoning to construct, evaluate, and validate conjectures and arguments, recognizing that patterns and relationships can assist in explaining and extending mathematical phenomena.	
M2.1a	A interpolate and extrapolate from data.	5, Ch. 1 H.O.T.S.
M2.1b	Quantity patterns and trends.	5
M3.1	Apply mathematical knowledge to solve real-world problems and problems that arise from the investigation of mathematical ideas, using representations such as pictures, charts, and tables.	
M3.1a	A use appropriate scientific tools to solve problems about the natural world.	4
Scientific Inquiry		
S1.1	Formulate questions independently with the aid of references appropriate for guiding the search for explanations of everyday observations.	
S1.1a	Formulate questions about natural phenomena.	2
S1.1b	Identify appropriate references to investigate a question.	2
S1.1c	Refine and clarify questions so that they are subject to scientific investigation.	2
S1.2	Construct explanations independently for natural phenomena, especially by proposing preliminary visual models of phenomena.	
S1.2a	A independently formulate a hypothesis.	2, Ch. 1 H.O.T.S., PT 1, PT 2, PT 5, PT 6
S1.2b	Propose a model of a natural phenomenon.	7
S1.2c	Differentiate among observations, inferences, predictions, and explanations.	5
S1.3	Represent, present, and defend their proposed explanations of everyday observations so that they can be understood and assessed by others.	5, PT 1, PT 2, PT 5, PT 6
S1.4	Seek to clarify, to assess critically, and to reconcile with their own thinking the ideas presented by others, including peers, teachers, authors, and scientists.	6
S2.1	Use conventional techniques and those of their own design to make further observations and refine their explanations, guided by a need for more information.	

Ch. = Chapter   PT = Performance Tasks   H.O.T.S. = Higher-Order Thinking Skills

New York State Learning Standards and Major Understandings	Measuring Up Express™ Lessons
S2.1a Demonstrate appropriate safety techniques.	1, PT 1, PT 2, PT 5, PT 6
S2.1b Conduct an experiment designed by others.	3, PT 1, PT 2, PT 5, PT 6
S2.1c Design and conduct an experiment to test a hypothesis.	3, Ch. 1 H.O.T.S.
S2.1d Use appropriate tools and conventional techniques to solve problems about the natural world, including: • Measuring • Observing • Describing • Classifying • Sequencing	3, PT 1, PT 2, PT 5, PT 6
S2.2 Develop, present, and defend formal research proposals for testing their own explanations of common phenomena, including ways of obtaining needed observations and ways of conducting simple controlled experiments.	
S2.2a Include appropriate safety procedures.	1
S2.2b Design scientific investigations (e.g., observing, describing, and comparing; collecting samples; seeking more information, conducting a controlled experiment; discovering new objects or phenomena; making models).	3, Ch. 1 H.O.T.S.
S2.2c Design a simple controlled experiment.	3, Ch. 1 H.O.T.S.
S2.2d Identify independent variables (manipulated), dependent variables (responding), and constants in a simple controlled experiment.	3, Ch. 1 H.O.T.S., PT 1, PT 2, PT 5, PT 6
S2.2e Choose appropriate sample size and number of trials.	3
S2.3 Carry out their research proposals, recording observations and measurements (e.g., lab notes, audiotape, computer disk, videotape) to help assess the explanation.	
S2.3a Use appropriate safety procedures.	1
S2.3b Conduct a scientific investigation.	3, PT 1, PT 2, PT 5, PT 6
S2.3c Collect quantitative and qualitative data.	3, PT 1, PT 2, PT 5, PT 6
S3.1 Design charts, tables, graphs, and other representations of observations in conventional and creative ways to help them address their research question or hypothesis.	
S3.1a Organize results, using appropriate graphs, diagrams, data tables, and other models to show relationships.	4
S3.1b Generate and use scales, create legends, and appropriately label axes.	4
S3.2 Interpret the organized data to answer the research question or hypothesis and to gain insight into the problem.	
S3.2a Accurately describe the procedures used and the data gathered.	5
S3.2b Identify sources of error and the limitations of data collected.	5
S3.2c Evaluate the original hypothesis in light of the data.	5
S3.2d Formulate and defend explanations and conclusions as they relate to scientific phenomena.	6
S3.2e Form and defend a logical argument about cause-and-effect relationships in an investigation.	6
S3.2f Make predictions based on experimental data.	6
S3.2g Suggest improvements and recommendations for further studying.	6

Ch. = Chapter   PT = Performance Tasks   H.O.T.S. = Higher-Order Thinking Skills

New York State Learning Standards and Major Understandings	Measuring Up Express™ Lessons
S3.2h Use and interpret graphs and data tables.	4, 5, Ch. 1 H.O.T.S.
S3.3 Modify their personal understanding of phenomena based on evaluation of their hypothesis.	6
Information Systems Students will access, generate, process, and transfer information, using appropriate technologies.	
IS 1.4 Collect data from probes to measure events and phenomena.	
IS 1.5 Use simple modeling programs to make predictions.	7
IS 3.2 Describe applications of information technology in mathematics, science, and other technologies that address needs and solve problems in the community.	34
STANDARD 6—Interconnectedness: Common Themes **Students will understand the relationships and common themes that connect mathematics, science, and technology and apply the themes to these and other areas of learning.**	
Systems Thinking	
ICT 1.3 Describe the differences between open- and closed-loop systems.	16
ICT 1.4 Describe how the output from one part of a system (which can include material, energy, or information) can become the input to other parts.	16, 39, Ch. 4 H.O.T.S.
Models	
ICT 2.1 Select an appropriate model to begin the search for answers or solutions to a question or problem.	7
ICT 2.2 Use models to study processes that cannot be studied directly (e.g., when the real process is too slow, too fast, or too dangerous for direct observation).	7
ICT 2.3 Demonstrate the effectiveness of different models to represent the same thing and the same model to represent different things.	7
Magnitude and Scale	
ICT 3.1 Cite examples of how different aspects of natural and designed systems change at different rates with changes in scale.	34
ICT 3.2 Use powers of ten notation to represent very small and very large numbers.	27
Equilibrium and Stability	
ICT 4.1 Describe how feedback mechanisms are used in both designed and natural systems to keep changes within desired limits.	10, 23
Patterns of Change	
ICT 5.1 Use simple linear equations to represent how a parameter changes with time.	18
ICT 5.2 Observe patterns of change in trends or cycles and make predictions on what might happen in the future.	4, 17, 28, 30, 39, 40, Ch. 1 H.O.T.S., Ch. 4 H.O.T.S., PT 4
STANDARD 7—Interdisciplinary Problem Solving **Students will apply the knowledge and thinking skills of mathematics, science, and technology to address real-life problems and make informed decisions.**	
Connections	
IPS 1.3 Design solutions to real-world problems of general social interest related to home, school, or community using scientific experimentation to inform the solution and applying mathematical concepts and reasoning to assist in developing a solution.	3, 5

Ch. = Chapter   PT = Performance Tasks   H.O.T.S. = Higher-Order Thinking Skills

New York State Learning Standards and Major Understandings	Measuring Up Express™ Lessons
IPS 1.4 Describe and explain phenomena by designing and conducting investigations involving systematic observations, accurate measurements, and the identification and control of variables; by inquiring into relevant mathematical ideas; and by using mathematical and technological tools and procedures to assist in the investigation.	3
Strategies	
IPS 2.1 Students participate in an extended, culminating mathematics, science, and technology project. The project would require students to: • Working Effectively: Contributing to the work of a brainstorming group, laboratory partnership, cooperative learning group, or project team; planning procedures; identify and managing responsibilities of team members; and staying on task, whether working alone or as part of a group. • Gathering and Processing Information: Accessing information from printed media, electronic data bases, and community resources and using the information to develop a definition of the problem and to research possible solutions. • Generating and Analyzing Ideas: Developing ideas for proposed solutions, investigating ideas, collecting data, and showing relationships and patterns in the data. • Common Themes: Observing examples of common unifying themes, applying them to a problem, and using them to better understand the dimensions of the problem. • Realizing Ideas: Constructing components or models, arriving at a solution, and evaluating the result. • Presenting Results: Using a variety of media to present the solution and to communicate the results.	3, 4, 5
STANDARD 4—The Living Environment **Students will understand and apply scientific concepts, principles, and theories pertaining to the physical setting and living environment and recognize the historical development of ideas in science.**	
Performance Indicator 1.1 Compare and contrast the parts of plants, animals, and one-celled organisms.	
LE 1.1a Living things are composed of cells. Cells provide structure and carry on major functions to sustain life. Cells are usually microscopic in size.	8, Ch. 2 H.O.T.S.
LE 1.1b The way in which cells function is similar in all living things. Cells grow and divide, producing more cells. Cells take in nutrients, which they use to provide energy for the work that cells do and to make the materials that a cell or an organism needs.	8
LE 1.1c Most cells have cell membranes, genetic material, and cytoplasm. Some cells have a cell wall and/or chloroplasts. Many cells have a nucleus.	8, Ch. 2 H.O.T.S.
LE 1.1d Some organisms are single cells; others, including humans, are multicellular.	8
LE 1.1e Cells are organized for more effective functioning in multicellular organisms. Levels of organization for structure and function of a multicellular organism include cells, tissues, organs, and organ systems.	9
LE 1.1f Many plants have roots, stems, leaves, and reproductive structures. These organized groups of tissues are responsible for a plant's life activities.	9
LE 1.1g Multicellular animals often have similar organs and specialized systems for carrying out major life activities.	9, Ch. 2 H.O.T.S.
LE 1.1h Living things are classified by shared characteristics on the cellular and organism level. In classifying organisms, biologists consider details of internal and external structures. Biological classification systems are arranged from general (kingdom) to specific (species).	9, Ch. 2 H.O.T.S.
Performance Indicator 1.2 Explain the functioning of the major human organ systems and their interactions.	
LE 1.2a Each system is composed of organs and tissues which perform specific functions and interact with each other, e.g., digestion, gas exchange, excretion, circulation, locomotion, control, coordination, reproduction, and protection from disease.	20, 21, 22, 23, 24, 25, 26, Ch. 3 H.O.T.S., PT 3

Ch. = Chapter   PT = Performance Tasks   H.O.T.S. = Higher-Order Thinking Skills

New York State Learning Standards and Major Understandings	Measuring Up Express™ Lessons
LE 1.2b Tissues, organs, and organ systems help to provide all cells with nutrients, oxygen, and waste removal.	21, 22, 25, Ch. 3 H.O.T.S.
LE 1.2c The digestive system consists of organs that are responsible for the mechanical and chemical breakdown for food. The breakdown process results in molecules that can absorbed and transported to cells.	22, Ch. 3 H.O.T.S
LE 1.2d During respiration, cells use oxygen to release the energy stored in food. The respiratory system supplies oxygen and removes carbon dioxide (gas exchange).	21
LE 1.2e The excretory system functions in the disposal of dissolved waste molecules, the elimination of liquid and gaseous wastes, and the removal of excess heat energy.	22, Ch. 3 H.O.T.S
LE 1.2f The circulatory system moves substances to and from cells, where they are needed or produced, responding to changing demands.	21, Ch. 3 H.O.T.S
LE 1.2g Locomotion, necessary to escape danger, obtain food and shelter, and reproduce, is accomplished by the interaction of the skeletal and muscular systems, and coordinated by the nervous system.	20, PT 3
LE 1.2h The nervous and endocrine systems interact to control and coordinate the body's responses to changes in the environment, and to regulate growth, development, and reproduction. Hormones are chemicals produced by the endocrine system; hormones regulate many body functions.	23
LE 1.2i The male and female reproductive systems are responsible for producing sex cells necessary for the production of offspring.	24, Ch. 3 H.O.T.S
LE 1.2j Disease breaks down the structures or functions of an organism. Some diseases are the result of failures of the system. Other diseases are the result of damage by infection from other organisms (germ theory). Specialized cells protect the body from infectious disease. The chemicals they produce identify and destroy microbes that enter the body.	26
Performance Indicator 2.1 Describe sexual and asexual mechanisms for passing genetic materials from generation to generation.	
LE 2.1a Hereditary information is contained in genes. Genes are composed of DNA that makes up the chromosomes of cells.	13
LE 2.1b Each gene carries a single unit of information. A single inherited trait of an individual can be determined by one pair or by many pairs of genes. A human cell contains thousands of different genes.	13
LE 2.1c Each human cell contains a copy of all the genes needed to produce a human being.	13
LE 2.1d In asexual reproduction, all the genes come from the single parent. Asexually produced offspring are genetically identical to the parent.	13
LE 2.1e In sexual reproduction typically half of the genes come from each parent. Sexually produced offspring are not identical to either parent.	13
Performance Indicator 2.2 Describe simple mechanisms related to the inheritance of some physical traits in offspring.	
LE 2.2a In all organisms, genetic traits are passed on from generation to generation.	13, Ch. 2 H.O.T.S.
LE 2.2b Some genes are dominant and some are recessive. Some traits are inherited by mechanisms other than dominance and recessiveness.	13, Ch. 2 H.O.T.S.
LE 2.2c The probability of traits being expressed can be determined using models of genetic inheritance. Some models of prediction and pedigree charts and Punnett squares.	13, Ch. 2 H.O.T.S.
Performance Indicator 3.1 Describe sources of variation in organisms and their structures and relate the variations to survival.	
LE 3.1a The processes of sexual reproduction and mutation have given rise to a variety of traits within a species.	15, Ch. 2 H.O.T.S.

Ch. = Chapter   PT = Performance Tasks   H.O.T.S. = Higher-Order Thinking Skills

New York State Learning Standards and Major Understandings	Measuring Up Express™ Lessons
LE 3.1b Changes in environmental conditions can affect the survival of individual organisms with a particular trait. Small differences between parents and offspring can accumulate in successive generations so that descendants are very different from their ancestors. Individual organisms with certain traits are more likely to survive and have offspring than individuals without those traits.	15, Ch. 2 H.O.T.S.
LE 3.1c Human activities such as selective breeding and advances in genetic engineering may affect the variations of species.	15
Performance Indicator 3.2 Describe factors responsible for competition within species and the significance of that competition.	
LE 3.2a In all environments, organisms with similar needs may compete with another for resources.	15
LE 3.2b Extinction of a species occurs when the environment changes and the adaptive characteristics of a species are insufficient to permit its survival. Extinction of species is common. Fossils are evidence that a great variety of species existed in the past.	15
LE 3.2c Many thousands of layers of sedimentary rock provide evidence for the long history of Earth and for the long history of changing lifeforms whose remains are found in the rocks. Recently deposited rock layers are more likely to contain fossils resembling existing species.	15
LE 3.2d Although the time needed for change in a species is usually great, some species of insects and bacteria have undergone significant change in just a few years.	15
Performance Indicator 4.1 Observe and describe the variations in reproductive patterns of organisms, including asexual and sexual reproduction.	
LE 4.1a Some organisms reproduce asexually. Other organisms reproduce sexually. Some organisms can reproduce both sexually and asexually.	12
LE 4.1b There are many methods of asexual reproduction, including division of a cell into two cells, or separation of part of an animal or plant from the parent, resulting in the growth of another individual.	12
LE 4.1c Methods of sexual reproduction depend upon the species. All methods involve the merging of sex cells to begin the development of a new individual. In many species, including plants and humans, eggs and sperm are produced.	12, 24
LE 4.1d Fertilization and / or development in organisms may be internal or external.	12
Performance Indicator 4.2 Explain the role of sperm and egg cells in sexual reproduction.	
LE 4.2a The male sex cell is the sperm. The female sex cell is the egg. The fertilization of an egg by a sperm results in a fertilized egg.	12, 24, Ch. 3 H.O.T.S
LE 4.2b In sexual reproduction, sperm and egg each carry one-half of the genetic information for the new individual. Therefore, the fertilized egg contains genetic information from each parent.	13, 24, Ch. 2 H.O.T.S., Ch. 3 H.O.T.S
Performance Indicator 4.3 Observe and describe developmental patterns in selected plants and animals (e.g., insects, frogs, humans, seed-bearing plants).	
LE 4.3a Mulitcellular organisms exhibit complex changes in development, which begin after fertilization. The fertilized egg undergoes numerous cellular divisions that will result in a multicellular organism, with each cell having identical genetic information.	11, 14, 24
LE 4.3b In humans, the fertilized egg grows into tissue which develops into organs and organ systems before birth.	14, 24
LE 4.3c Various body structures and functions change as an organism goes through its life cycle.	14

Ch. = Chapter   PT = Performance Tasks   H.O.T.S. = Higher-Order Thinking Skills

New York State Learning Standards and Major Understandings	Measuring Up Express™ Lessons
LE 4.3d Patterns of development vary among animals. In some species the young resemble the adult, while in others they do not. Some insects and amphibians undergo metamorphosis as they mature.	14
LE 4.3e Patterns of development vary among plants. In seed-bearing plants, seeds contain stored food for early development. Their later development into adulthood is characterized by varying patterns of grown from species to species.	14
LE 4.3f As an individual organism ages, various body structures and functions change.	14
Performance Indicator 4.4 Observe and describe cell division at the microscopic level and its macroscopic effects.	
LE 4.4a In multicellular organisms, cell division is responsible for growth, maintenance, and repair. In some one-celled organisms, cell division is a method of asexual reproduction.	11
LE 4.4b In one type of cell division, chromosomes are duplicated and then separated into two identical and complete sets to be passed to each of the two resulting cells. In this type of cell division, the hereditary information is identical in all the cells that result.	11
LE 4.4c Another type of cell division accounts for the production of egg and sperm cells in sexually reproducing organsisms.	11
LE 4.4d Cancers are a result of abnormal cell division.	11
Performance Indicator 5.1 Compare the way a variety of living specimens carry out basic life functions and maintain dynamic equilibrium.	
LE 5.1a Animals and plants have a great variety of body plans and internal structures that contribute to their ability to maintain a balanced condition.	10
LE 5.1b An organism's overall body plan and its environment determine the way that the organism carries out the life processes.	10
LE 5.1c All organisms require energy to survive. The amount of energy needed and the method for obtaining this energy vary among cells. Some cells use oxygen to release the energy stored in food.	17
LE 5.1d The methods for obtaining nutrients vary among organisms. Producers, such as green plants, use light energy to make their food. Consumers, such as animals, take in energy-rich foods.	17
LE 5.1e Herbivores obtain energy from plants. Carnivores obtain energy from animals. Omnivores obtain energy from both plants and animals. Decomposers, such as bacteria and fungi, obtain energy by consuming wastes and / or dead organisms.	17
LE 5.1f Regulation of an organism's internal environment involves sensing the internal environment and changing physiological activities to keep conditions within the range required for survival. Regulation includes a variety of nervous and hormonal feedback systems.	10
LE 5.1g The survival of an organism depends on its ability to sense and respond to its external environment.	10
Performance Indicator 5.2 Describe the importance of major nutrients, vitamins, and minerals in maintaining health and promoting growth, and explain the need for a constant input of energy for living organisms.	
LE 5.2a Food provides molecules that serve as fuel and building material for all organisms. All living things, including plants, must release energy from their food, using it to carry on their life processes.	25, Ch. 3 H.O.T.S
LE 5.2b Foods contain a variety of substances, which include carbohydrates, fats, vitamins, proteins, minerals, and water. Each substance is vital to the survival of the organism.	25, Ch. 3 H.O.T.S
LE 5.2c Metabolism is the sum of all chemical reactions in an organism. Metabolism can be influenced by hormones, exercise, diet, and aging.	25

Ch. = Chapter   PT = Performance Tasks   H.O.T.S. = Higher-Order Thinking Skills

New York State Learning Standards and Major Understandings	Measuring Up Express™ Lessons
LE 5.2d Energy in foods is measured in Calories. The total caloric value of each type of food varies. The number of Calories a person requires varies from person to person.	25, Ch. 3 H.O.T.S
LE 5.2e In order to maintain a balanced state, all organisms have a minimum daily intake of each type of nutrient based on species, size, age, activity, etc. An imbalance in any of the nutrients might result in weight gain, weight loss, or a diseased state.	25, Ch. 3 H.O.T.S
LE 5.2f Contraction of infectious disease, and personal behaviors such as use of toxic substances and some dietary habits, may interfere with one's dynamic equilibrium. During pregnancy these conditions may also affect the development of the child. Some effects of these conditions are immediate; others may not appear for many years.	26
Performance Indicator 6.1 Describe the flow of energy and matter through food chains and food webs.	
LE 6.1a Energy flows through ecosystems in one direction, usually from the Sun, through producers to consumers and then to decomposers. This process may be visualized with food chains or energy pyramids.	17, PT 2
LE 6.1b Food webs identify feeding relationships among producers, consumers, and decomposers in an ecosystem.	17
LE 6.1c Matter is transferred from one organism to another and between organisms and their physical environment. Water, nitrogen, carbon dioxide, and oxygen are examples of substances cycled between the living and nonliving environment.	16
Performance Indicator 6.2 Provide evidence that green plants make food and explain the significance of this process to other organisms.	
LE 6.2a Photosynthesis is carried on by green plants and other organisms containing chlorophyll. In this process, the Sun's energy is converted into and stored as chemical energy in the form of a sugar. The quantity of sugar molecules increases in green plants during photosynthesis in the presence of sunlight.	17, PT 2
LE 6.2b The major source of atmospheric oxygen is photosynthesis. Carbon dioxide is removed from the atmosphere and oxygen is released during photosynthesis.	16, PT 2
LE 6.2c Green plants are the producers of food which is used directly or indirectly by consumers.	17, PT 2
Performance Indicator 7.1 Describe how living things, including humans, depend upon the living and nonliving environment for their survival.	
LE 7.1a A population consists of all individuals of a species that are found together at a given place and time. Populations living in one place form a community. The community and the physical factors with which it interacts compose an ecosystem.	18
LE 7.1b Given adequate resources and no disease or predators, populations (including humans) increase. Lack of resources, habitat destruction, and other factors such as predation and climate limit the growth of certain populations in the ecosystem.	18, Ch. 2 H.O.T.S.
LE 7.1c In all environments, organisms interact with one another in many ways. Relationships among organisms may be competitive, harmful, or beneficial. Some species have adapted to be dependent upon each other with the result that neither could survive without the other.	18, Ch. 2 H.O.T.S.
LE 7.1d Some microorganisms are essential to the survival of other living things.	18
LE 7.1e The environment may contain dangerous levels of substances (pollutants) that are harmful to organisms. Therefore, the good health of environments and individuals requires the monitoring of soil, air, and water, and taking steps to keep them safe.	19
Performance Indicator 7.2 Describe the effects of environmental changes on humans and other populations.	
LE 7.2a In ecosystems, balance is the result of interactions between community members and their environment.	18, Ch. 2 H.O.T.S.

Ch. = Chapter   PT = Performance Tasks   H.O.T.S. = Higher-Order Thinking Skills

New York State Learning Standards and Major Understandings		Measuring Up Express™ Lessons
LE 7.2b	The environment may be altered through the activities of organisms. Alterations are sometimes abrupt. Some species may replace others over time, resulting in long-term gradual changes (ecological succession).	18
LE 7.2c	Overpopulation by any species impacts the environment due to the increased use of resources. Human activities can bring about environmental degradation through resource acquisition, urban growth, land-use decisions, waste disposal, etc.	18, 19, Ch. 2 H.O.T.S.
LE 7.2d	Since the Industrial Revolution, human activities have resulted in major pollution of air, water, and soil. Pollution has cumulative ecological effects such as acid rain, global warming, or ozone depletion. The survival of living things on our planet depends on the conservation and protection of Earth's resources.	19
STANDARD 4: The Physical Setting		
Performance Indicator 1.1 Explain daily, monthly, and seasonal changes on Earth.		
PS 1.1a	Earth's Sun is an average-sized star. The Sun is more than a million times greater in volume that Earth.	27
PS 1.1b	Other star's are like the Sun but are so far away that they look like points of light. Distances between stars are vast compared to distances within our solar system.	27
PS 1.1c	The Sun and the planets that revolve around it are the major bodies in the solar system. Other members include comets, moons, and asteroids. Earth's orbit is nearly circular.	30
PS 1.1d	Gravity is the force that keeps planets in orbit around the Sun and the Moon in orbit around the Earth.	30
PS 1.1e	Most objects in the solar system have a regular and predictable motion. These motions explain such phenomena as a day, a year, phases of the Moon, eclipses, tides, meteor showers, and comets.	28, 29, 30, Ch. 4 H.O.T.S., PT 4
PS 1.1f	The latitude/longitude coordinate system and our system of time are based on celestial observations.	31
PS 1.1g	Moons are seen by reflected light. Our moon orbits Earth, while Earth orbits the Sun. The moon's phases as observed from Earth are the result of seeing different portions of the lighted area of the Moon's surface. The phases repeat in a cyclic pattern in about one month.	29
PS 1.1h	The apparent motions of the Sun, Moon, planets, and stars across the sky can be explained by Earth's rotation and revolution. Earth's rotation causes the length on one day to be approximately 24 hours. This rotation also causes the Sun and Moon to appear to rise along the eastern horizon and to set along the western horizon. Earth's revolution around the Sun defines the length of the year as 365 ¼ days.	28, 29, Ch. 4 H.O.T.S., PT 4
PS 1.1i	The tilt of Earth's axis of rotation and the revolution of Earth around the Sun cause seasons on Earth. The length of daylight varies depending on latitude and season.	28, Ch. 4 H.O.T.S., PT 4
PS 1.1j	The shape of Earth, the other planets, and stars is nearly spherical.	30
Performance Indicator 2.1 Explain how the atmosphere (air), hydrosphere (water), and lithosphere (land) interact, evolve, and change.		
PS 2.1a	Nearly all the atmosphere is confined to a thin shell surrounding Earth. The atmosphere is a mixture of gases, including nitrogen and oxygen with small amounts of water vapor, carbon dioxide, and other trace gases. The atmosphere is stratified into layers, each having distinct properties. Nearly all weather occurs in the lowest layer of the atmosphere.	32
PS 2.1b	As altitude increases, air pressure decreases.	32
PS 2.1c	The rock at Earth's surface forms a nearly continuous shell around Earth called the lithosphere.	36
PS 2.1d	The majority of the lithosphere is covered by a relatively thin layer of water called the hydrosphere.	35

Ch. = Chapter   PT = Performance Tasks   H.O.T.S. = Higher-Order Thinking Skills

New York State Learning Standards and Major Understandings	Measuring Up Express™ Lessons
PS 2.1e Rocks are composed of minerals. Only a few rock-forming minerals make up most of the rocks of Earth. Minerals are identified on the basis of physical properties such as streak, hardness, and reaction to acid.	36
PS 2.1f Fossils are usually found in sedimentary rocks. Fossils can be used to study past climates and environments.	36
PS 2.1g The dynamic processes that wear away Earth's surface include weathering and erosion.	37
PS 2.1h The process of weathering breaks down rocks to form sediment. Soil consists of sediment, organic material, water, and air.	37
PS 2.1i Erosion is the transport of sediment. Gravity is the driving force behind erosion. Gravity can act directly or through agents such as moving water, wind, and glaciers.	37
PS 2.1j Water circulates through the atmosphere, lithosphere, and hydrosphere in what is known as the water cycle.	35
Performance Indicator 2.2 Describe volcano and earthquake patterns, the rock cycle, and weather and climate changes.	
PS 2.2a The interior of Earth is hot. Heat flow and movement of material within Earth cause sections of Earth's crust to move. This may result in earthquakes, volcanic eruption, and the creation of mountains and ocean basins.	38, 40, 41, Ch. 4 H.O.T.S.
PS 2.2b Analysis of earthquake wave data (vibrational disturbances) leads to the conclusion that there are layers within Earth. These layers-the crust, mantle, outer core, and inner core-have distinct properties.	38, Ch. 4 H.O.T.S.
PS 2.2c Folded, tilted, faulted, and displaced rock layers suggest past crustal movement.	40
PS 2.2d Continents fitting together like puzzle parts and fossil correlations provided initial evidence that continents were once together.	40
PS 2.2e The Theory of Plate Tectonics explains how the "solid" lithosphere consists of a series of plates that "float" on the partially molten section of the mantle. Convection cells within the mantle may be the driving force for the movement of the plates.	40
PS 2.2f Plates may collide, move part, or slide past one another. Most volcanic activity and mountain building occur at the boundaries of these plates, often resulting in earthquakes.	40, 41
PS 2.2g Rocks are classified according to their method of formation. The three classes of rocks are sedimentary, metaphoric, and igneous. Most rocks show characteristics that give clues to their formation conditions.	39
PS 2.2h The rock cycle model shows how types of rock or rock material may be transformed from one type of rock to another.	39, Ch. 4 H.O.T.S.
PS 2.2i Weather describes the conditions of the atmosphere at a given location for a short period of time.	33, Ch. 4 H.O.T.S.
PS 2.2j Climate is the characteristic weather that prevails from season to season and year to year.	33, Ch. 4 H.O.T.S.
PS 2.2k The uneven heating of Earth's surface is the cause of weather.	33
PS 2.2l Air masses form when air remains nearly stationary over a large section of Earth's surface and takes on the conditions of temperature and humidity from that location. Weather conditions at a location are determined primarily by temperature, humidity, and pressure of air masses over that location.	34
PS 2.2m Most local weather condition changes are caused by movement of air masses.	34
PS 2.2n The movement of air masses is determined by prevailing winds and upper air currents.	34
PS 2.2o Fronts are boundaries between air masses. Precipitation is likely to occur at these boundaries.	34

Ch. = Chapter   PT = Performance Tasks   H.O.T.S. = Higher-Order Thinking Skills

New York State Learning Standards and Major Understandings	Measuring Up Express™ Lessons
PS 2.2p High-pressure systems generally bring fair weather. Low-pressure systems usually bring cloudy, unstable conditions. The general movement of highs and lows is from west to east across the United States.	34
PS 2.2q Hazardous weather conditions include thunderstorms, tornadoes, hurricanes, ice storms, and blizzards. Humans can prepare for and respond to these conditions if given sufficient warning.	34
PS 2.2r Substances enter the atmosphere naturally and from human activity. Some of these substances include dust from volcanic eruptions and greenhouse gases such as carbon dioxide, methane, and water vapor. These substances can affect weather, climate, and living things.	34
Performance Indicator 3.1 Observe and describe properties of materials, such as density, conductivity, and solubility.	
PS 3.1a Substances have characteristic properties. Some of these properties include color, odor, phase at room temperature, density, solubility, heat, and electrical conductivity, hardness, and boiling and freezing points.	45, Ch. 5 H.O.T.S.
PS 3.1b Solubility can be affected by the nature of the solute and solvent, temperature, and pressure. The rate of solution can be affected by the size of the particles, stirring, temperature, and the amount of solute already dissolved.	45
PS 3.1c The motion of particles helps to explain the phases (states) of matter as well as changes from one phase to another. The phase in which matter exists depends on the attractive forces among its particles.	44, Ch. 5 H.O.T.S.
PS 3.1d Gases have neither a determined shape nor a definite volume. Gases assume the shape and volume of a closed container.	44
PS 3.1e A liquid has definite volume, but it takes the shape of a container.	44, Ch. 5 H.O.T.S.
PS 3.1f A solid has definite shape and volume. Particles resist a change in position.	44, Ch. 5 H.O.T.S.
PS 3.1g Characteristic properties can be used to identify different materials, and separate a mixture of substances into its components. For example, iron can be removed from a mixture by means of a magnet. An insoluble substance can be separated from a soluble substance by such processes as filtration, settling, and evaporation.	45, Ch. 5 H.O.T.S.
PS 3.1h Density can be described as the amount of matter that is in a given amount of space. If two have equal volume, but one has more mass, the one with more mass is denser.	45, Ch. 5 H.O.T.S.
PS 3.1i Buoyancy is determined by comparative densities.	45
Performance Indicator 3.2 Distinguish between chemical and physical changes.	
PS 3.2a During a physical change a substance keeps its chemical composition and properties. Examples of physical changes include freezing, melting, condensation, boiling, evaporation, tearing, and crushing.	45
PS 3.2b Mixtures are physical combinations of materials and can be separated by physical means.	45
PS 3.2c During a chemical change, substances react in characteristic ways to form new substances with different physical and chemical properties. Examples of chemical changes include burning of wood, cooking of an egg, rusting of iron, and souring of milk.	46, PT 5
PS 3.2d Substances are often placed in categories if they react in similar ways. Examples include metals, nonmetals, and noble gases.	43, 46
PS 3.2e The Law of Conservation of Mass states that during an ordinary chemical reaction matter cannot be created or destroyed. In chemical reactions, the total mass of the reactants equals the total mass of the products.	46, PT 5
Performance Indicator 3.3 Develop mental models to explain common chemical reactions and changes in states of matter.	
PS 3.3a All matter is made up of atoms. Atoms are too far small to see with a light microscope.	42

Ch. = Chapter   PT = Performance Tasks   H.O.T.S. = Higher-Order Thinking Skills

New York State Learning Standards and Major Understandings	Measuring Up Express™ Lessons
PS 3.3b Atoms and molecules are perpetually in motion. The greater the temperature, the greater the motion.	42, 44
PS 3.3c Atoms may join together in well-defined molecules or may be arranged in regular geometric patterns.	42
PS 3.3d Interactions among atoms and/ or molecules result in chemical reactions.	46, 50
PS 3.3e The atoms of any one element are different from the atoms of other elements.	42
PS 3.3f There are more than 100 elements. Elements combine in a multitude of ways to produce compounds that account for all living and nonliving substances. Few elements are found in their pure form.	43
PS 3.3g The periodic table is one useful model for classifying elements. The periodic table can be used to predict properties of elements (metals, nonmetals, noble gases).	43
Performance Indicator 4.1 Describe the sources and identify the transformations of energy observed in everyday life.	
PS 4.1a The Sun is a major source of energy of Earth. Other sources of energy include nuclear and geometrical energy.	47
PS 4.1b Fossil fuels contain stored solar energy and are considered nonrenewable resources. They are major source of energy in the United States. Solar energy, wind, moving water, and biomass are some examples of renewable energy resources.	47
PS 4.1c Most activities in everyday life involve one form of energy being transformed into another. For example, the chemical energy in gasoline is transformed into mechanical energy in an automobile engine. Energy, in the form of heat, is almost always one of the products of energy transformations.	48
PS 4.1d Different forms of energy include heat, light, electrical, mechanical, sound, nuclear, and chemical. Energy is transformed in many ways.	48, Ch. 5 H.O.T.S.
PS 4.1e Energy can be considered to be either kinetic energy, which is the energy of motion, or potential energy, which depends on relative position.	48, Ch. 5 H.O.T.S.
Performance Indicator 4.2 Observe and describe heating and cooling events.	
PS 4.2a Heat moves in predictable ways, flowing from warmer objects to cooler ones, until both reach the same temperature.	49
PS 4.2b Heat can be transferred through matter by the collisions of atoms and / or molecules (conduction) or through space (radiation). In a liquid or gas, currents will facilitate the transfer of heat (convection).	49
PS 4.2c During a phase change, heat energy is absorbed or released. Energy is absorbed when a solid changes to a liquid and when a liquid changes to a gas. Energy is released when a gas changes to a liquid and when a liquid changes to a solid.	49, Ch. 5 H.O.T.S.
PS 4.2d Most substances expand when heated and contract when cooled. Water is an exception, expanding when changing to ice.	49
PS 4.2e Temperature affects the solubility of some substances in water.	49
Performance Indicator 4.3 Observe and describe energy changes as related to chemical reactions.	
PS 4.3a In chemical reactions, energy is transformed into or out of a system. Light, electricity, or mechanical motion may be involved in such transfers in addition to heat.	50
Performance Indicator 4.4 Observe and describe the properties of sound, light, magnetism, and electricity.	
PS 4.4a Different forms of electromagnetic energy have different wavelengths. Some examples of electromagnetic energy are microwaves, infrared light, visible light, ultraviolet light, X-rays, and gamma rays.	51

Ch. = Chapter   PT = Performance Tasks   H.O.T.S. = Higher-Order Thinking Skills

New York State Learning Standards and Major Understandings	Measuring Up Express™ Lessons
PS 4.4b Light passes through some materials, sometimes refracting in the process. Materials absorb and reflect light, and may transmit light. To see an object, light from that object, emitted by or reflected from it, must enter the eye.	51, Ch. 5 H.O.T.S.
PS 4.4c Vibrations in materials set up wave-like disturbances that spread away from the source. Sound waves are an example. Vibrational waves move at different speeds in different materials. Sound cannot travel in a vacuum.	51
PS 4.4d Electrical energy can be produced from a variety of energy sources and can be transformed into almost any other form of energy.	52
PS 4.4e Electrical circuits provide a means of transferring electrical energy.	52
PS 4.4f Without touching them, material that has been electrically charged attracts uncharged material, and may either attract or repel other charged material.	52
PS 4.4g Without direct contact, a magnet attracts certain materials and either attracts or repels other magnets. The attractive force of a magnet is greatest at its poles.	52
Performance Indicator 4.5 Describe situations that support the principle of conservation of energy.	
PS 4.5a Energy cannot be created or destroyed, but only changed from one form into another.	48, 50, Ch. 5 H.O.T.S.
PS 4.5b Energy can change from one form to another, although in the process some energy is always converted to heat. Some systems transform energy with less loss of heat than others.	48, 50
Performance Indicator 5.1 Describe different patterns of motions of objects.	
PS 5.1a The motion of an object is always judged with respect to some other object or point. The idea of absolute motion or rest is misleading.	53
PS 5.1b The motion of an object can be described by its position, direction of motion, and speed.	53, Ch. 6 H.O.T.S.
PS 5.1c An object's motion is the result of the combined effect of all forces acting on the object. A moving object that is not subjected to a force will continue to move at a constant speed in a straight line. An object at rest will remain at rest.	54 Ch. 6 H.O.T.S.
PS 5.1d Force is directly related to an object's mass and acceleration. The greater the force, the greater the change in motion.	54 Ch. 6 H.O.T.S.
PS 5.1e Force is directly related to an object's mass and acceleration. The greater the force, the greater the change in motion.	54
Performance Indicator 5.2 Observe, describe, and compare effects of forces (gravity, electric current, and magnetism) on the motion of objects.	
PS 5.2a Every object exerts gravitational force on every other object. Gravitational force depends on how much mass the objects have and on how far apart they are. Gravity is one of the forces acting on orbiting objects and projectiles.	55 Ch. 6 H.O.T.S.
PS 5.2b Electric currents and magnets can exert a force on each other.	55
PS 5.2c Machines transfer mechanical energy from one object to another.	56, PT 6
PS 5.2d Friction is a force that opposes motion.	54, PT 6
PS 5.2e A machine can be made more efficient by reducing friction. Some common ways of reducing friction include lubricating or waxing surfaces.	56, PT 6
PS 5.2f Machines can change the direction or amount of force, or the distance or speed of force required to do work.	56 Ch. 6 H.O.T.S., PT 6
PS 5.2g Simple machines include a lever, a pulley, a wheel, and axle, and an inclined plane. A complex machine uses a combination of interacting simple machines, e.g., a bicycle.	56 Ch. 6 H.O.T.S., PT 6

Ch. = Chapter   PT = Performance Tasks   H.O.T.S. = Higher-Order Thinking Skills

New York State Process Skills Based on Standard 4

Process Skills Based on Standard 4	Measuring Up Express™ Lessons
General Skills	
1. follow safety procedures in the classroom and laboratory	1
2. safely and accurately use the following measurement tools: – metric ruler – balance – stopwatch – graduated cylinder – thermometer – spring scale – voltmeter	PT1, PT2, PT3, PT4, PT5, PT6
3. use appropriate units for measured or calculated values	4, 27, 33, 53, 54, PT1, PT2, PT3, PT4, PT5, PT6
4. recognize and analyze patterns and trends	5, 18, 27, 28, 29, 34
5. classify objects according to an established scheme and a student-generated scheme	8, 9, 27, 30, 39, 56
6. develop and use a dichotomous key	9
7. sequence events	11, 28, 29, 35, 39, 40, 41
8. identify cause-and-effect relationships	10, 28, 29, 32, 33, 34, 40, 41, 45, 46, 49
9. use indicators and interpret results	PT1, PT2, PT3, PT4, PT5, PT6
Living Environment Skills	
1. manipulate a compound microscope to view microscopic objects	N/A
2. determine the size of a microscopic object, using a compound microscope	N/A
3. prepare a wet mount slide	N/A
4. use appropriate staining techniques	N/A
5. design and use a Punnett square or pedigree chart to predict the probability of certain traits	13
6. classify living things according to a student-generated scheme and an established scheme	9
7. interpret and/or illustrate the energy flow in a food chain, energy pyramid, or food web	17
8. identify pulse points and pulse rates	21
9. identify structure and function relationships in organisms	8, 20, 21, 22, 23, 24
Physical Setting Skills	
1. given the latitude and longitude of a locate, indicate its position on a map and determine the latitude and longitude of a given location on a map	31
2. using identification tests and a flow chart, identify mineral samples	36
3. use a diagram of the rock cycle to determine geological processes that led to the formation of a specific rock type	39
4. plot the location of recent earthquake and volcanic activity on a map and identify patterns of distribution	41
5. use a magnetic compass to find cardinal directions	31
6. measure the angular elevation of an object, using appropriate instruments	31

Ch. = Chapter   PT = Performance Tasks   H.O.T.S. = Higher-Order Thinking Skills

Process Skills Based on Standard 4	Measuring Up Express™ Lessons
7. generate and interpret field maps including topographic and weather maps	34
8. predict the characteristics of an air mass based on the origin of the air mass	34
9. measure weather variables such as wind speed and direction, relative humidity, barometric pressure, etc.	33
10. determine the density of liquids, and regular- and irregular-shaped solids.	45
11. determine the volume of a regular- and irregular-shaped solid, using water displacement	44
12. using the periodic table, identify an element as a metal, nonmetal, or noble gas	43
13. determine the identity of an unknown element, using physical and chemical properties	45, 46
14. using appropriate resources, separate the parts of a mixture	45
15. determine the electrical conductivity of a material, using a simple circuit	52
16. determine the speed and acceleration of a moving object	53, 54

Ch. = Chapter   PT = Performance Tasks   H.O.T.S. = Higher-Order Thinking Skills

Correlation to the New York City Grade 8 Science Scope and Sequence

This worktext is customized to the *New York City Science Scope and Sequence* and will help you prepare for the *New York City Test* in Science for Grade 8.

NYC Scope and Sequence	NYS Learning Standard(s)	Measuring Up Express™ Lessons
UNIT 1: Reproduction, Heredity, and Revolution		
How does life on Earth continue and adapt in response to environmental change?		
Reproductive Patterns and the Continuity of Life		
• Asexual Reproduction, e.g., Binary fission in unicellular organisms, budding, and vegetative propagation.	LE 2.1d LE 4.1a,b	13 12
• Sexual Reproduction- formation of gametes	LE 2.1e, LE 4.1a,c,d LE 4.2b LE 4.4c	13 12 13,24 11
• Compare and contrast results, contexts, advantages and disadvantages of each method.	LE 4.1a	12
Patterns of Development and the Continuity of Life		
• Patterns of development in plants	LE 4.3a,b,c,e,f	11, 14, 24
• Patterns of development in animals	LE 4.3a,b,c,d,f	11, 14, 24
• Cell division-growth, maintenance, and repair – Cancer is the result of abnormal cell division	LE 4.4a,b LE 4.4d	11 11
Heredity		
• Genes and DNA	LE 2.1a-e	13
• Mendelian genetics	LE 2.2a-c	13
• Mutations	LE 3.1a	15
Roles of Sexual and Asexual Reproduction in Human Growth and Development		
• The role of the sperm and egg	LE 4.2a,b	12, 13, 24
• Human reproductive system	LE 1.2i	24
• Hormonal regulation: Endocrine system	LE 1.2h	23
• Patterns of development: cell division and genetic expression	LE 4.3b	24
• Genetic diseases	LE 1.2j, LE 2.2a	26
• Genetic engineering, esp. cloning	LE 3.1c IPS 1.2, 1.3	15 3, 5
Natural Selection: The Driving Mechanism Behind Evolution		
• Sources of variation in organisms	LE 3.1a	15
• Adaptations	LE 3.1a-c	15
• Competition	LE 3.2a	15
• Extinction	LE 3.2b, LE 7.2d	15, 19
• Evidence for evolution	LE 3.2c,d	15

Ch. = Chapter   PT = Performance Tasks   H.O.T.S. = Higher-Order Thinking Skills

NYC Scope and Sequence	Process Skills Based on Standard 4	Measuring Up Express™ Lessons
General Skills (from NYS Core Curriculum)		
• Follow safety procedures in the classroom and laboratory.	G1	1
• Recognize and analyze patterns and trends.	G4	5, 18, 27, 28, 29, 34
• Sequence events.	G7	11, 28, 29, 35, 39, 40, 41
Living Environment Skills (from NYS Core Curriculum)		
• Manipulate a compound microscope to view microscopic objects (*e.g., look at cells undergoing mitosis*).	LE1	N/A
• Determine the size of a microscopic object using a compound microscope.	LE2	N/A
• Design and use a Punnett square or a pedigree chart to predict the probability of certain traits.	LE5	13
• Classify living things (*evolutionary relationships*).	LE6	9
• Identify cause-and-effect relationships.	G8	10, 28, 29, 32, 33, 34, 40, 41, 45, 46, 49
• Identify structure and function relationships in organisms.	LE9	8
UNIT 2: Forces and Motion on Earth		
How do we apply the laws of motion to explain the movement of objects on Earth?		
Motion and Newton's Laws		
• Patterns of motion, frame of reference and position, direction, and speed	PS 5.1a,b	53
• Newton's First Law of Motion: Inertia	PS 5.1c	54
• Newton's Second Law: F = ma (*conceptual understanding as opposed to teaching the formula*)	PS 5.1d	54
• Newton's Third Law: For every action there is an equal and opposite reaction; Force as an interaction	PS 5.1e PS5.2b	54, 55
General Skills (from NYS Core Curriculum)		
• Follow safety procedures in the classroom and laboratory.	G1	1
• Safely and accurately use the following measurement tools: – Metric ruler – Balance – Stop watch – Spring scale.	G2	PT 1, PT 2, PT 3, PT 4, PT 5, PT 6
• Use appropriate units for measured or calculated values.	G3	4, 27, 33, 53, 54, PT 1, PT 2, PT 3, PT 4, PT 5, PT 6
• Recognize and analyze patterns and trends.	G4	5, 18, 27, 28, 29, 34
• Identify cause-and-effect relationships.	G8	10, 28, 29, 32, 33, 34, 40, 41, 45, 46, 49
Physical Setting Skills (from NYS Core Curriculum)		
• Determine the speed and acceleration of a moving object.	PS16	53, 54

Ch. = Chapter   PT = Performance Tasks   H.O.T.S. = Higher-Order Thinking Skills

NYC Scope and Sequence	Process Skills Based on Standard 4	Measuring Up Express™ Lessons
UNIT 3: Earth, Sun, Moon System		
What roles do forces play in the patterns and stability of the Solar System?		
Seasons and Cycles: Relationships Among the Sun, Earth, and Moon		
• Day: rotation	PS 1.1e,h	28, 29, 30
• Year: revolution	PS 1.1e,h	28, 29, 30
• Seasons: tilt of Earth's axis of rotation	PS 1.1i	28
• Phases of the Moon	PS 1.1g	29
• Eclipses	PS 1.1e	28, 29, 30
• Tides	PS 1.1e	28, 29, 30
Solar System		
• Classification of celestial objects: stars including the sun; planets; comets; moons; and asteroids.	PS 1.1a-c,j	27, 30
• Patterns of motion, frame of reference and position, direction, and speed.	PS 1.1c-i PS 5.1a-c	28, 29, 30, 31 53, 54
• Observe, describe, and compare the effects of balanced and unbalanced forces on the motion of objects. – Newton's First Law of Motion: Inertia – Gravity	PS 1.1c,e,g,h PS 5.1c PS 1.1d, PS 5.2a	28, 29, 30 54 30, 55
General Skills (from NYS Core Curriculum)		
• Follow safety procedures in the classroom and laboratory.	G1	1
• Safely and accurately use the following measurement tools: – Metric ruler – Stopwatch – Spring scale.	G2	PT 1, PT 2, PT 3, PT 4, PT 5, PT 6
• Use appropriate units for measured or calculated values.	G3	4, 27, 33, 53, 54, PT 1, PT 2, PT 3, PT 4, PT 5, PT 6
• Recognize and analyze patterns and trends.	G4	5, 18, 27, 28, 29, 34
• Classify objects.	G5	8, 9, 27, 30, 39, 56
• Identify cause-and-effect relationships.	G8	10, 28, 29, 32, 33, 34, 40, 41, 45, 46, 49
Physical Setting Skills (from NYS Core Curriculum)		
• Given the latitude and longitude of a location, indicate its position on a map and determine the latitude and longitude of a given location on a map.	PS1	31
UNIT 4: Humans in their environment: Needs and tradeoffs		
How does human consumption of resources impact the environment and our health?		
Natural Resources and Energy		
• Energy needs	LE 3.2a; PS 4.1a-d; PS 4.4d,e; ICT 1.1-1.4, 2.1-2.3, 4.1, 4.2, 5.1, 5.2, 6.1, 6.2; IPS 1.1-1.4; IPS 2.1	15, 47, 48, 52,16, 38, 39, 40, 7, 10, 23, 24, 3, 4, 5

Ch. = Chapter   PT = Performance Tasks   H.O.T.S. = Higher-Order Thinking Skills

xxiv

NYC Scope and Sequence	Process Skills Based on Standard 4	Measuring Up Express™ Lessons
• Renewable and non-renewable sources of energy	PS 4.1a,b ICT 5.1, 5.2	47, 28, 30, 17, 18, 4
• Material needs	LE 3.2a; ICT 1.1-1.4, 2.1-2.3, 4.1, 4.2, 5.1, 5.2, 6.1, 6.2; IPS 1.1-1.4; IPS 2.1	10, 23, 24, 28, 15, 7, 16, 17, 18, 39, 40, 30, 3, 4, 5
• Renewable and nonrenewable sources of materials	LE 6.1c; ICT 5.1, 5.2	16, 4, 17, 18, 28, 30
• Environmental concerns: Acquisition and depletion of resources: Waste disposal; Land use and urban growth; Overpopulation; Global Warming; Ozone depletion; Acid rain; Air pollution; Water pollution; Impact on other organisms	LE 3.2b; LE 7.1e; LE 7.2c,d; ICT 1.2, 1.4, 2.1-2.3, 4.1, 4.2, 5.1, 5.2, 6.1, 6.2; IPS 1.1-1.4; IPS 2.1	15, 19, 18, 3, 4, 5, 7, 10, 17, 18, 30, 40, 39, 24
• Energy conservation	PS 4.5a,b; ICT 1.1-1.4, 2.1-2.3, 4.1, 5.1, 5.2, 6.1, 6.2; IPS 1.1-1.4; IPS 2.1	48, 50, 7, 4, 5, 3, 16, 17, 18, 28, 30, 39, 40
Nutrition and Food Choices: Impact on the Environment and our Health		
Environment: • Environmental Toxins: pesticides and herbicides; fertilizers; organic waste	LE 7.2c,d; ICT 6.1; IPS 1.1-1.4; IPS 2.1	18, 19, 3, 4, 5,
• Endangered species: Habitat destruction, overfishing	LE 7.2b,c,d; ICT 5.2; IPS 1.1-1.4; IPS 2.1	18, 19, 3, 4, 5, 17, 28, 30, 39, 40
• Packaging and solid waste	ICT 5.2; IPS 1.1-1.4; IPS 2.1	3, 4, 5, 17, 28, 30, 39, 40
• Water issues: depletion; pollution	LE 7.2c,d; ICT 5.2; IPS 1.1-1.4; IPS 2.1	18, 19, 3, 4, 5, 17, 28, 30, 39, 40
Homeostasis and Health: • Analyzing nutritional value	LE 5.2a,b; ICT 6.1	25
• Food-borne illness: Infectious disease and the immune system (bacteria, parasites)	LE 1.2j; LE 5.2f; IPS 1.1-1.4; IPS 2.1	26, 3,4,5
• System failures: heart disease, high blood pressure; colon cancer; epidemics of childhood obesity and diabetes; osteoporosis	LE 1.2j; LE 4.4d; LE 5.2f; IPS 1.1-1.4; IPS 2.1	3,4,5, 26, 11
General Skills (from NYS Core Curriculum)		
• Follow safety procedures in the classroom and laboratory.	G1	1
• Safely and accurately use the following measurement tools: (*depends on project*).	G2	3
• Use appropriate units for measured or calculated values.	G3	4, 27, 33, 53, 54, PT 1, PT 2, PT 3, PT 4, PT 5, PT 6
• Recognize and analyze patterns and trends.	G4	5, 18, 27, 28, 29, 34
• Sequence events.	G7	11, 28, 29, 35, 39, 40, 41

Ch. = Chapter   PT = Performance Tasks   H.O.T.S. = Higher-Order Thinking Skills

NYC Scope and Sequence	Process Skills Based on Standard 4	Measuring Up Express™ Lessons
• Identify cause-and-effect relationships.	G8	10, 28, 29, 32, 33, 34, 40, 41, 45, 46, 49
• Use indicators and interpret results.	G9	??
Living Environment Skills (from NYS Core Curriculum)		
• Interpret and/ or illustrate the energy flow in a food chain, energy pyramid, or food web.	LE7	17
• Identify structure and function relationships in organisms (within the study of system failures).	LE9	8
Physical Setting Skills (from NYS Core Curriculum)		
• Look for opportunities to address density, as this is a significant concept for the ILSE.	PS10	45

How to Answer NYS Test Questions

This book was created for New York students like you. Each lesson, question, and problem will help you review the tested New York State Learning Standards and do well on the Grade 8 Intermediate-Level Science Test. In this section you will learn about the Grade 8 Intermediate-Level Science Test, test taking tips, and how to answer questions just like those on the test.

About the Grade 8 Intermediate-Level Science Test

New York educators have developed the New York State Learning Standards for Science. These standards spell out what all students at each grade level should know as well as what will be tested on the Grade 8 Intermediate-Level Science Test. The Grade 8 Intermediate-Level Science Test will show how well you have mastered the New York State Learning Standards for Science.

The Grade 8 Intermediate-Level Science Test will be administered in two parts. Part I consists of 45 multiple-choice questions. Part II consists of 36 open-ended questions. You will have two hours to complete the whole test.

Check out the Commonly Used Units page in the back of the book. Also check out the grading rubric in this book for the open-ended questions so you know what is expected of you on test day. This rubric explains what is expected of you on each open-ended question. Understanding this rubric will increase your score on the Grade 8 Intermediate-Level Science Test!

NYS Test Tips

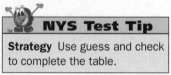

NYS Test Tip

Strategy Use guess and check to complete the table.

Throughout this book, you will find little boxes that look like this:

These **NYS Test Tips** help you think about the test and focus on certain lesson skills. Here are some other things you should keep in mind, both on and before test day:

✓ Get a good night's sleep and make sure you eat a healthy breakfast.

✓ Make sure to read through all directions and questions and identify important facts.

✓ Skip questions you don't know and then go back—and remember, there is no penalty for guessing.

✓ Use workspace to draw pictures, if necessary.

✓ Understand the grading rubric for open-ended questions.

✓ Wear a watch. Keep track of time so that you finish the whole test.

How to Answer Multiple-Choice Questions

A multiple-choice question has two parts. The first part is the stem, or question. It has a number in front of it. The second part is made up of the answer choices. Each answer choice has a number in parentheses, (1), (2), (3), or (4), in front of it. You will be asked to read each question and then circle the number for the best answer.

Some of the multiple-choice questions have a graph or table. You will need to read information from the graph or table to solve the problem. Other questions may have a picture or diagram. You will need to take a careful look at the image to help answer the question.

Hydroelectric Power Plant

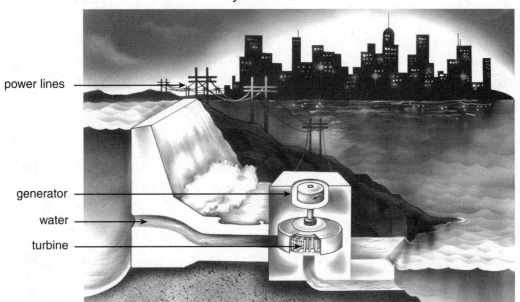

In this system, when does motion occur so that energy is produced?

(1) when the force of the dam is greater than the force of the water

(2) when gravity releases the pressure to power the generator

(3) when water flows through a duct in the dam and around the turbine

(4) when gravity allows the turbine to pull water to power the generator

By studying the image, you can see that the water is flowing through a duct around the turbine, causing it to turn. So (3) is the correct answer.

How to Answer NYS Test Questions

Here are some specific NYS Test tips for answering multiple-choice questions:

- Try to answer the question without looking at the answer choices. Once you have answered the question, compare your answer with the answer choices.

- Eliminate answer choices you know are wrong. Then choose from the answers that are left.

- Some questions will be more difficult than others. The problem may require an extra step, or you may need to eliminate the answer choices that do not apply.

- Even if you don't know the answer, you can get the right answer by making a good guess based on what you know.

- Check and double-check your answers before you turn in the test. Be sure of your answers.

Higher-Order Thinking Skills

The Grade 8 Intermediate-Level Science Test is designed to tap your higher-order thinking skills. When you use higher-order thinking skills, you do more than just recall information. For example, instead of being asked to name the parts of the circulatory system, you might need to describe how this system functions and affects the body of a living organism.

Measuring Up Express™ helps you develop and apply your higher-order thinking skills by providing questions like those you will see on the Grade 8 Intermediate-Level Science Test on every NYS Test Practice page. In addition, extra practice for H.O.T.S. pages are included in each chapter to build your stamina to answer tough Grade 8 Intermediate-Level Science Test-like questions.

How to Answer Open-Ended Questions

The open-ended questions on the Grade 8 Intermediate-Level Science Test require that you use your science and critical-thinking skills to develop an in-depth response. It is very important that you read the question carefully and completely before you begin to answer it. You may need to draw conclusions about science, show your work, and explain why and how you found your answers.

Here is an example of an open-ended question and how it should be answered.

How does the pancreas play a role in more than one body system? [2]

As part of the digestive system, the pancreas secretes digestive enzymes. The enzymes are involved in the breakdown of starches, fats, and proteins. As part of the endocrine system, the pancreas secretes hormones. The hormones, insulin and glucagon, regulate the level of glucose (sugar) in the blood.

Here are specific NYS Test tips for answering open-ended questions.

- Read the question carefully and completely. Make sure you understand what the question is asking. Think about what information you need to answer the question.

- Draw a picture to help you model the problem.

- Check the directions to be sure that you are doing what is required, such as showing your work, explaining how you found your answer, or writing your answer in the correct form.

- Reread the question to make sure you are answering what is asked. This is especially important if the question has more than one step.

- When you show your work, include labels such as measurement units. This helps you keep track of what you are doing and makes it easier to check your work when you are finished. When you explain how you found your answer or why you did each step, make the explanation complete, clear, and easy to understand.

- If you can't answer the whole question, answer any parts that you can. Partial credit is usually given even if you don't explain everything. Explain everything you can.

- When you are finished, reread the question, your answer, and your explanation. Be sure you have answered all parts of the question completely and correctly.

- Check that your explanation is easy to understand. Will someone else understand what you wrote? Did you leave anything out? Use all the time you have left to check and recheck your work and your explanation.

Higher-Order Performance Tasks

There is a section in each chapter called Higher-Order Performance Tasks. In this section, you will be performing short hands-on experiments, based on skills you have learned throughout that particular chapter. Higher-Order Performance Tasks give you practice in performing classroom experiments using short-response questions and data tables and creating drawings. Higher-Order Performance Tasks assess your skills in using hands-on equipment and materials and safety precautions in your responses to the questions posed.

You will learn a lot in Measuring Up Express™ *for the New York State Test*. You will review and practice the tested New York State Learning Standards. You will practice for the Grade 8 Intermediate-Level Science Test. Finally, you will build your confidence in being able to answer tough questions. You will more than measure up. You'll be a smashing success!

SAFETY FIRST

This book contains various investigations and activities that demonstrate the concepts in Measuring Up Express™ *for the New York State Test*. Following standard safety practices is an important laboratory procedure.

Before You Experiment

1. Make sure your teacher or another adult is present to supervise your work.

2. Read the instructions for each science activity before you begin.

3. Wear the safety equipment that your teacher tells you to. If your hair is long, tie your hair back.

During an Experiment

4. Follow the instructions step-by-step in the order that they are presented.

5. Never run in a lab or play games during an experiment.

6. Do not bring food or drink into the lab or classroom.

7. Check to see that all containers are labeled so you know what substances they hold.

8. Substances used in experiments can be dangerous. Only taste them or smell them if your teacher tells you to.

9. Mix ingredients only as your activity instructs. Playing with these ingredients may create dangerous substances.

10. Remember, knives and scissors are sharp. Move the knife or scissors away from your body when you are cutting.

11. Accidents do occur. Someone may be hurt or something may be broken. Immediately tell your teacher or the adult supervising your work.

After the Experiment Is Done

12. Ask your teacher what to do with unused ingredients and containers.

13. Follow your teacher's instructions to clean up your work area.

14. Make sure you turn off all lights, switches, burners, and faucets.

Common Safety Equipment Symbols

	Safety goggles must be worn		Use electrical safety guidelines
	Gloves must be worn		Do not use an open flame
	Protective clothing must be worn		Poisonous chemicals

Chapter 1

Focus on the NYS Learning Standards

Lesson 1   Lab Safety

S2.1a	Demonstrate appropriate safety techniques.
S2.2a	Include appropriate safety procedures.
S2.3a	Use appropriate safety procedures.

It is important to use chemicals and equipment safely while conducting field and laboratory investigations.

An **investigation** is a study or experiment done to learn more about a natural object or event. Some investigations can be dangerous if they are not done safely. There are risks in handling some types of chemicals, hot objects, and glass equipment. Always get your teacher's permission before starting an investigation. If an accident happens during an investigation, immediately tell your teacher. Many investigations have instructions that include safety symbols. Some important symbols are shown in the table.

Common Safety Equipment Symbols

	Safety goggles must be worn		Use electrical safety guidelines
	Gloves must be worn		Do not use an open flame
	Protective clothing must be worn		Poisonous chemicals

You should also follow these general guidelines when you are doing an investigation:

1. Wear required safety equipment for a lab (goggles, apron, gloves, etc.) at all times unless you are told to remove them. Follow your teacher's instructions.

2. Know where safety equipment, such as fire blankets, fire extinguishers, and eyewash fountains, is located. Be sure you know how to operate the equipment.

3. Avoid loose clothing and dangling jewelry to avoid knocking over equipment. Tie back long hair. Do not wear sandals or other open shoes in the laboratory.

4. Check equipment for damage before using it. Chipped or cracked glassware could break when heated. Check electrical equipment for frayed cords. Choose appropriate tools for the investigation. For example, if you are asked to heat a beaker, the beaker must be tempered glass, not plastic.

5. When working with chemicals, follow each step in the investigation carefully. Never mix chemicals unless specifically instructed by your teacher. Never taste, touch, or smell any chemical unless your teacher tells you to do so. If you must record the odor of a reaction, use your hand to waft the odor to your nose. Do not eat or drink anything in the science lab. Food may be contaminated with chemicals.

6. When working in the field, do not approach any animal or touch any animal or plant without your teacher's permission.

7. Always wash your hands with soap and warm water after completing an investigation.

Directions (1–8): Decide which choice is the best answer. Circle the number of the answer you have chosen.

1   While a student is using a thermometer during an investigation, the thermometer breaks. What is the first thing the student should do?

(1) Wearing gloves, the student should carefully sweep up and discard the glass.

(2) The student should immediately notify the teacher.

(3) The student should warn classmates about the broken glass on the floor.

(4) The student should get a new thermometer for the investigation.

2   While doing a field investigation, a student notices an unusual insect. What should the student do?

(1) Trap the insect under a jar in order to identify it.

(2) Show the insect to other students.

(3) Carefully pick up the insect and take it to the teacher.

(4) Do not touch it, and notify the teacher.

3   A lamp you need to use during a science investigation has a loose plug. What should you do?

(1) Use it anyway, but be careful not to touch the loose plug.

(2) Wrap some electrical tape around the plug.

(3) Take it to your teacher and get another lamp.

(4) Exchange it for a lamp from another lab group.

4   A student reads the instructions for an investigation. The investigation has the safety symbol shown below.

What precautions should the student take during the investigation?

(1) The student should not use an open flame during the investigation.

(2) The student should wear the fire blanket while doing the investigation.

(3) The student should not use any chemicals in the investigation.

(4) The student should keep a fire extinguisher nearby during the investigation.

5   A student is doing an investigation that involves heating chemicals. Which behavior should the student avoid while working in the laboratory?

NYS Test Tip

Safety Before starting any science investigation, first read all the steps.

(1) wearing protective latex gloves

(2) using a hand to waft the odor to the nose

(3) eating a breath mint

(4) choosing glass test tubes

6   A student is writing the steps to a laboratory investigation and does not include a symbol for safety goggles. Which items will the investigation most likely involve?

(1) paper and pencil

(2) sharp objects

(3) chemicals

(4) heating devices

7   A student is conducting an investigation that involves the use of chemicals. While in the laboratory, the student should avoid

(1) asking the teacher for help

(2) taking notes with a pen

(3) drinking a soda

(4) using water to wash glassware

8   A student reads the instructions for an investigation. The investigation has the safety symbol shown below.

The safety symbol tells the student to

(1) dim the lights in the laboratory

(2) follow electrical safety guidelines

(3) avoid using electricity during the investigation

(4) plug in the electrical equipment at the lab station

Directions (9–11): Record your answers on the lines provided below each question.

9   Why is it important to understand safety symbols?   [1]

_____

_____

10   What should you do after completing an investigation?   [1]

> **NYS Test Tip**
> **Comprehension** Pay attention to each symbol and make sure you know what each symbol stands for.

_____

11   Describe the safety symbol that should be included in the directions for an investigation that involves poisonous chemicals.   [1]

_____

_____

Focus on the NYS Learning Standards

Lesson 2 Scientific Processes

M1.1a	Identify independent and dependent variables.
S1.1a	Formulate questions about natural phenomena.
S1.1b	Identify appropriate references to investigate a question.
S1.1c	Refine and clarify questions so that they are subject to scientific investigation.
S1.2a	Independently formulate a hypothesis.

Understand that a scientific process is an organized way to answer questions about nature that includes making observations and conducting experiments.

Scientific processes describe the procedures scientists use to learn more about the natural world. Such processes begin with **observations**. When you make an observation, you use your senses to gather information about the world.

Observations often lead to questions. A question that can be investigated through scientific processes is a **scientific question.** Unlike other questions, a scientific question has an answer that can be discovered through investigation. The answer to a scientific question does not depend on opinions and it is not a fact that can be researched in a book.

To begin investigating a scientific question, you should conduct research. You can begin your research by visiting the reference section of your library. There are encyclopedias and scientific periodicals such as magazines and journals. Periodicals are published regularly, so new information is always available. You will be able to find published works of scientists because they share their results with each other. These articles will provide detailed examples of investigations that other scientists have performed.

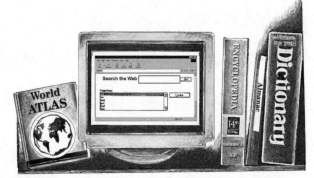

The Internet is another resource you can use to conduct research. You will be able to find a lot of information on the Internet, but not all of it will be useful or correct information. It can be difficult to determine which sources are reliable because anyone can post information there. Web sites ending in -.org or -.edu usually contain trustworthy information because they are maintained by government organizations or schools. Academic journals online are also reliable. However, blogs, forums, and personal Web sites are not always reliable because there is no way to know if the information they present is accurate.

Based on what you discover, you may refine or clarify your question to be more specific. Then you can use your research to try to formulate a **hypothesis,** or a possible answer to the question you have asked. A hypothesis relates to factors, or **variables,** that you want to consider. For example, a possible hypothesis might be "Crickets chirp more frequently as temperature rises." This hypothesis relates the frequency of chirps to temperature.

The variable that you change is known as the **independent variable**. In this case, the independent variable is temperature. The variable that changes in response to the independent variable is the **dependent variable.** The number of chirps is the dependent variable. Once you have your hypothesis, you can design an investigation to test your hypothesis.

Copying is illegal. Measuring Up Express™ for the New York State Test

Directions (1–8): Decide which choice is the best answer. Circle the number of the answer you have chosen.

1 When you formulate a hypothesis to answer a scientific question, you do not necessarily

  (1) make an educated guess

  (2) provide a possible answer

  (3) come up with a correct answer

  (4) relate independent and dependent variables

2 Which is not a reliable source of information related to a scientific question?

  (1) a newspaper article

  (2) a novel

  (3) a scientific magazine

  (4) a research journal

3 Which sentence could be a valid hypothesis?

  (1) Scientists like to perform experiments to find out about nature.

  (2) Sponges are the only animals that do not have emotions.

  (3) The heart pumps blood throughout the body.

  (4) The speed of sound through metal increases with temperature.

4 A student hypothesizes that polishing a bowling ball will cause it to roll faster. What is the dependent variable in this hypothesis?

  (1) the speed of the bowling ball

  (2) the length of the bowling lane

  (3) the shininess of the bowling ball

  (4) the surface of the bowling lane

5 Which is a good scientific question related to observations about ice melting?

  (1) Does juice taste better with ice in it?

  (2) Does the size of an ice cube affect how long it takes to melt?

  (3) Do people prefer round ice to square ice?

  (4) How does a freezer cause water to form ice?

6 You might refine or clarify a question you have asked about the natural world so that

  (1) it can be subject to scientific investigation

  (2) you can find the answer in a textbook

  (3) there is no single answer

  (4) no one else will ask the same question

7 What is the common goal of all scientists?

  (1) to learn how to build colonies in space

  (2) to write articles about plants and animals

  (3) to build trains that use magnets to move

  (4) to learn more about some part of the natural world

8 Which sentence could be a valid hypothesis?

  (1) Why do Canada geese fly south for the winter?

  (2) Two objects dropped from the same height will hit the ground simultaneously.

  (3) Put 30 mL of sulfuric acid into a beaker.

  (4) An electric motor involves electricity and magnetism.

Directions (9–11): Record your answers on the lines provided below each question.

9 How is a hypothesis related to a scientific question? [1]

_____

_____

10 You observe that your dog barks when someone knocks on the door, but not when your mother opens the door with a key. Write a question and a hypothesis you might formulate based on this observation. [2]

_____

_____

11 A student wants to test the following hypothesis:

"A tomato plant that receives warm water will grow taller than a tomato plant that receives cold water."

Identify the independent and dependent variables. [1]

_____

_____

Focus on the NYS Learning Standards

Lesson 3 — Designing and Performing Experiments

S2.1c	Design and conduct an experiment to test a hypothesis.
S2.2b	Design scientific investigations.
S2.2c	Design a simple controlled experiment.
S2.2d	Identify independent variables, dependent variables, and constants in a simple controlled experiment.

S2.1b, S2.1d, S2.2e, S2.3b, S2.3c, IPS 1.3, IPS 1.4, IPS 2.1

In order to test a hypothesis, you need to design and perform a controlled experiment.

Recall from Lesson 2 that a hypothesis is a possible answer to a scientific question. To design an experiment to test your hypothesis, you need to change the independent variable and observe the dependent variable. An experiment in which you change only the independent variable is known as a **controlled experiment**. Every other factor must be held constant.

Consider an experiment in which you are investigating how temperature affects the growth rate of bacteria. You would change the temperature during the experiment. Temperature would be your manipulated variable. As you change temperature, you might measure the number of bacteria in a culture. The number of bacteria at each temperature is the dependent variable. Every other factor would be held constant. These might include the amount of light the bacteria receive, the nutrients they receive, and the container in which they are held. Factors that are kept the same are called **constants**.

To be sure any changes you observed in the dependent variable were because of the independent variable, you need to have a group with which you can compare your results. The group used for comparison is known as the **control group**.

Any information that you collect during a controlled experiment is known as **data**. Some data, known as **quantitative data**, consists of numbers resulting from measurements. Quantitative data might include the number of bacteria at a certain temperature. Other data, known as **qualitative data**, is made up of general descriptions. Qualitative data might describe the color or appearance of the bacteria.

Once you design the experiment, you need to repeat each trial several times to be sure you have not made an error. You can then average the results. You must also decide on the size of your sample. Whether you choose a large sample or a smaller sample may affect your results.

In order to collect your data, you need to choose the appropriate tools. For example, you might choose a microscope to observe small objects. You would choose a thermometer to measure temperature, a ruler to measure length, a graduated cylinder to measure volume, and a balance to measure mass. You would also have to choose the correct units of measurement. Your choices depend on the kinds of variables you are measuring.

NYS Test Practice

Directions (1–8): Decide which choice is the best answer. Circle the number of the answer you have chosen.

1   A student wants to find out whether tomato plants grow better under different kinds of artificial light than in sunlight. Which table would have resulted from the setup providing the most useful results?

(1)
Type of Light	Amount of Light per Day	Amount of Water per Day	Air Temp
sunlight	16 hours	$\frac{1}{4}$ cup	25°C
fluorescent light	16 hours	$\frac{1}{4}$ cup	25°C
ultraviolet light	16 hours	$\frac{1}{4}$ cup	25°C

(2)
Type of Light	Amount of Light per Day	Amount of Water per Day	Air Temp
sunlight	16 hours	$\frac{1}{2}$ cup	25°C
fluorescent light	16 hours	$\frac{1}{4}$ cup	25°C
ultraviolet light	16 hours	$\frac{1}{8}$ cup	25°C

(3)
Type of Light	Amount of Light per Day	Amount of Water per Day	Air Temp
sunlight	16 hours	$\frac{1}{4}$ cup	30°C
fluorescent light	16 hours	$\frac{1}{4}$ cup	25°C
ultraviolet light	16 hours	$\frac{1}{4}$ cup	20°C

(4)
Type of Light	Amount of Light per Day	Amount of Water per Day	Air Temp
sunlight	16 hours	$\frac{1}{2}$ cup	30°C
fluorescent light	16 hours	$\frac{1}{4}$ cup	25°C
ultraviolet light	16 hours	$\frac{1}{8}$ cup	20°C

2   You are conducting an investigation about the Moon. Which tool would be the most useful in observing the craters on the Moon?

(1) microscope

(2) telescope

(3) hand lens

(4) computer

3   Which is an example of qualitative data?

(1) The rock is smooth.

(2) The rock is black.

(3) The rock has a mass of 124 g.

(4) The rock is made up of layers.

4   How can you make the results of an investigation more reliable?

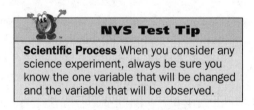

NYS Test Tip

Scientific Process When you consider any science experiment, always be sure you know the one variable that will be changed and the variable that will be observed.

(1) Use several independent variables.

(2) Repeat trials of an investigation.

(3) Do not prevent any variables from changing.

(4) Do not measure the dependent variable.

5 You are conducting an investigation to test the hypothesis, "Oranges from indoor trees produce more juice than outdoor trees do." Which tool can you use to measure the dependent variable?

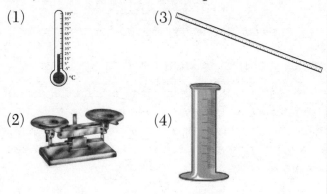

(1)

(3)

(2)

(4)

6 You want to find out how temperature affects the rate of dissolving sugar. Which is a variable that should not be held constant during the experiment?

(1) the amount of sugar

(2) the amount of water

(3) the temperature of the water

(4) the type of sugar

7 A student hypothesizes that the rate at which a plant grows is directly related to the length of sunlight it receives. What would be the independent variable in an experiment to test her hypothesis?

(1) the number of hours of sunlight the plant receives

(2) the type of plant used

(3) the height of the plant over time

(4) the amount of water the plant receives

8 A student conducts an experiment to find out if the density of liquids changes with temperature. The student performs the experiment twice, but gets very different results. What should the student do?

(1) Use the lower measurement.

(2) Accept the results of the first trial.

(3) Choose the expected results.

(4) Perform the experiment more times.

Directions (9–10): Record your answers on the lines provided below each question.

9 Why is it important for scientists to choose the proper tools when conducting experiments? [1]

_____

_____

_____

_____

10 You hypothesize that warm water freezes faster than cold water. Describe an experiment you could perform to test your hypothesis. [1]

_____

_____

Lesson 4 — Displaying Data

S3.1a	Organize results, using appropriate graphs, diagrams, data tables, and other models to show relationships.
S3.1b	Generate and use scales, create legends, and appropriately label axes.
S3.2h	Use and interpret graphs and data tables.

M3.1a, ICT 5.2, IPS 2.1

Learn to display data in the way that makes it easiest to interpret.

In your investigation, you will collect data to test your hypothesis. Data is a crucial part of an investigation. After you collect and record data, you will analyze the information collected, to draw conclusions that will tell you whether or not your hypothesis is correct. Most scientists find it very helpful to present their data visually with graphs. The graphs help make it easier to observe any patterns or trends in the data.

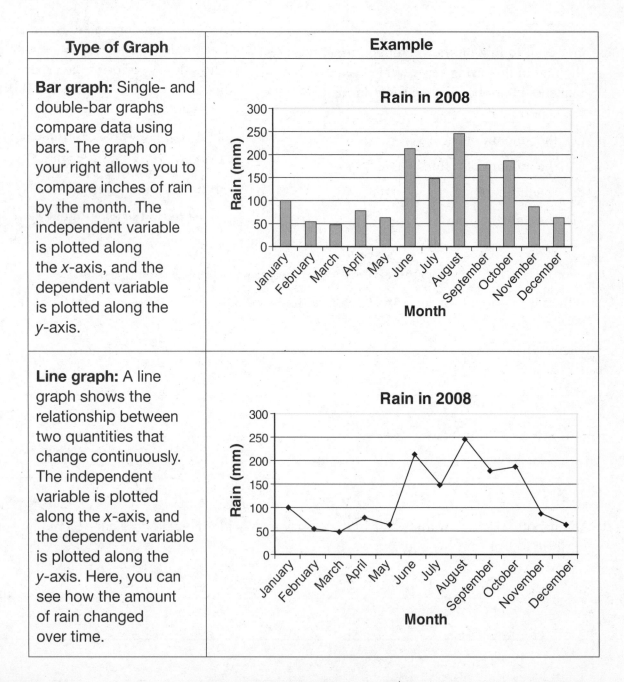

Type of Graph	Example
Bar graph: Single- and double-bar graphs compare data using bars. The graph on your right allows you to compare inches of rain by the month. The independent variable is plotted along the *x*-axis, and the dependent variable is plotted along the *y*-axis.	*Rain in 2008* (bar graph showing Rain (mm) by Month)
Line graph: A line graph shows the relationship between two quantities that change continuously. The independent variable is plotted along the *x*-axis, and the dependent variable is plotted along the *y*-axis. Here, you can see how the amount of rain changed over time.	*Rain in 2008* (line graph showing Rain (mm) by Month)

Type of Graph	Example
Scattergram: A scattergram shows how two variables relate to each other. All data in a scattergram needs to be quantitative, or numerical, so in the graph on your right, the months are expressed numbers, from 1 to 12. Unlike a bar graph, which shows differences in data, a scattergram is used to show any similarities that may exist.	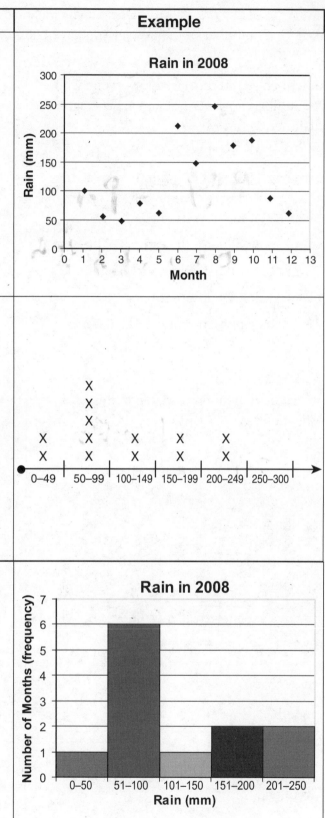
Line plot: Frequency tells how often something happens. Scientists often use frequency to organize data, and a line plot is one way to show frequency. However, line plots are usually used only when there are less than 50 data points and they can only show the frequency of data for one variable. The line plot on your right shows frequency of data in terms of rain.	
Histogram: A histogram is another way to show frequency. Histograms can be used to summarize huge amounts of data and they can show frequency for two variables. One variable is put into groups. In the graph on your right, the millimeters of rain have been grouped, making it easier to summarize data. Looking at the histogram, you can see that most months receive between 51 mm and 100 mm of rain.	

Directions (1–6): Decide which choice is the best answer. Circle the number of the answer you have chosen.

1   A student collected the ages of everyone who signed up for a yoga class at a gym. The ages in the data set consist of:

10, 8, 15, 19, 14, 22, 45, 25, 17

The student makes a histogram to display the data. If the student used intervals of 5 years of age, which statement is true?

(1) Four bars will have the same height.

(2) Every bar will have the same height.

(3) There will be 9 different bars.

(4) Two bars will each represent one person.

2   Which is the dependent variable in this investigation?

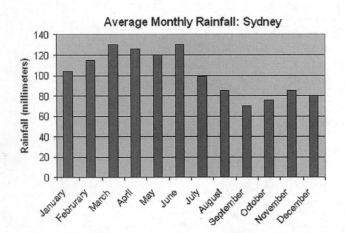

Average Monthly Rainfall: Sydney

(1) month

(2) Sydney

(3) amount of rainfall

(4) frequency of rain

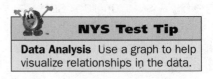

NYS Test Tip

Data Analysis Use a graph to help visualize relationships in the data.

3   The table below shows data zoologists collected when they tracked a group of wildebeests over several years.

Year	Average Distance Traveled (miles)
2003	500
2004	452
2005	546
2006	515
2007	25
2008	487

The zoologists want to make a line graph of the data. What might they conclude from the graph?

(1) Wildebeests like to travel.

(2) Data was incorrectly recorded in 2007.

(3) Data was incorrectly recorded in 2005.

(4) Wildebeests didn't travel too much in 2007.

4   A group of students participate in an extended project to study the health of a group of patients. The scatterplot below is part of their results.

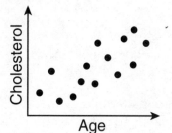

What does each point on the scatterplot represent?

(1) the number of students who conducted the study

(2) the number of people in the study and their cholesterol levels

(3) the number of people in the study and their ages

(4) the cholesterol level and age of each person

5   Which type of graph would be best to display the distance traveled by a turtle over the course of 15 minutes?

(1) line graph   (3) scatterplot

(2) histogram   (4) line plot

6   A student displayed the data she collected in a double bar graph. Which data might she have collected?

(1) the amount of water vapor the atmosphere can hold at different temperatures

(2) the length of daylight during each of 12 months

(3) the average temperature in two cities during four months

(4) the chemical elements that make up a sample of ocean water

Directions (7–8): Record your answers on the lines provided below each question.

7   A student recorded the data in the table.

Sample	Mass (g)	Volume (g³)
1	1	0.14
2	5	0.70
3	10	1.40
4	15	2.10
5	20	2.80
6	25	3.5

Which type of graph would be best for displaying the data? Why? [1]

_____

_____

8   In what way can a computer be useful in displaying data? [1]

_____

M1.1b	Identify relationships among variables including: direct, indirect, cyclic, constant.
M1.1c	Apply mathematical equations to describe relationships among variables in the natural world.
S1.2c	Differentiate among observations, inferences, predictions, and explanations.
S3.2h	Use and interpret graphs and data tables.

M2.1a, M2.1b, S1.3, S3.2a, S3.2b, S3.2c, IPS 1.3, IPS 2.1

Explain how scientists analyze and interpret data to make inferences, draw conclusions, and make predictions.

To **analyze** means to interpret and evaluate data by breaking down its elements. For example, suppose you repeat an investigation several times and get different results each time. You might analyze each step in your procedure and decide which step could have caused the differences.

After analyzing data, scientists **draw conclusions** or make decisions about whether the data supports the hypothesis. A *conclusion* is a data-based decision to accept or reject a hypothesis.

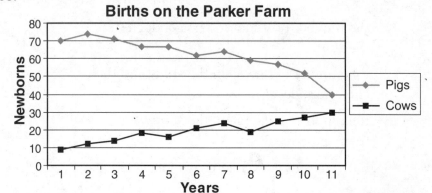

Scientists try to identify relationships among variables. In a **direct** relationship, one variable changes in the same direction as another. As one variable increases, the other increases. In an **indirect** relationship, the variables change in opposite ways. As one variable increases, the other decreases. In a **cyclic** relationship, one variable increases and then decreases in a repeating pattern. In a **constant** relationship, one variable stays the same as the other increases.

Sometimes scientists can use an **equation** to describe a mathematical relationship among variables. For example, speed $= \frac{\text{distance}}{\text{time}}$ is an equation that relates the speed of an object to the distance it travels in a certain amount of time.

An **inference** is a logical conclusion based on evidence. Scientists limit their inferences and conclusions to the tested conditions.

Evidence is proof or information on which a conclusion can be based. *Direct* evidence is clear and requires no assumptions about cause and effect. For example, a rise in temperature is direct evidence. *Indirect* evidence relies on an inference. For example, the temperature rose because a chemical reaction took place.

To **extrapolate** means to estimate or infer data beyond a given set of data. Extrapolation is often used to make predictions. To **interpolate** means to estimate or infer data between given data points. A **prediction** is a statement about what will happen in the future based on observations and experiences.

An **explanation** is a description of why or how something occurred, based on the data. Scientists must understand how the data was obtained in order to develop an explanation. Keep in mind that scientists must look for any errors in the data and be aware of its limitations as they develop an explanation. Scientists communicate their results in science journals, Web sites, or books to inform other scientists around the world so that the results can be further verified or expanded.

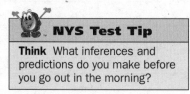

NYS Test Practice   *Directions* (1–6): Decide which choice is the best answer. Circle the number of the answer you have chosen.

1   A student counts the number of earthworms on the surface of a plot of grass each day for several months. The student notices that there are more earthworms after rainy days than after dry days. Which inference can the student make based on his observation?

> **NYS Test Tip**
>
> **Think** What inferences and predictions do you make before you go out in the morning?

(1)   Dry weather causes earthworms to reproduce.

(2)   Dry weather causes earthworms to eat more soil.

(3)   Rain causes earthworms to hide underground.

(4)   Rain causes earthworms to come to the surface.

2   While sitting under a certain lamp, a student observes that the teacher's voice is louder and clearer. After the student moves to another seat, the teacher's voice is not as loud and clear. The student does this several times with the same result. The student concludes that the lamp affects the sound of the teacher's voice. How would you evaluate this conclusion?

(1)   It is probably correct because the student did the test several times.

(2)   It is correct, assuming that the teacher always stood in the same place.

(3)   It may be incorrect because the student didn't consider the distance from the teacher.

(4)   It is incorrect because light and sound are energy.

Base your answers to questions 3 and 4 on the information below and on your knowledge of science.

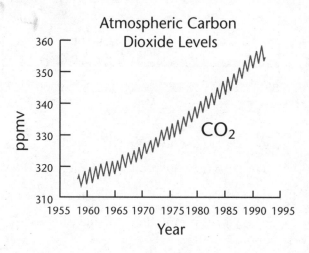

3   Which is a valid conclusion you might draw from the data on the graph?

(1)   The levels of carbon dioxide will continue to rise in coming years.

(2)   Some variable caused an increase in carbon dioxide levels between 1955 and 1995.

(3)   Carbon dioxide is the most abundant gas in the atmosphere.

(4)   There was no carbon dioxide in the atmosphere before 1955.

4   Based on the graph, a scientist states that, unless factors change, carbon dioxide levels in the atmosphere will continue to rise. Which steps in the scientific process led directly to this statement?

(1)   observation and analysis

(2)   measurement and communication

(3)   organizing data and evaluation

(4)   extrapolation and prediction

5   The graph below shows world population growth over the last 300 years. What will occur if the trend continues?

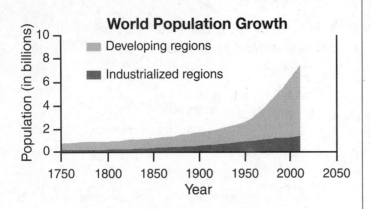

World Population Growth

Developing regions

Industrialized regions

Population (in billions)

Year

(1) The world population will increase.

(2) The world population will decrease.

(3) The world population will rise and then fall.

(4) The world population will stay the same.

6   A group of students participated in a study of bacteria. They used electronic probes and computers to collect the data shown in the table.

Temperature (degrees Celsius)	Time for population to double (minutes)
10	124
15	55
20	39
25	23
30	14
35	12
40	17

Based on the trend shown in the data, what conclusion can the students reach?

(1) Bacteria multiply most slowly at 20°.

(2) Bacteria multiply most rapidly at 35°.

(3) Bacteria multiply most rapidly at 40°.

(4) Bacteria multiply most slowly at 15°.

Directions (7–8): Record your answers on the lines provided below each question.

7   Why is it important to accurately describe the procedures used to gather data?   [1]

_____

_____

_____

_____

8   How does a direct relationship differ from an indirect relationship? Give an example of each.   [2]

_____

_____

_____

_____

_____

Focus on the NYS Learning Standards | Lesson 6 — Evaluating Scientific Conclusions

S1.4	Seek to clarify, to assess critically, and to reconcile with their own thinking the ideas presented by others.
S3.2d	Formulate and defend explanations and conclusions as they relate to scientific phenomena.
S3.2e	Form and defend a logical argument about cause-and-effect relationships in an investigation.
S3.2f, S3.2g, S3.3	

Use critical thinking to evaluate scientific explanations and to analyze scientific claims.

A **theory** is a widely accepted scientific explanation for something that happens in nature. A scientific theory is not an opinion or a guess. Scientists develop theories based on large amounts of data over a long period of time. An opinion is based on someone's feelings or state of mind. A theory can be tested, but an opinion cannot. Scientific theories cannot be proven right. They often change as new data or evidence becomes available.

A **bias** is an opinion or a point of view that is highly personal or based on a belief that is not supported by evidence. A person with a bias might distort information or evidence in order to support his or her interests or beliefs. There are even some scientists who have changed their data to support a hypothesis in which they strongly believed. There is no place for biases in science.

Reproducibility describes how alike the results of an experiment are when reproduced by different scientists using the same method and substances. One important way to avoid bias is to have several people repeat an experiment. Scientists should be able to reproduce the results. Experiments in which scientists changed their data were discovered when other scientists tried to reproduce their results and could not.

A **claim** is a statement about what a product can do. It is not always a fact.

Empirical evidence is evidence acquired through direct observation in a controlled experiment. The results are reported in well-defined units of measure. Quantitative data is preferred to qualitative data. In critiquing a scientific claim, the most important question is what empirical evidence supports the claim.

Skepticism is an attitude of questioning or doubt. A *skeptic* is a person who requires empirical evidence and proof before believing a claim.

Critical thinking includes analyzing, reviewing, and critiquing scientific explanations you come across before you accept the explanations as fact. Many advertisements are biased. Some make claims that sound scientific but are not. For example, advertisers will make claims such as "Tests have shown that Product A is twice as effective as Product B." Ask questions such as "What tests?", "Who did them?", "How were the tests conducted?", and "Twice as effective as what?"

NYS Test Practice

Directions (1–5): Decide which choice is the best answer. Circle the number of the answer you have chosen.

1 Which is *not* an example of a scientific theory?

(1) Gravity keeps the planets orbiting the Sun.

(2) The Moon formed when an asteroid collided with Earth.

(3) Earth is the best planet in the solar system.

(4) Earth's crust contains plates that move.

2 A beverage company advertises that its product is good for people on a diet because it contains only 100 calories per serving.

Nutrition Info

Serving size 8 fl oz (240 mL)
Servings per 20 fl oz container: 25

	Per Serving		Per Container	
	8 fl oz	%DV*	20 fl oz	%DV*
Calories	100	-	250	-
Total Fat (g)	0	0	0	0
Sodium (mg)	20	1	50	2
Total Carbs (g)	28	9	69	23
Sugars (g)	28	-	69	-
Protein (g)	0	-	0	-
Potassium (mg)	10	0	20	1
Phosphorus (mg)	36	-	89	-

Not a significant source of other nutrients.
* Percent Daily Values (DV) are based on a 2,000 calorie diet.

Based on the label above, how would you evaluate the company's claim?

(1) The claim is not deceptive because it's up to the person to count calories.

(2) The claim is not deceptive because one serving does contain 100 calories.

(3) The claim is deceptive because the beverage actually contains 250 calories per serving.

(4) The claim is deceptive because many people assume that a bottle is one serving.

3 Which question would be the least helpful in deciding if a scientist's claims are true?

(1) Have any other scientists reproduced the experiment?

(2) Where was the experiment performed?

(3) What procedure did the scientist use?

(4) What will the scientist gain from the experiment?

4 A television advertisement claims that a new pill will help people lose weight without changing their diet or exercising. Which type of scientific thinking will be most valuable in evaluating this claim?

(1) open-mindedness

(2) prediction

(3) inference

(4) skepticism

5   At one time, scientists believed that objects expanded when heated because heat was a fluid that took up space. Today, scientists believe that matter expands because particles in matter move faster when heated. Which statement is true?

NYS Test Tip

Strategy Monitor your own biases when doing an investigation.

(1) The first idea must have been an opinion because no one experimented.

(2) The first idea was a hypothesis because it was proved to be false.

(3) The first idea was a scientific theory that changed when new information became available.

(4) The second idea was the only scientific theory because experiments proved it true.

Directions (6–7): Record your answers on the lines provided below each question.

6   What should scientists do when similar investigations give different results? [1]

_____

_____

_____

_____

7   What would cause part or all of a theory to change? [1]

_____

_____

Lesson 7   Making Scientific Models

S1.2b	Propose a model of a natural phenomenon.
ICT 2.1	Select an appropriate model to begin the search for answers or solutions to a question or problem.
ICT 2.2	Use models to study processes that cannot be studied directly.
ICT 2.3	Demonstrate the effectiveness of different models to represent the same thing and the same model to represent different things.
IS 1.5	Use simple modeling programs to make predictions.

Explain how scientists use models to study, describe, and understand the natural world.

There are different types of models in science. In general, a **model** is a representation of an object or a system. All types of models are useful to study processes that cannot be studied directly because they are too large, too small, too complex, too expensive, or too dangerous.

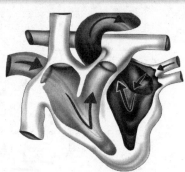

Type of Model	Description	Examples
Physical model	A physical model is an object that represents an event, a system, or another object. Many physical models are scale models.	globe; toy car; diagram of a human heart
Mathematical model	A mathematical model is made up of data and equations. Mathematical models may also involve graphs or charts. Many mathematical models are used to make predictions.	weather forecasting software, economic predictions; software; chemical equations
Computer model	A computer model is made up of data and equations. Many computer models include a visual of a physical structure or natural event. Computer models can illustrate change.	weather forecasting; geological events; structural drawings
Conceptual model	A conceptual model is a group or system of ideas. Many conceptual models explain observations. **Scientific theories** are conceptual models.	the theory of general relativity; the theory of evolution; the theory of plate tectonics

All types of models have some limitations. A **limitation** is a restriction, or limit, on the usefulness of a model. For example, a skeleton shows the bones in the body, but not the muscles that move the bones. A physical model of the solar system shows the distances among the Sun and planets, but doesn't show the forces that act on those bodies. Therefore, some conclusions, inferences, or predictions based on the model might be incorrect when applied to the actual structure.

NYS Test Practice

Directions (1–7): Decide which choice is the best answer. Circle the number of the answer you have chosen.

Base your answers to questions 1 and 2 on the diagram below and on your knowledge of science.

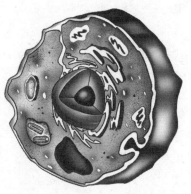

1   This model makes it easier to understand an animal cell because it shows

   (1) the exact shape and size of the cell

   (2) how every animal cell functions

   (3) what all animal cells look like

   (4) a larger version of something very small

2   Which is *not* a limitation of this cell model?

   (1) It shows the relative size of the cell parts.

   (2) It shows how the parts of a cell interact.

   (3) It doesn't have labels on the cell parts.

   (4) It shows only one type of predator.

3   Which statement about models is true?

   (1) Models always look exactly like what they represent.

   (2) Only one model is necessary to understand a particular object or process.

   (3) Models are always smaller than what they represent.

   (4) Models make it easier to study an object or process.

4   Physicists often describe electric current as being similar to water running through a pipe. Which aspect of electric current does this analogy model?

   (1) its consistency

   (2) its strength

   (3) its motion

   (4) its source

5   An engineer needs to make a model in order to test a new car design. She needs to test whether the new design will tip over when the car turns a corner. Which does the engineer's model probably *not* need to include?

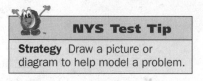

NYS Test Tip

Strategy Draw a picture or diagram to help model a problem.

   (1) the size of the car's tires

   (2) the shape of the car's body

   (3) the material that the car's seat covers are made of

   (4) the amount of force the car's engine can produce

6   A scientist wants to make a model that shows changes a scuba diver experiences while descending in ocean water. Which factor is most important to show in this model?

   (1) wind speed

   (2) water pressure

   (3) air temperature

   (4) soil thickness

7   How might using a computer help a scientist
     develop a more accurate model for the life cycle
     of a star?

     (1) A computer can show exactly how a star will
          change in the future.

     (2) A computer can represent long processes in
          short amounts of time.

     (3) A computer can determine what events
          occurred in the past.

     (4) A computer can bring objects closer so they
          can be viewed.

Directions (8–9): Record your answers on the lines provided below each question.

8   The diagram below shows a model of a helium atom.

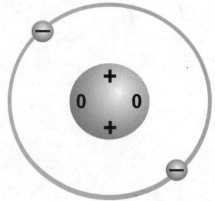

     Describe another way to make a model of a helium atom.   [1]

     _____

     _____

     _____

     _____

9   Why do scientists change models over time? Give an example.   [2]

     _____

     _____

     _____

     _____

Practice for H.O.T.S.

Directions (1–3): Decide which choice is the best answer. Circle the number of the answer you have chosen.

Base your answers to questions 1 and 2 on the information below and on your knowledge of science.

A scientist named Ivan Pavlov conducted an experiment in which he rang a bell each time food was presented to a group of dogs. He repeated this many times. Then, he rang the bell without presenting the food. Each time he observed the dogs to determine if they were drooling. After a while, the dogs drooled at the sound of the bell alone. Today, Pavlov's method is known as *classical conditioning*.

1 What might have been Pavlov's hypothesis?

   (1) Dogs can be trained to respond to a specific stimulus.

   (2) Dogs prefer dog food with meat rather than vegetables.

   (3) Dogs cannot hear the frequency of a bell ringing.

   (4) Dogs always drool before they eat.

2 What was the independent variable in Pavlov's experiment?

   (1) the type of dog food he used

   (2) the presence or absence of food

   (3) the ringing of a bell

   (4) the drooling of the dogs

3 A scientist would like to find out which color flower is most attractive to bees. The scientist designed an experiment where he placed potted flowers in a room with white walls, released twenty bees into the room, and counted how many times each bee visits each flower. A problem with the experiment's design is that

   (1) using more than one bee will cause the study to be biased

   (2) the experiment should be performed outside in natural light

   (3) using different flower types introduces more than one variable

   (4) the experiment is not controlled if more than one flower is used

Directions (4): Record your answer on the lines provided below the question.

4 The table shows data collected about the volcanoes in the Hawaiian Islands.

Ages and Locations of Hawaiian Island Volcanoes

Volcano	Distance from Kilauea (km)	Age (millions of years)
1	500	5
2	1,000	10
3	2,600	28
4	3,100	39

What would most likely be the age of a volcano that is 2,500 kilometers from Kilauea? [2]

Higher-Order Performance Task
Conduct an Investigation

Task:
You will conduct an investigation to see if salt affects the rate at which water boils.
To do this, you will use scientific tools, measure materials, and record data.

Materials:
- water
- graduated cylinder
- 2 beakers
- balance
- salt
- stirrer
- 2 hot plates
- timer

Directions:

1. Work with a partner to write a hypothesis to answer this question: Does salt affect the rate at which water boils?

   _____

2. Which of the materials listed for this activity would be best for measuring water?

   _____

   Work with a partner to measure exactly 200 mL of water into each beaker.
   Why is accuracy important when measuring the amount of water in each beaker?

   _____

   _____

3. Which of the materials listed for this activity would be best for measuring grams of salt?

   _____

   Work with a partner to measure 5 grams of salt. Add the salt to one beaker of water and stir the mixture.

4. Place the beaker of water without salt on one hot plate and the beaker of water with salt on the other hot plate. Turn on both hot plates at the same time. Have your partner start the timer as you turn on the hot plates. Do not touch the beakers, the water, or the surfaces of the hot plates once you have turned on the hot plates.

Copying is illegal.   Measuring Up Express™ for the New York State Test

5. Record the times at which the water in each beaker begins to boil in the table below under the head "Time Trial 1". Turn off the hot plates. Do not touch the beakers, the water, or the surfaces of the hot plates until they have cooled. Repeat the experiment two more times and record the data in the table. Then find the mean (average) of the three trials and record it in the last column.

Beaker	Time Trial 1	Time Trial 2	Time Trial 3	Time Average
Water without salt				
Water with salt				

Why is it important to keep honest and accurate data during an investigation?

_____

_____

_____

Why do you think you needed to repeat the experiment three times?

_____

6. Check the unit of time measurement (seconds or minutes) that you used in the chart. If it is not the most appropriate unit of measurement to use for this data, adjust it. Be sure to use the same unit of measurement for both beakers.

7. What was the outcome of this investigation?

_____

Did your findings support your hypothesis?

_____

_____

Why is a hypothesis valuable even if it is not completely correct?

_____

_____

_____

8. When you have finished, put all the materials back the way you found them. Clean up any spills.

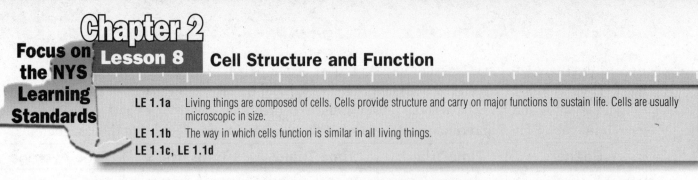

LE 1.1a	Living things are composed of cells. Cells provide structure and carry on major functions to sustain life. Cells are usually microscopic in size.
LE 1.1b	The way in which cells function is similar in all living things.
LE 1.1c, LE 1.1d	

Understand the cell and how it functions in living organisms.

Cells are the basic units of life. Cells provide structure to an organism and carry on the functions necessary to sustain life. The way in which cells function is similar in all living things. They grow and reproduce. They obtain energy from the nutrients they take in, and they use the nutrients to make the materials they need. Cells release any wastes they do not need.

Unicellular organisms are made of only one cell. All of the life functions of the organism are carried out in that one cell. They are also known as single-celled organisms. Examples of unicellular organisms include a euglena, paramecium, and amoeba.

Multicellular organisms are made of many cells. Different cells are specialized to perform different functions within the organism. Multicellular organisms include plants and animals.

Cells are made up of different structures:

Organelle	Function
Nucleus	controls cell activities; contains the cell's genetic material
Mitochondria	powerhouse of the cell; breaks sugars down into energy
Ribosome	joins together amino acids to make proteins, which are used to build and repair cells
Endoplasmic reticulum	packages proteins; makes lipids (fats); breaks down some materials
Golgi complex	processes and moves proteins around the cell; transports some proteins out of the cell
Lysosome	traps and digests waste materials and foreign invaders
Vacuole	stores water and other materials; plant cells often have one large vacuole
Chloroplast	contains the green pigment *chlorophyll*, which gathers energy from the Sun so plant cells can make food
Cell membrane	surrounds the cell and separates the inside of the cell from the environment
Cell wall	stiff covering over the cell membrane that protects and gives structure to plant cells

PLANT CELL

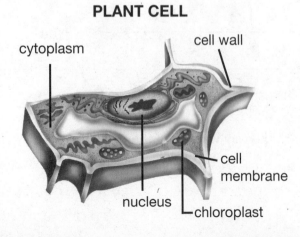

cytoplasm · cell wall · cell membrane · nucleus · chloroplast

ANIMAL CELL

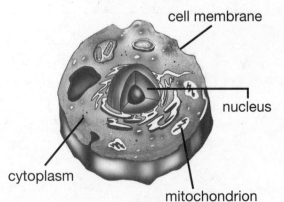

cell membrane · nucleus · cytoplasm · mitochondrion

Measuring Up Express™ for the New York State Test

NYS Test Practice   *Directions* (1–7): Decide which choice is the best answer. Circle the number of the answer you have chosen

1   Which cell structure is responsible for providing the energy you need to run?

   (1) cell membrane

   (2) mitochondria

   (3) nucleus

   (4) ribosome

2   An example of a unicellular organism is

   (1) an amoeba

   (2) mushroom

   (3) jellyfish

   (4) weed

3   The arrow in the picture points to a structure in a plant cell that contains chlorophyll.

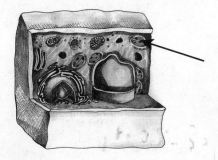

What is the function of this structure?

   (1) to make food

   (2) to store water

   (3) to move proteins around

   (4) to make fats

4   Which would you expect to find in both animal and plant cells?

   (1) cell wall   (3) nucleus

   (2) chloroplast   (4) chlorophyll

5   What function do all cells have in common?

   (1) They reproduce.

   (2) They make food.

   (3) They produce oxygen.

   (4) They form blood.

6   Which structure can carry out all of the functions of life?

   (1) nucleus

   (2) cell

   (3) chloroplast

   (4) membrane

7   A student is looking at different samples under a microscope. The student would expect to find cells when looking at a sample from

NYS Test Tip

Strategy   Use process of elimination when you're unsure of the answer.

   (1) a marble

   (2) a rock

   (3) a leaf

   (4) a raindrop

Directions (8–10): Record your answers on the lines provided below each question.

8   Why do plants need chloroplasts? [1]

_____

_____

9   How is a unicellular organism different from a multicellular organism? [1]

_____

_____

_____

10   Which organelle controls the activities of most cells? [1]

_____

     Measuring Up Express™ for the New York State Test

Focus on the NYS Learning Standards

Lesson 9 — Levels of Organization and Classification

LE 1.1e	Cells are organized for more effective functioning in multicellular organisms.
LE 1.1f	Many plants have roots, stems, leaves, and reproductive structures.
LE 1.1g	Multicellular animals often have similar organs and specialized systems for carrying out major life activities.
LE 1.1h	Living things are classified by shared characteristics on the cellular and organism level.

Understand that cells are organized into specialized structures that enable organisms to survive.

A **system** is a group of independent but interrelated parts that form a more complex whole. The levels of organization for living things are cells, tissues, organs, organ systems, and organisms.

A **tissue** is a group of similar cells that perform a specific function.

An **organ** is a group of tissues that work together to perform a specific function.

An **organ system** is a group of organs that work together to perform a body function.

cell → tissue → organ → organ system → organism

Living things are often classified by the characteristics they share, both on a cellular level and an organism level.

In plants, cells are organized into structures such as roots, stems, and leaves, as well as reproductive structures. Plant **roots** keep a plant anchored in the soil and take in nutrients and water. **Stems** hold the leaves upright and transport materials throughout the plant. **Leaves** collect sunlight and carbon dioxide, which they use to produce food.

The table below summarizes some of the major functions of organs and organ systems in multicellular animals.

Major Organs	Organ System	Major Function
Heart, blood, blood vessels	Circulatory System	Delivers oxygen and nutrients to cells; removes wastes from cells.
Mouth, esophagus, stomach, intestines	Digestive System	Breaks down food into nutrients that are usable by the body.
Endocrine glands	Endocrine System	Sends chemical messages (hormones) that help to regulate body functions and growth.
Lungs, skin, and kidneys	Excretory System	Lungs remove carbon dioxide; skin releases water, salt, and heat; kidneys filter blood and release water and dissolved wastes in urine.
Tonsils, lymph nodes, red bone marrow	Lymphatic System	Searches for and destroys bacteria, viruses, and other foreign invaders in the body; removes excess fluid around cells and returns it to the bloodstream.
Muscles	Muscular System	Allows the body to move; allows the heart to beat.
Brain, spinal cord, nerves	Nervous System	Sends electrical messages through the body to help your body move and avoid danger.
Ovaries, testes	Reproductive System	Ovaries produce eggs and testes produce sperm to allow the creation of a new organism.
Lungs, trachea, larynx, bronchi	Respiratory System	Obtains oxygen for cells and removes carbon dioxide from the body.
Bones	Skeletal System	Supports the body and protects internal organs.

Directions (1–8): Decide which choice is the best answer. Circle the number of the answer you have chosen.

1 A group of similar tissues that work together to perform a function in the body make up

(1) a cell

(2) an organ

(3) an organ system

(4) an organism

2 Which organ system's main purpose does *not* help to maintain body functions?

(1) cardiovascular system

(2) endocrine system

(3) reproductive system

(4) respiratory system

3 Scientists often use dichotomous keys, such as this one, to classify organisms into groups.

1a. Butterfly has "tail" on hind wings	Go to step 2
1b. Butterfly does not have "tail" on hind wings	Go to step 3
2a. Butterfly is black with yellow spots	Black Swallowtail
2b. Butterfly is yellow with black stripes	Tiger Swallowtail
3a. Butterfly is blue	Go to step 4
3b. Butterfly is not blue	Go to step 5
4a. Butterfly has black edge around wings	Spring Azure
4b. Butterfly has orange dots at edge of wing	Eastern-tailed Blue
5a. Butterfly has a black edge around wings	Northern Crescent
5b. Butterfly is black, orange, and white	Checkerspot

Which statement is true about the Spring Azure butterfly?

(1) It has a "tail" on its hind wing.

(2) It has white on it.

(3) It is blue.

(4) It has yellow spots.

4 Which two organ systems are involved in removing carbon dioxide from the body?

(1) digestive and cardiovascular systems

(2) muscular and respiratory systems

(3) respiratory and cardiovascular systems

(4) urinary and digestive systems

5 Which plant organ is most directly responsible for producing the food on which plants and animals depend?

(1) roots

(2) flowers

(3) stems

(4) leaves

6 Which characteristic would be best for classifying plants into different groups?

(1) Some plants produce flowers, but others produce cones.

(2) Some plants are short when they are young, but grow tall over time.

(3) Some plants are light green, but others are dark green.

(4) Some plants are made of cells, but others are not.

7 Which is an example of how an organ system affects your body's growth?

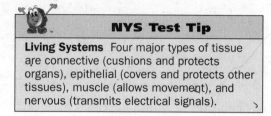

NYS Test Tip

Living Systems Four major types of tissue are connective (cushions and protects organs), epithelial (covers and protects other tissues), muscle (allows movement), and nervous (transmits electrical signals).

(1) The endocrine system controls the rate of cell division in the body.

(2) The urinary system removes wastes from the body.

(3) The respiratory system maintains oxygen levels.

(4) The integumentary system maintains body temperature.

8 The drawing shows a neuron, or nerve cell. Neurons are a unique kind of cell because they are long and thin. One end receives a message, the other end transmits the message, and the message must then "jump" across a gap called a synapse to the next neuron.

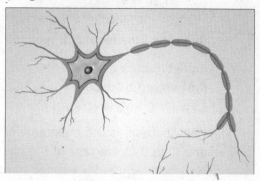

What is the most important feature of a nerve cell that helps it function to carry messages to the brain?

(1) It has a cell membrane.

(2) It has a nucleus.

(3) It is long and thin.

(4) It is an organ.

Directions (9–10): Record your answers on the lines provided below each question.

9 Why is it effective for multicellular organisms to have different levels of organization? [1]

_____

_____

_____

10 Lions, zebras, wildebeests, tigers, crocodiles, giraffes, and gazelles are just some of the many animals that live in the African savanna. Suggest one way to classify these animals into different groups. [1]

_____

_____

_____

_____

Focus on the NYS Learning Standards

Lesson 10   Homeostasis

LE 5.1a	Animals and plants have a great variety of body plans and internal structures that contribute to their ability to maintain a balanced condition.	
LE 5.1f	Regulation of an organism's internal environment involves sensing the internal environment and changing physiological activities to keep conditions within the range required for survival.	
ICT 4.1	Describe how feedback mechanisms are used in both designed and natural systems to keep changes within desired limits.	
LE 5.1b, LE 5.1g		

Describe how feedback mechanisms help maintain conditions within systems.

Equilibrium is a stable, balanced condition within a system. All forces acting within the system are balanced. For example, when you run, your body constantly adjusts to balance the force of gravity and keep you upright.

Homeostasis is the maintenance of a stable environment within a system. For example, the enzymes that are part of the chemical systems in a warm-blooded animal must remain within a certain temperature range to operate correctly. Water and chemical concentrations in a cell must remain at a certain level for normal cellular processes to occur.

A **feedback mechanism** is a process that is controlled by receptors that can stop or start an action. **Feedback loops** adjust and self regulate to maintain the input and output of the system to achieve homeostasis. The flowchart shows a feedback mechanism that regulates human body temperature. It involves the hypothalamus, which is a structure in the brain.

The feedback mechanism to control temperature is an example of a *negative feedback mechanism.* In this type of mechanism, a response decreases the original stimulus. When the temperature becomes too high, the mechanism responds to lower it. A *positive feedback mechanism* enhances the original stimulus. For example, as an apple ripens, it

Body Temperature Feedback Mechanism

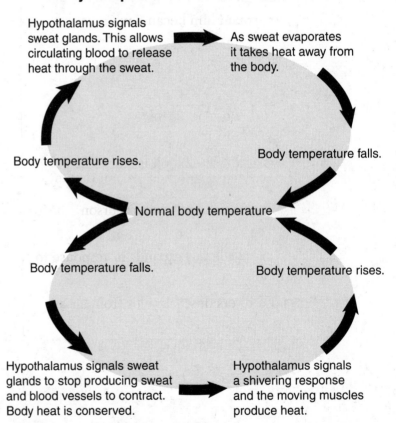

Hypothalamus signals sweat glands. This allows circulating blood to release heat through the sweat.

As sweat evaporates it takes heat away from the body.

Body temperature rises.

Body temperature falls.

Normal body temperature

Body temperature falls.

Body temperature rises.

Hypothalamus signals sweat glands to stop producing sweat and blood vessels to contract. Body heat is conserved.

Hypothalamus signals a shivering response and the moving muscles produce heat.

releases a substance that speeds up the ripening process. This causes nearby fruit to ripen and release the same substance. All the fruit becomes ripe together.

Animals and plants have a great variety of body plans and internal structures that help them maintain a balanced condition. For example, sweating and shivering in humans is just one example. Dogs can pant to stay cool. Plant leaves can close up to conserve water. The key to maintaining homeostasis is being able to sense the internal environment and change activities within an organism to keep conditions within the range needed for survival.

NYS Test Practice

Directions (1–7): Decide which choice is the best answer. Circle the number of the answer you have chosen.

1   A student went to school in a short sleeve shirt. A cold front blew in while he was in school. On his way home from school, he began shivering as he walked. When he started running, his shivering stopped. Which statement best explains this?

(1) He couldn't shiver and run at the same time.

(2) The muscle activity of running raised his temperature.

(3) He got home so fast that he didn't notice the cold.

(4) The air around him became warmer as he ran.

2   Which example does not involve a feedback mechanism?

(1) Excess sugar in the blood is stored in the liver.

(2) Blood pressure drops when a person is inactive.

(3) The pupil of the eye expands in response to light intensity.

(4) The nose filters dust particles from air as you breathe.

3   What device in a home is most like the feedback mechanism that controls temperature in the human body?

(1) vacuum cleaner

(2) dishwasher

(3) water meter

(4) thermostat

4   The diagram shows the feedback mechanism that controls blood pressure.

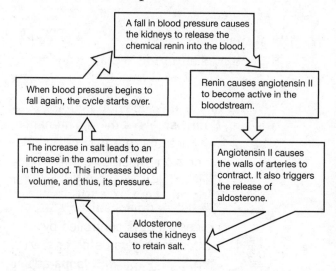

Based on the feedback mechanism, what would you expect to happen in response to a rise in blood pressure?

(1) The amount of water in the blood will increase.

(2) The level of renin in the blood will increase.

(3) More salt will be retained by the kidneys.

(4) The walls of the arteries will expand.

5   Homeostasis is best described as

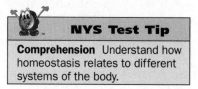

NYS Test Tip

Comprehension Understand how homeostasis relates to different systems of the body.

(1) taking in information through the senses

(2) the regulation of a stable internal environment

(3) the ability of an organism to change location

(4) a constant change of internal conditions

6 A plant seed sprouts when it is placed in a moist environment. What is the most likely reason that the moist environment causes the seed to sprout?

(1) Water combines with chemicals inside the seed, causing a root and shoot to grow from the seed.

(2) Water dissolves the seed coat, freeing the tiny plant inside and allowing it to start growing.

(3) Water enters the seed and increases pressure, forcing the seed to split and allowing the plant to grow.

(4) Water surrounds the seed, attracting the plant inside and causing it to sprout.

7 Turgor pressure is the force exerted on a plant's cell wall by the cell's contents. This pressure supports the cells. When a carrot is left out on the counter, it becomes limp. If it is placed in water, it remains firm. What feedback mechanism might account for this?

(1) As the carrot dries out, water enters the cells to keep the turgor pressure constant.

(2) As the carrot dries out, water leaves the cells to keep the water level constant.

(3) When the carrot is in water, the cells don't require as much turgor pressure to support them.

(4) The turgor pressure remains the same whether the carrot is in or out of the water.

Directions (8–9): Record your answers on the lines provided below each question.

8 Why does the survival of an organism depend on its ability to sense changes in its external environment? [1]

_____

_____

_____

_____

9 During a long run on a hot day, an athlete produces a large amount of sweat. The kidneys are responsible for releasing excess water from the body in the form of urine. How will the activity of the kidneys change as a result of the run? [1]

_____

_____

Focus on the NYS Learning Standards

Lesson 11 **Mitosis and Meiosis**

LE 4.4b In one type of cell division, chromosomes are duplicated and then separated into two identical and complete sets to be passed to each of the two resulting cells.

LE 4.4c Another type of cell division accounts for the production of egg and sperm cells in sexually reproducing organisms.

LE 4.3a, LE 4.4a, LE 4.4d

Understand the processes of mitosis and meiosis, and how they are related to cell division.

The nucleus of a cell contains genetic material called **DNA.** Molecules of DNA are long, tightly coiled structures that are bundled into structures called **chromosomes.**

Cell division is the process in which a cell divides to form two new cells. In multicellular organisms, cell division is responsible for growth, maintenance, and repair. In some one-celled organisms, cell division is a method of reproduction.

Before a cell divides, the chromosomes must be copied and separated into two complete sets. This is so both the resulting cells, called *daughter cells*, will have the exact same genetic material as the original cell, called the *parent cell*. **Mitosis** is the process of cell division in which both daughter cells are genetically identical to the parent cell.

Stages of Mitosis:

1. The parent cell has a complete set of chromosomes.

2. The chromosomes are copied so there are two of each.

3. The membrane around the nucleus dissolves and the chromosomes line up in the center of the cell.

4. The two sets of chromosomes are pulled apart and each one becomes surrounded by a nuclear membrane.

5. A cell membrane forms between the two nuclei.

6. The cells separate and two new daughter cells are formed that have the same number of chromosomes as the parent cell.

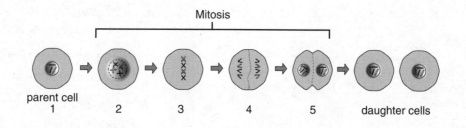

Mitosis

parent cell
1   2   3   4   5   daughter cells

Meiosis is the process that occurs to produce cells involved in reproduction—sperm and egg cells. Meiosis includes all of the stages of mitosis. However, each daughter cell then divides again to produce a total of four daughter cells. During the second division, the genetic material divides in half a second time. Therefore, each daughter cell formed contains only half the number of chromosomes found in the parent cell. The reason is that when two reproductive cells combine during **fertilization,** they will form a **zygote** with a complete set of genetic material that is different from either of its parents. This cell will then divide by mitosis to produce more cells like itself as it grows into an **embryo** and then a fully-developed organism.

NYS Test Practice   *Directions* (1–8): Decide which choice is the best answer. Circle the number of the answer you have chosen.

1   The process of meiosis occurs to

(1) replace damaged cells

(2) allow an organism to grow larger

(3) add tissue to developing organs

(4) produce reproductive cells

2   Which process requires mitosis?

(1) breathing

(2) eating

(3) growing

(4) walking

3   A wolf's body cells each have 78 chromosomes. How many chromosomes does a wolf's sperm or egg cells contain?

(1) 20

(2) 39

(3) 78

(4) 156

4   Which process can directly lead disease in a body?

(1) the genetic material of a cell dividing in half

(2) a parent cell dividing to form two daughter cells

(3) a cell dividing without any limit of control

(4) the cells of an embryo separating into layers

5   Which type of cell might be produced form the process shown in the diagram?

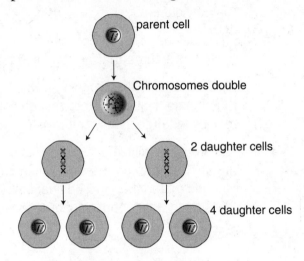

(1) sperm cell

(2) heart cell

(3) liver cell

(4) nerve cell

6   Which process occurs after fertilization as a multicellular organism grows larger?

(1) The genetic material within cells increases so the organism becomes more complex.

(2) The size of each cell becomes larger so the organism can grow.

(3) Each cell continues to divide by meiosis so the organism can form different parts.

(4) Cells divide by mitosis so the number of cells increases.

7 What type of organism might use mitosis for reproduction?

(1) a mushroom

(2) a paramecium

(3) a fern

(4) a jellyfish

8 What must happen in a cell before it can divide?

(1) It must be removed from an organism.

(2) It must release all of its water.

(3) It must form a cell wall.

(4) Its genetic material must be copied.

Directions (9–10): Record your answers on the lines provided below each question.

9 How are the daughter cells produced by mitosis different from the daughter cells produced during meiosis? [1]

NYS Test Tip

Comprehension Be able to compare and contrast mitosis with meiosis.

_____

_____

_____

10 How are both meiosis and mitosis involved in the birth and development of a puppy? [2]

_____

_____

_____

_____

Lesson 12 Asexual and Sexual Reproduction

LE 4.1a	Some organisms reproduce asexually. Other organisms reproduce sexually. Some organisms can reproduce both sexually and asexually.
LE 4.1b	There are many methods of asexual reproduction.
LE 4.1c	Methods of sexual reproduction depend upon the species. All methods involve the merging of sex cells to begin the development of a new individual.
LE 4.1d, LE 4.2a	

Describe and compare the different ways that organisms reproduce.

Reproduction is the process by which organisms make offspring like themselves.

Sexual reproduction is the process during which sex cells from two individuals unite to begin the development of a new individual. The male sex cell is the *sperm*. The female sex cell is the *egg*. During the process of *fertilization*, a sperm cell joins with an egg cell to produce a fertilized egg, or *zygote*. Fertilization may be internal or external, depending on the species.

Meiosis is necessary for sexual reproduction. The zygote acquires half its genetic material from the sperm cell and half from the egg cell.

Asexual reproduction is the process in which only one parent produces offspring. The offspring are genetically identical to the parent. There are many methods of asexual reproduction. **Binary fission** is the process through which some unicellular organisms without a nucleus, such as bacteria, reproduce. Other forms of asexual reproduction are summarized in the table.

Some Methods of Asexual Reproduction

Animals	Plants
In **budding,** an offspring grows out of the body of the parent and then breaks off. Hydras reproduce in this way.	Some plants send up new stems from their roots. These stems include bulbs, tubers, and rhizomes. In time, the stems form separate plants. Dandelions and poplar trees reproduce in this way.
In **fragmentation,** the body of the parent breaks into pieces, each of which can grow into a new offspring. A planarian can reproduce in this way.	Some plants produce stems above the ground that grow into new plants. These are known as **runners.** Strawberry plants reproduce in this way.
In **regeneration,** a piece of the parent can break off and grow into a completely new individual. A sea star can reproduce in this way.	Some plants produce **plantlets,** which are smaller plants that grow along the plant's leaves. The plantlets then fall off and grow on their own. Bryophyllum reproduce in this way.

Asexual reproduction is more efficient than sexual reproduction. It avoids the need to combine cells from different organisms, and it can allow an organism to produce many copies of itself in a relatively short period of time. However, the advantage of sexual reproduction is that it results in offspring with new combinations of genetic material. This enables individual organisms to adapt to changes in the environment.

NYS Test Practice

Directions (1–7): Decide which choice is the best answer. Circle the number of the answer you have chosen.

1 Which process is most like the development of plantlets in plants?

(1) binary fission in bacteria

(2) budding in animals

(3) zygote production in animals

(4) seed production in plants

2 Unicellular organisms, such as bacteria, undergo binary fission to reproduce. This process is most like

(1) mitosis

(2) sexual reproduction

(3) meiosis

(4) production of sperm

3 Which process does *not* result in offspring that are genetically identical to the parent?

(1) fragmentation

(2) binary fission

(3) seed production

(4) formation of runners

4 What do all methods of sexual reproduction have in common?

(1) They produce genetically identical offspring.

(2) They produce many offspring at once.

(3) They produce a seed.

(4) They involve merging two cells.

5 Why type of reproduction is shown in the diagram?

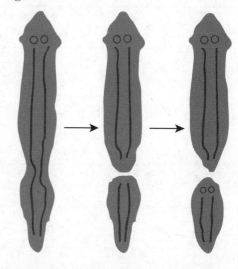

NYS Test Tip

Life Science Know some organisms that reproduce through asexual reproduction and some that reproduce through sexual reproduction.

(1) fragmentation

(2) formation of a zygote

(3) production of tubers

(4) binary fission

6   The male sex cell is called the

  (1) egg

  (2) tuber

  (3) sperm

  (4) nucleus

7   Female salmon deposit their eggs. Then male salmon swims by and fertilizes them. Salmon exhibit

  (1) internal fertilization for sexual reproduction

  (2) external fertilization for sexual reproduction

  (3) internal fertilization for asexual reproduction

  (4) external fertilization for asexual reproduction

Directions (8–9): Record your answers on the lines provided below each question.

8   What is one advantage of sexual reproduction over asexual reproduction?   [2]

_____

_____

9   What is sexual reproduction?   [1]

_____

_____

_____

LE 2.1a	Hereditary information is contained in genes. Genes are composed of DNA that makes up the chromosomes of cells.
LE 2.1b	Each gene carries a single unit of information. A single inherited trait of an individual can be determined by one pair or by many pairs of genes. A human cell contains thousands of different genes.
LE 2.2a	In all organisms, genetic traits are passed on from generation to generation.
LE 2.2b	Some genes are dominant and some are recessive.

LE 2.1c, LE 2.1d, LE 2.1e, LE 2.2c, LE 4.2b

Understand how the exchange of genetic information occurs and how it causes variation in species.

Reproduction is the process by which living things produce offspring. During reproduction, information about traits and characteristics of the parents are passed to the offspring.

Genes are sections of *chromosomes* (structures that contain DNA) that carry the information for a single trait. Human cells contain thousands of different genes located within 46 chromosomes. Sperm and egg cells have 23 chromosomes. In sexual reproduction, sperm and egg cells combine during fertilization to produce a zygote with 46 chromosomes. Half come from the mother, and half are from the father. In asexual reproduction, all the genes come from a single parent.

Inherited traits are characteristics that are received from the genes of the organism's parents, such as hair color, the shape of a bird's body, or a dog's instinct to sniff after a scent. Dyed hair, suntans, and pierced ears are not inherited traits but are *acquired* traits.

Heredity is the way in which traits are passed from parent to offspring.

An **allele** is a version of a gene that determines a particular trait, such as height or color. Each body cell has two alleles for each trait. A **dominant** allele is expressed or visible in the organism. A **recessive** allele is not expressed when paired with a dominant allele.

Incomplete dominance refers to alleles that are neither dominant nor recessive. The expression of the trait is a blending of the two, such as a cross between red and white flower plants producing pink flowers.

Homozygous means two alleles for a trait are the same, resulting in a *purebred*.

Heterozygous means two alleles for a trait are different, resulting in a *hybrid*.

A **genotype** is an individual's inherited combination of alleles.

A **phenotype** is an individual's inherited appearance.

A **Punnett square** is a graphic organizer used to predict the possible results of a genetic cross. An uppercase letter represents the dominant allele. The same letter, but lowercase, represents the recessive allele for the same trait.

The Punnett square on the right shows a cross between a homozygous tall plant (*TT*) and a homozygous short plant (*tt*). Notice that the probability that all the offspring will be tall is 100%. All of the offspring will be hybrids, (*Tt*), masking an allele for short height.

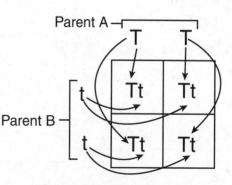

Directions (1–8): Decide which choice is the best answer. Circle the number of the answer you have chosen.

1   The uppercase letter *E* represents the dominant allele for red eyes in a fruit fly. The recessive allele for white eyes is represented by the lowercase *e*. All the offspring of two fruit flies are hybrids with red eyes. What is the genotype of these offspring?

(1) *ee*   (3) *EE*

(2) *Ee*   (4) white

2   The Punnett square shows the genotypes of pea plants. *Y* represents the allele for the dominant yellow trait. The allele for the recessive green trait is represented by *y*.

	Y	y
y	?	?
y	?	?

What are the possible genotypes of the two plants' offspring?

(1) *Yy* only   (3) *Yy* and *yy*

(2) *yy* only   (4) *YY* and *yy*

3   Which does *not* result in variations in phenotype?

(1) self-pollination

(2) cross breeding two hybrids

(3) incomplete dominance of a trait with the parent alleles

(4) exchange of genetic materials

4   A hitchhiker's thumb is one where the thumb bends down when extended. It is a recessive trait. If you have a hitchhiker's thumb and you marry someone who is a hybrid for the trait, what is the probability that your offspring will have a hitchhiker's thumb?

(1) 100% chance all will have it

(2) 100% chance none will have it

(3) 75% chance they will have it

(4) 50% chance they will have it

5   Which is *not* an inherited trait?

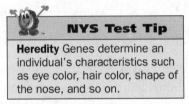

NYS Test Tip

Heredity Genes determine an individual's characteristics such as eye color, hair color, shape of the nose, and so on.

(1) color of corn kernels on an ear of corn

(2) fire scar on the bark of a tree

(3) shape and color of the scales of a fish

(4) length of a dog's tail and ears

6   In which structures is hereditary information contained in cells?

(1) genes

(2) membranes

(3) vacuoles

(4) mitochondria

7   How many traits does each gene contain information about?

(1) 1

(2) 2

(3) 23

(4) 46

8   An individual inherits a dominant allele and a recessive allele. How will the trait be expressed in the individual?

(1) The recessive trait will appear.

(2) The dominant trait will appear.

(3) Both traits will appear.

(4) Neither trait will appear.

Directions (9–10): Record your answers on the lines provided below each question.

9   How do the genes of an offspring depend on whether it was produced through asexual reproduction or sexual reproduction?   [1]

_____

_____

10   How are genes related to chromosomes?   [1]

_____

_____

_____

Focus on the NYS Learning Standards

Lesson 14 Patterns of Development

LE 4.3a	Multicellular organisms exhibit complex changes in development, which begin after fertilization.
LE 4.3d	Patterns of development vary among animals.
LE 4.3e	Patterns of development vary among plants.
LE 4.3b, LE 4.3c, LE 4.3f	

Describe patterns of development that occur among plants and animals.

After fertilization, multicellular organisms go through complex changes in development. The series of changes that occur from the beginning to the end of an organism's life is known as its **life cycle.**

A flowering plant produces **pollen,** which contains sperm cells. If pollen fertilizes an egg cell in a flower, a zygote is formed. The zygote divides by mitosis until a seed is formed. A seed contains a plant **embryo.** If conditions are right, the seed **germinates** and the embryo begins to grow. A seedling develops and then grows into a mature plant. When the plant grows flowers, the plant makes seeds and the process begins again.

Some plants, including mosses and ferns, produce **spores.** Each spore can grow into a new plant without being fertilized by another cell. The plants that grow from a spore then produce sperm and egg cells and reproduce through sexual reproduction. The two processes alternate from one generation to the next.

Humans develop from a fertilized egg cell. The single cell divides through mitosis and forms three layers of tissue. Before a baby is born, organs and organ systems form from those tissues. After birth, the body structures and functions change as the baby grows into a child, an adolescent, and then an adult.

Humans, and many other animals, keep the same basic shape throughout their lives. Other organisms undergo more dramatic changes. **Complete metamorphosis** is a developmental change in which the adult form looks very different from the young stage, or **larva.** The adult lays an egg, which hatches into the larva. The larva becomes a pupa, which becomes the adult. Butterflies, beetles, moths, and flies go through complete metamorphosis. **Incomplete metamorphosis** is a developmental change in which the adult form looks similar to the young form. The adult lays eggs that hatch into *nymphs*. The nymphs look much like the adults without wings. Gradually, the nymphs grow and develop wings. Grasshoppers and damselflies go through incomplete metamorphosis.

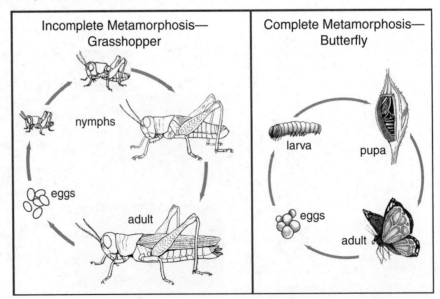

Incomplete Metamorphosis—
Grasshopper

nymphs

eggs

adult

Complete Metamorphosis—
Butterfly

larva

pupa

eggs

adult

NYS Test Practice   *Directions* (1–7): Decide which choice is the best answer. Circle the number of the answer you have chosen.

1   Through what process does a fertilized egg develop into an embryo?

(1) It grows larger in size.

(2) It duplicates through meiosis.

(3) It divides through mitosis.

(4) It develops organelles inside.

2   How are sperm cells carried to egg cells in flowering plants?

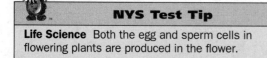

NYS Test Tip

Life Science Both the egg and sperm cells in flowering plants are produced in the flower.

(1) They are contained in pollen.

(2) They are contained in seeds.

(3) They are contained in spores.

(4) They are contained in cones.

3   Spores are part of the life cycle of

(1) oak trees

(2) rose bushes

(3) pine trees

(4) ferns

4   When do the organs and organ systems of humans first begin to develop?

(1) during adulthood

(2) during adolescence

(3) during childhood

(4) before birth

5   The diagram shows the development of a flower bug.

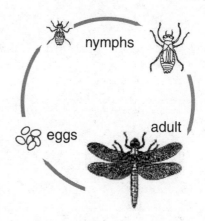

How can you tell from the diagram that the flower bug goes through incomplete metamorphosis rather than complete metamorphosis?

(1) The life cycle begins with an egg.

(2) The flower bug changes during its life cycle.

(3) The adult stage looks similar to the nymph stage.

(4) The life cycle does not involve seeds or flowers.

6   What occurs during germination?

(1) The embryo in a seed begins to grow.

(2) A fertilized egg divides into two new cells.

(3) A sperm cell unites with an egg cell.

(4) A spore grows into a mature plant.

7   The larval stage of a butterfly's life cycle is also known as the

(1) chrysalis   (3) egg

(2) caterpillar   (4) nymph

Directions (8–9): Record your answers on the lines provided below each question.

8   What stage follows the larval stage of a butterfly?   [1]

_____

9   In what way is reproduction in animals similar to reproduction in flowering plants?   [2]

_____

_____

_____

_____

_____

       Measuring Up Express™ for the New York State Test

Lesson 15 Diversity and Evolution

LE 3.1a   The processes of sexual reproduction and mutation have given rise to a variety of traits within a species.
LE 3.1b   Changes in environmental conditions can affect the survival of individual organisms with a particular trait.
LE 3.1c   Human activities such as selective breeding and advances in genetic engineering may affect the variations of species.
LE 3.2a, LE 3.2b, LE 3.2c, LE 3.2d

Understand the factors that lead to changes in organisms over time.

Diversity describes the differences among the traits and genetic material of organisms. The processes of sexual reproduction and mutations give rise to diversity within a species.

A **mutation** is a random change in an organism's genes or chromosomes. Genes, which are located on chromosomes, carry instructions for the traits of an organism. A mutation causes a change in some of those traits. Many mutations are harmless and do not affect the survival of the organism. Some mutations are actually helpful and enhance an organism's ability to survive. Other mutations are harmful and prevent an organism from surviving.

Organisms with similar needs compete with each other for resources. **Natural selection** is the process through which organisms best adapted to their environment survive to reproduce. In this way, they pass on their favorable traits to their offspring.

Over time, the traits of an entire species can change. This is especially true if an environment changes. Organisms not adapted to survive the change may become **extinct.** A species is extinct when it no longer exists on Earth in any location. Generally, it takes many generations for a change in a species to become noticeable. Some species of insects and bacteria, however, have undergone significant change in just a few years.

Evidence for changes in life forms over time is found in **fossils** trapped in sedimentary rocks. When organisms die, their bodies can become buried in layers of sediment. The fleshy parts of the organisms decay, but harder parts such as bones and teeth may become fossils. Over many years, high pressure can cause the layers of sediment to form solid rock with fossils trapped inside. Scientists can use fossils to trace changes in organisms over time.

Humans can affect the variations among species in different ways. **Selective breeding** is the process through which only plants or animals with desirable traits are allowed to breed and produce offspring. **Genetic engineering** is the process through which genes from one organism are transferred into the DNA of another organism.

NYS Test Practice

Directions (1–6): Decide which choice is the best answer. Circle the number of the answer you have chosen.

1   Which factor increases the diversity of a species?

(1) natural selection

(2) competition

(3) mutations

(4) mitosis

2   Which organism might show evidence of change in just a few years rather than a much longer period of time?

(1) elephants

(2) bacteria

(3) redwood trees

(4) cats

3   The differences among the varieties of dogs at a dog show are the result of

(1) selective breeding

(2) mutations

(3) regeneration

(4) budding

4   The process through which organisms best adapted to their environment survive to reproduce is known as

(1) extinction

(2) diversity

(3) mutation

(4) natural selection

5   What happens to a species if it is not adapted to changes in its environment?

NYS Test Tip

Life Science Many species are endangered because of human destruction of their environment.

(1) It will become extinct.

(2) It will alter its genes to survive.

(3) It will develop traits that it needs.

(4) It will change the environment to meet its needs.

6   Where should a scientist look for evidence of the history of change in organisms over time?

(1) soil along riverbeds

(2) ocean water near islands

(3) rock along ocean trenches

(4) layers of sedimentary rock

Directions (7–9): Record your answers on the lines provided below each question.

7   What is genetic engineering?   [1]

_____

_____

8   How does sexual reproduction give rise to diversity within a species?   [2]

_____

_____

_____

9   How can changes in environmental conditions affect the survival of individual organisms with a particular trait?   [2]

_____

_____

Focus on the NYS Learning Standards

Lesson 16 **Matter in Ecosystems**

LE 6.1c	Matter is transferred from one organism to another and between organisms and their physical environment.
ICT 1.4	Describe how the output from one part of a system can become the input to other parts.
LE 6.2b, ICT 1.3	

Understand how matter cycles between organisms and their physical environment.

The **water cycle** is the continuous movement of water between organisms and their environment. In the water cycle, energy from the Sun heats water in lakes and oceans, causing the water to *evaporate*, or change into water vapor. Water also evaporates from the pores of plants and animals. As water vapor rises in the atmosphere, it cools and *condenses* into liquid water droplets that form clouds. When these droplets become heavy enough, they fall to Earth as *precipitation*—rain, snow, sleet, or hail. Most precipitation falls into the oceans. The water that falls onto land can run off into lakes and streams, or seep into the soil and become *groundwater*.

Nitrogen is an essential element for building proteins and nucleic acids (such as DNA) in organisms. Nitrogen is always moving between living organisms and their environment in the **nitrogen cycle**. In this cycle, **nitrogen-fixing bacteria** in soil or water convert, or "fix," nitrogen gas in the atmosphere into a form that is usable by plants. Lightning strikes can also fix nitrogen. Plants take up this fixed nitrogen through their roots and store some of it in their tissues. Animals must eat plants or other organisms to obtain usable nitrogen.

When plants or animals die, decomposers such as bacteria and fungi break down the dead organisms. This releases nitrogen back into the soil. Some of this nitrogen is used by plants to build tissue. Some is converted back to nitrogen gas by bacteria, and released into the atmosphere.

Carbon is another essential element for living organisms. Molecules that contain carbon, called *organic molecules,* are found in every living thing—proteins, fats, and sugars are all types of organic molecules. The **carbon cycle** is the continuous movement of carbon between organisms and their environment.

You can find illustrations of these three cycles in the back of this book.

During **photosynthesis**, a plant uses carbon dioxide from the atmosphere, energy from sunlight, and water to make sugars. Oxygen is released in the process. In fact, photosynthesis is the major source of oxygen in the atmosphere. When plant and animal cells break down these sugars, carbon dioxide is released back into the atmosphere through the process of *respiration*.

$$CO_2 + H_2O + sunlight \rightarrow C_6H_{12}O_6 + O_2$$

When organisms die, bacteria and fungi break down their bodies. This process of decomposition releases carbon dioxide into the atmosphere and adds carbon to the soil, increasing soil fertility.

If buried for millions of years, carbon in the soil can become fossil fuel, such as oil, coal, and natural gas. When wood or fossil fuels are burned—through the process of combustion—they release stored carbon back into the atmosphere as carbon dioxide.

Directions (1–7): Decide which choice is the best answer. Circle the number of the answer you have chosen.

1 What happens to the carbon in grass after a deer eats the grass?

(1) It is released into the atmosphere as carbon dioxide.

(2) It is stored in the deer's tissues.

(3) It is used up to provide energy to cells.

(4) Some is stored and some is released into the atmosphere.

2 Examine the diagram of the carbon cycle below.

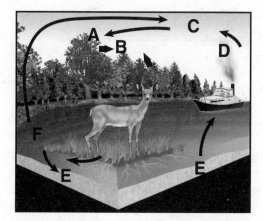

Which process does arrow D represent?

(1) combustion

(2) respiration

(3) decomposition

(4) photosynthesis

3 Which uses nitrogen gas?

(1) plant

(2) animals

(3) bacteria

(4) fungi

4 What initially happens to water vapor as it cools in the atmosphere?

(1) It falls to Earth as precipitation.

(2) It remains a vapor and forms clouds.

(3) It freezes into ice crystals.

(4) It condenses into water droplets.

5 Which process is found in both the carbon and nitrogen cycles?

(1) Combustion releases gases into the atmosphere.

(2) Photosynthesis converts gases into usable substances in soil.

(3) Decomposition releases substances into the soil.

(4) Bacteria convert gases into usable nitrogen in the soil.

6   What is the major source of atmospheric oxygen?

(1) cellular respiration

(2) combustion

(3) decomposition

(4) photosynthesis

7   What organisms return carbon trapped in the tissues of dead organisms to the carbon cycle?

(1) green plants

(2) decomposers

(3) carnivores

(4) herbivores

Directions (8–9): Record your answers on the lines provided below each question.

8   Scientists believe that high levels of carbon dioxide in the atmosphere can enhance Earth's natural *greenhouse effect*. The carbon dioxide traps energy from the Sun, which causes temperatures to increase worldwide. From your knowledge of the carbon cycle, what human activity might enhance the greenhouse effect? How might the effects be lessened?   [2]

_____

_____

_____

_____

9   How are the outputs from photosynthesis and respiration related to the inputs?   [1]

_____

_____

_____

Focus on the NYS Learning Standards

Lesson 17 Food Chains and Food Webs

LE 6.1a	Energy flows through ecosystems in one direction, usually from the Sun, through producers to consumers and then to decomposers.
LE 6.1b	Food webs identify feeding relationships among producers, consumers, and decomposers in an ecosystem.
LE 6.2c	Green plants are the producers of food which is used directly or indirectly by consumers.

LE 5.1c, 5.1d, 5.1e, LE 6.2a, ICT 5.2

Understand how energy flows through an ecosystem.

All organisms require energy to survive. The methods of obtaining energy and nutrients vary among organisms.

Photosynthesis is the process by which green plants and other organisms containing chlorophyll use energy from the Sun to convert water and carbon dioxide into sugar and oxygen. The Sun's radiant energy is stored as chemical energy in the sugar.

Chlorophyll is a green material in plant cells that traps the energy in sunlight.

A **producer** is an organism that makes its own food using radiant energy from the Sun. A producer uses some of the food it makes for its own life processes and stores the rest.

A **consumer** is an organism that gets its energy from eating other organisms. When a consumer eats a producer or another consumer, it gets any energy stored in its tissues. During **cellular respiration**, plants and animals break down food to release energy and nutrients in the presence of oxygen. Carbon dioxide and water are released during this process.

- **Herbivores** are consumers that get their energy from eating only plants. Cows, rabbits, and some insects are herbivores.

- **Carnivores** are consumers that get their energy from eating only other consumers. Lions, wolves, hawks, robins, frogs, and snakes are carnivores.

- **Omnivores** are consumers that get their energy from eating both plants and other consumers. Omnivores include bears, pigs, chickens, raccoons, and mosquitoes. Humans who are not vegetarians are omnivores.

Decomposers are organisms that break down dead plant or animal matter. Fungi (molds, mildew, and mushrooms), bacteria, and worms are decomposers. Decomposers break down waste from other organisms and decompose dead animal and plant matter into nutrients that can be used by producers.

Transfer of Energy and Matter Through an Ecosystem

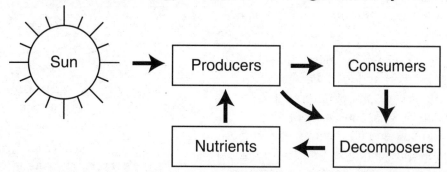

The diagram summarizes how the Sun's energy is transferred through an ecosystem.

A **food chain** is a model that describes the way energy passes from one organism to another in an ecosystem. The producers form the first link in the food chain. For example, energy passes from grass to a grasshopper that eats the grass. A frog eats the grasshopper. A snake eats the frog. An owl eats the snake.

grass ➔ grasshopper ➔ frog ➔ snake ➔ owl

A **primary consumer** eats only producers. Primary consumers are herbivores. A **secondary consumer** eats primary consumers. A **tertiary consumer** eats secondary consumers. Secondary and tertiary consumers are carnivores or omnivores.

A **food web** shows many different interactions among plants and animals. It consists of many food chains connected together. The diagram shows a food web. The organisms in italics represent one food chain in the web.

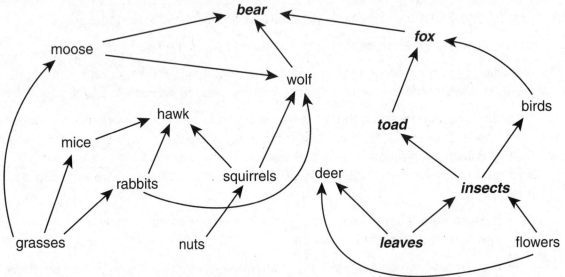

An **energy pyramid** shows how the available energy for consumers decreases at each level of a food chain. Only 10% of the energy in a lower level is available as energy for the next higher level. The diagram to the right shows this relationship. The pyramid is wider at the bottom because the greatest amount of available energy is at the producer level. The least amount of available energy is at the top consumer level.

Biomass is organic waste and matter from dead plants and animals that can be used as a source of energy. Decomposers work at all levels of a food web. They use some of the chemical energy to live and recycle the rest into chemical nutrients that are released back into the soil, air, and water.

Composting is a process in which organic wastes, such as food and yard wastes, decompose naturally. Composting results in a mineral-rich product that is ideal as a fertilizer for farming and gardening. New plants absorb nutrients and chemical energy from the compost. This energy then passes to herbivores and through the food web.

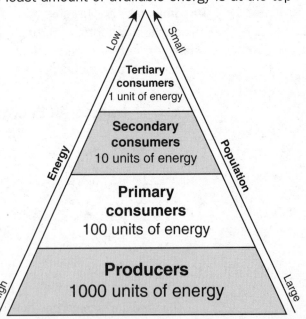

Producers provide the most available energy.

Measuring Up Express™ for the New York State Test

NYS Test Practice

Directions (1–8): Decide which choice is the best answer. Circle the number of the answer you have chosen.

1   Which best describes the energy transfer that takes place during photosynthesis?

   (1) Heat energy changes to light energy.

   (2) Light energy changes to sugar and carbon dioxide.

   (3) Radiant energy changes to chemical energy.

   (4) Solar energy changes to chlorophyll energy.

2   In what way do producers and consumers depend on one another?

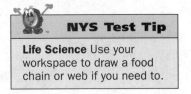

NYS Test Tip

Life Science Use your workspace to draw a food chain or web if you need to.

   (1) Producers get their energy by eating consumers and consumers get their energy by eating producers.

   (2) Producers use carbon dioxide given off by consumers and consumers use oxygen given off by producers.

   (3) Consumers produce sugar for producers to use in the process of photosynthesis.

   (4) Both producers and consumers change the energy from the Sun into energy they can use.

3   Which organism gets its energy from the waste of other organisms?

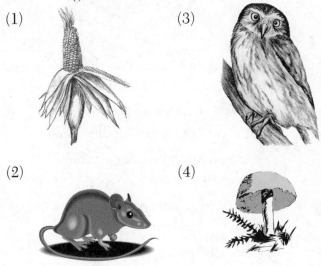

4   Which best expresses how consumers get the energy they need to live?

   (1) Consumers combine food with oxygen to release energy, water, and carbon dioxide.

   (2) Consumers combine radiant energy with carbon dioxide and water to produce food and oxygen.

   (3) Consumers decompose dead plants and animals to produce energy and nutrients.

   (4) Consumers absorb their energy from their environment for their own use.

5   From where does the energy that a herbivore uses come?

   (1) radiant energy directly from the Sun

   (2) chemical energy stored in producers

   (3) its own process of photosynthesis

   (4) a chemical reaction when it eats other herbivores

6 The original source of energy for a food web is

(1) producers

(2) the Sun

(3) herbivores

(4) soil

7 Few food chains have more than five levels. This is because

(1) there are too many types of producers to separate them into another level

(2) tertiary consumers can eat only secondary consumers

(3) most secondary consumers have only one type of predator

(4) very little energy is available for a consumer's use beyond four levels

8 Which occurs during the composting process?

(1) Decomposers break down dead plant and animal matter into nutrients that provide chemical energy to plants.

(2) Decomposers make the chemical energy in biomass available to plants.

(3) Biomass changes the Sun's energy to chemical energy.

(4) Biomass decays and rots, so its energy is no longer useful.

Directions (9–10): Record your answers on the lines provided below each question.

9 What is represented by a food chain? [1]

_____

_____

10 How do all organisms in a land ecosystem depend on green plants? [1]

_____

_____

Focus on the NYS Learning Standards

Lesson 18 **Communities and Populations**

LE 7.1a   A population consists of all individuals of a species that are found together at a given place and time. Populations living in one place form a community. The community and the physical factors with which it interacts compose an ecosystem.

LE 7.1b   Given adequate resources and no disease or predators, populations (including humans) increase.

LE 7.1c, LE 7.1d, LE 7.2a, LE 7.2b, LE 7.2c, ICT 5.1

Understand the relationship between populations and communities.

A **population** is made up of all the individuals of a species that live at a given place and time.

A **community** is made up of all the populations living in one place.

An **ecosystem** is the community of organisms that live in an area along with their nonliving surroundings.

A population can change in size when new members join the population or members leave the population. The **birth rate** is the number of births in a population in a certain amount of time. The **death rate** is the number of deaths in a population in a certain amount of time. If the birth rate is greater than the death rate, the population grows. If the death rate is greater than the birth rate, the population decreases.

In all environments, organisms interact with one another in many ways. One way is through the predator-prey relationship. A **predator** is an organism that hunts and eats other organisms for food. The **prey** is the organism that is eaten by a predator. Another way is through the parasite-host relationship. A **parasite** is an organism that lives on or in another organism, known as the **host,** to survive. Parasites hurt or kill their hosts over time. Organisms may also **compete** for resources, such as space, food, and water. Some interactions are helpful, such as when bacteria help other organisms to digest food or when decomposers return nutrients to the soil for plants to use.

Given adequate resources and no disease, parasites, or predators, populations will increase. The **carrying capacity** is the largest population that an area can support given the available resources. If the population grows beyond the carrying capacity, **overpopulation** occurs. The organisms use more resources than the ecosystem can replace. In time, the resources will be depleted and the population will not be able to survive. The carrying capacity can be affected by the activities of organisms, including humans.

Population size is often shown as a line graph of change over time. The population generally increases and decreases as the organisms interact with their environment until balance is established at the carrying capacity of the ecosystem.

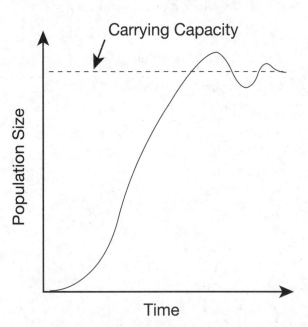

Carrying Capacity

Population Size

Time

Directions (1–7): Decide which choice is the best answer. Circle the number of the answer you have chosen.

1 All of the pine trees in a forest represent a

(1) community

(2) population

(3) ecosystem

(4) organism

2 How would you describe the relationship between a parasite and a host?

> **NYS Test Tip**
>
> **Life Science** A close relationship between two species is known as *symbiosis*.

(1) Both species benefit.

(2) One species benefits and the other is unharmed.

(3) One species benefits and the other is harmed.

(4) Neither species benefits.

3 Which describes a pond community?

(1) all of the koi fish that live in the pond

(2) all of the plants that grow in the pond

(3) all of the species of living things in the pond

(4) all of the living and nonliving things in the pond

4 The graph represents the population of brown bears in a forest over time.

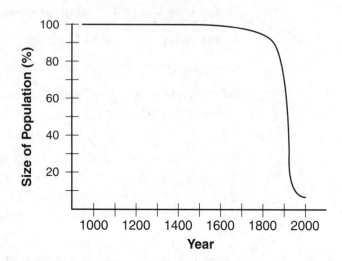

What factor has most likely affected the bear population?

(1) Diseases have been eliminated from the bears.

(2) The prey populations of the bears have increased.

(3) Humans have provided food resources for the bears.

(4) Much of its ecosystem has been destroyed.

5 When overpopulation by a species occurs,

(1) the rate at which renewable resources are produced increases

(2) there are not enough resources to meet the needs of all the organisms

(3) the ecosystem increases in size to fit the additional organisms

(4) the death rate exceeds the birth rate for a species

6   Which example describes microorganisms that help other organisms to survive?

   (1) Plants produce food through the process of photosynthesis.

   (2) Predators hunt prey as a source of food.

   (3) Bacteria in the intestines of cows help them digest plant materials.

   (4) Parasites absorb nutrients from the hosts in which they live.

7   Which factor will limit the growth of a population?

   (1) the introduction of a disease

   (2) a lack of predators

   (3) an adequate supply of water

   (4) plenty of space

Directions (8–9): Record your answers on the lines provided below each question.

8   What will happen if a species is introduced into a new ecosystem in which it has no natural predators?   [1]

_____

_____

9   In some regions, local communities of people drain water for ecosystems for drinking or irrigation. Explain how this can affect the populations of plants and animals in the ecosystem.   [1]

_____

_____

_____

Focus on the NYS Learning Standards

Lesson 19 **Human Effects on Ecosystems**

LE 7.2d Pollution has cumulative ecological effects such as acid rain, global warming, or ozone depletion. The survival of living things on our planet depends on the conservation and protection of Earth's resources.

LE 7.1e, LE 7.2c

Analyze the impact of human activities on ecosystems.

Natural resources are substances that occur naturally and are useful to people. These include living things and nonliving things, such as plants, fish, soil, water, and air. As populations of people grow, more resources are used. There are three general types of resources.

- **Renewable resources,** such as trees used to make lumber and paper, are replaced in a fairly short time.

- **Nonrenewable resources,** such as fossil fuels, may take millions of years to form. Minerals, gas, oil, and coal are nonrenewable. Mined resources, such as metal ores, are also nonrenewable resources.

- **Inexhaustible resources,** such as solar energy and wind, can be used over and over without being used up.

Sustainable management of a resource occurs when a renewable resource is managed in such a way that it can be used indefinitely. Sustainable forest management, for example, includes balancing the need for logging with the recreational use of the forest. New trees are planted to replace those removed.

Pollution occurs when resources are contaminated with harmful substances. For example, agricultural pesticides, herbicides, and fertilizers may flow into streams and rivers, which can kill off producers and primary consumers in the ecosystem.

Greenhouse gases are gases in the atmosphere that absorb heat that would otherwise escape to space. This warming is called the **greenhouse effect.**

Global warming is the increase of the average temperature of Earth's atmosphere. Many scientists believe that excess amounts of greenhouse gases in the atmosphere enhance Earth's natural greenhouse effect, causing global warming. A global rise in temperature of several degrees could cause widespread changes in the environment.

The combustion of fossil fuels also leads to **acid rain**, which is precipitation containing higher than normal amounts of certain kinds of acids. Gases released during combustion combine with water in the atmosphere to produce acid rain. Acid rain can damage ecosystems.

Other gases released by humans can cause **ozone depletion**, which is a loss of part of the protective layer of ozone that shields Earth from some of the Sun's harmful radiation.

Conservation is a reduction in the amount of a natural resource a person uses. **Recycling** is a form of conservation. Recycling conserves raw materials by reusing them to make new products. Reducing the use of resources is also a form of conservation. Fossil fuels are often used to produce electricity. The less electricity used, the fewer fossil fuels will be burned.

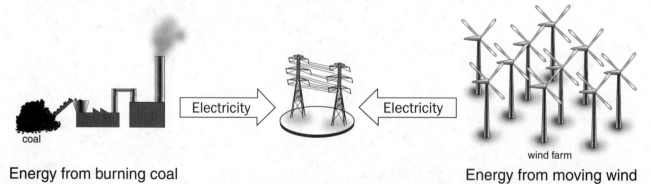

coal

Electricity ▷   ◁ Electricity

wind farm

Energy from burning coal   Energy from moving wind

NYS Test Practice

Directions (1–7): Decide which choice is the best answer. Circle the number of the answer you have chosen.

1   Which is *not* a sustainable management practice in the production of agricultural crops?

(1) clearing more land for crop production

(2) rotating crops to provide natural fertilizers

(3) plowing fields in patterns that avoid erosion

(4) irrigation that reduces the evaporation of water

2   Which conservation practice is the best way to conserve some of Earth's nonrenewable resources?

(1) recycling newspapers

(2) turning off lamps, televisions, and computers when not in use

(3) reusing a paper sack as wrapping paper

(4) turning off the water while brushing your teeth

3   Tires are a major source of pollution because they take up a lot of space in landfills and do *not* decompose easily. One method of dealing with unwanted tires is to shred them and then use the shredded tires to form roadbeds and soft ground coverings for playgrounds. Shredding tires is an example of

(1) conservation

(2) pollution

(3) regulation

(4) recycling

4   Which part of the diagram of the greenhouse effect is first affected by the combustion of fossil fuels?

Greenhouse Effect

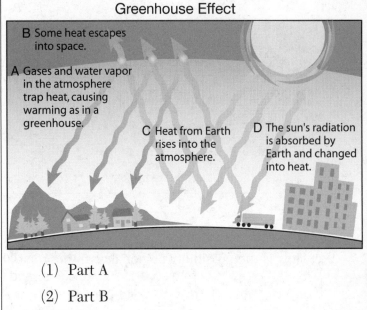

B Some heat escapes into space.

A Gases and water vapor in the atmosphere trap heat, causing warming as in a greenhouse.

C Heat from Earth rises into the atmosphere.

D The sun's radiation is absorbed by Earth and changed into heat.

(1) Part A

(2) Part B

(3) Part C

(4) Part D

5   Decaying waste in landfills sometimes produces methane gas (CH_4). Methane is a flammable greenhouse gas. The most useful way to reduce the methane pollution of the atmosphere would be to

NYS Test Tip

Environmental Studies Greenhouse gases exist naturally, but some are considered pollutants because they are emitted as a result of human, actions such as burning fossil fuels.

(1) burn the gas as it comes out of the ground

(2) capture the gas and use it as a source of fuel

(3) add chemicals that react with the methane

(4) make smaller landfills that don't produce as much gas

6   Toxic substances that are harmful to organisms are known as

(1) resources

(2) pollutants

(3) recycling

(4) radiation

7   Acid rain is produced by gases released by

(1) the combustion of fossil fuels

(2) plants during photosynthesis

(3) fertilizers spread on crops

(4) water when it changes state

Directions (8–9): Record your answers on the lines provided below each question.

8   How does overpopulation impact an environment?   [1]

_____

_____

9   How is the possibility of global warming related to the greenhouse effect?   [2]

_____

_____

_____

Practice for H.O.T.S. ★

Directions (1–4): Decide which choice is the best answer. Circle the number of the answer you have chosen.

1   Most likely, mitochondria would be most numerous in

(1) cells producing sugars in the leaves of a tree

(2) muscle cells in the arms of a swimmer

(3) bacterial cells growing on sugars

(4) cardiac cells in the tissues of the heart

2   Both tuna fish and sharks have gills, eat smaller fish, and have similarly shaped fins in the same places. However, scientists classify sharks and tuna in different groups. Which of these most likely explains why scientists classify tuna and sharks in different groups?

(1) Tuna have bones, but sharks have cartilage.

(2) Sharks are more aggressive than tuna.

(3) Sharks can swim in deeper waters than tuna can.

(4) Tuna weigh less, on average, than sharks.

3   Which is an example of variation?

(1) Tigers have stripes that make them difficult to see in a forest.

(2) Sea turtles lay as many as 150 eggs at a time because only a small number will survive.

(3) Some gypsy moths are light gray, and others are dark gray.

(4) Poison dart frogs are brightly colored to advertise the fact that they are poisonous to predators.

4   A population of bats in a forest ecosystem experiences a high birth rate. How will this most likely affect the insect populations in the forest?

(1) The insect populations will increase.

(2) The insect populations will decrease.

(3) The insect populations will not be affected.

(4) The insect populations will move to other areas.

Directions (5):   Record your answer on the lines provided below the question.

5   In dachshunds, the allele S for short hair is dominant over the allele for long hair s. If a dachshund with the genotype Ss mates with a dachshund with the genotype SS, what could be the phenotype(s) and genotype(s) of their offspring? [2]

_____

_____

_____

Higher-Order Performance Task
Photosynthesis

Task:

You will investigate how changes in environmental conditions such as temperature and amount of light affect individual elodea plants.

Materials:

- 2 test tubes
- 2 plastic funnels that will fit into the test tubes
- modeling clay
- water
- sprigs of elodea
- 2 beakers that are wider than the funnels
- labels
- watertight plastic container that is wider than a beaker
- 2 lamps
- paper bag
- metric ruler

Directions:

1. Place a funnel in a test tube as shown in the diagram below. Secure and seal the funnel to the test tube with clay.

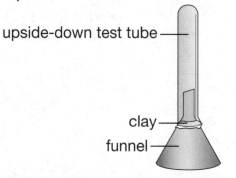

upside-down test tube

clay

funnel

2. Fill the test tube halfway with water. Place a sprig of elodea in the tube. Then fill the tube completely with water. Make sure that the water goes all the way to the top of the funnel.

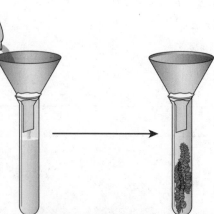

Copying is illegal.   Measuring Up Express™ for the New York State Test

3. Turn a beaker upside down and place it on top of the funnel. Press the funnel and test tube into the bottom of the beaker as you turn the beaker right-side up. Make sure that none of the water escapes from the test tube.

4. Fill the beaker halfway with water.

5. Repeat steps 1–4 to prepare another beaker for the experiment. Label the beakers 1 and 2.

6. Place a lamp next to beaker 1. Place a paper bag over beaker 2. Turn on each lamp and shine each on one beaker for 30 minutes.

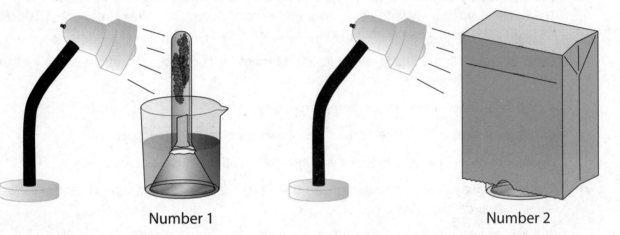

Number 1   Number 2

7. Turn off the lamp and remove the bag. How has the amount of water in each test tube changed? The test tube in beaker 1 has a space at the top and less water. The test tube in beaker 2 is still full of water.

8. What has taken the place of the water in beaker 1?

_____

9. What kind of an effect does light have on photosynthesis? Support your answer, based on the results from the experiment.

_____

_____

_____

10. How does photosynthesis help plants to survive?

_____

_____

11. When you are finished, put all your materials back the way you found them. Wipe up any spills. Wash your hands. Discard the plants.

LE 1.2a	Each system is composed of organs and tissues which perform specific functions and interact with each other.
LE 1.2g	Locomotion, necessary to escape danger, obtain food and shelter, and reproduce, is accomplished by the interaction of the skeletal and muscular systems, and coordinated by the nervous system.

Many organ systems work together to protect and help an organism move.

The **integumentary system** is made up of skin, hair, and nails. The system protects the body and helps regulate body temperatures.

The **skeletal system** is a system made up of bones, cartilage, ligaments, and tendons. The skeletal system gives the body shape, protects the organs, allows movement, stores minerals, and produces new blood cells.

Bone marrow fills the spongy bone inside the hard, or compact, part of the bone. It is the site where new red blood cells are produced.

A **joint** is a place where two or more bones meet.

Cartilage is softer and more flexible than bone but also gives support.

Ligaments connect bones together and **tendons** connect muscles to bones.

The **muscular system** is a system made up of three different types of muscles: *skeletal*, *smooth*, and *cardiac*.

Skeletal muscles are *voluntary* muscles because you can control them when you move.

Smooth and **cardiac muscles** are *involuntary* muscles because they work without your control. Smooth muscles include the linings of your digestive tract and blood vessels, and muscles needed for breathing. Cardiac muscles are found in the heart.

The **nervous system** is the body's control system and is composed of the brain, spinal cord (central nervous system), and nerves (peripheral nervous system).

Neurons are nerve cells that carry electrical messages. Neurons are made up of *axons* that carry messages away from a cell and *dendrites* that carry messages to a cell separated by a gap called a *synapse*. Chemicals produced by the endocrine system carry messages across synapses.

The **brain** is the control center of the nervous system and is made up of billions of neurons. The brain is divided into three sections, the *cerebrum*, the *cerebellum*, and the *medulla*. The cerebrum functions in thinking and interpreting sense signals from the body. The cerebellum coordinates muscle and balance. The medulla controls involuntary functions, such as breathing, coughing, and sneezing, as well as heart rate and muscular movements in the digestive system.

Muscles contract and relax to move bones

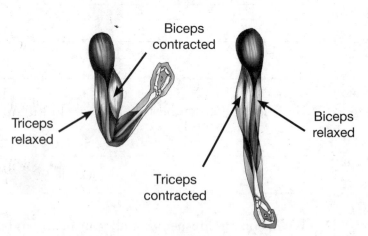

Biceps contracted

Triceps relaxed

Biceps relaxed

Triceps contracted

NYS Test Practice

Directions (1–9): Decide which choice is the best answer. Circle the number of the answer you have chosen.

1   Alcohol, sleeping pills, and pain killers, called *depressants*, slow down the central nervous system. How does the body react to depressants?

(1) Information received through the senses is altered.

(2) Heartbeat and breathing rate decrease.

(3) Heartbeat and breathing rate increase.

(4) White blood cells will increase.

2   Predict what might be the result if you injured your hand and destroyed all the nerve cells.

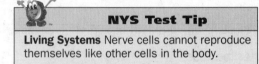

NYS Test Tip

Living Systems Nerve cells cannot reproduce themselves like other cells in the body.

(1) The central nervous system would take over.

(2) Your hand would swell.

(3) You could lose control of your hand.

(4) Your hand would become infected.

3   Which muscles shown above are relaxing?

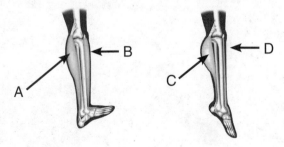

(1) A and B

(2) B and C

(3) C and D

(4) D and A

4   Which body system provides support and structure to the body and helps it to move?

(1) skeletal

(2) muscular

(3) nervous

(4) circulatory

5   The skeletal and nervous systems are analogous to which parts of a house?

(1) water pipes and roof

(2) wooden framework and electrical wires

(3) electrical wires and insulation

(4) vinyl siding and roof

6   What would happen if bone marrow stopped functioning?

(1) The body would lose red blood cells.

(2) The body would lose calcium.

(3) The body would lose vitamin D.

(4) The body's water supply would dry up.

7   Which body system coordinates the other body systems?

(1) skeletal

(2) muscular

(3) digestive

(4) nervous

8   In which structure are red blood cells produced?

   (1) heart

   (2) brain

   (3) bone

   (4) spinal cord

9   Suppose you touch a sharp tack. Which system coordinates the movement of your bicep muscle so it contracts and pulls your hand away?

   (1) skeletal

   (2) muscular

   (3) digestive

   (4) nervous

Directions (10–11):   Record your answers on the lines provided below each question.

10   How do the muscular system, nervous system, and skeletal system work together to enable the human body to move?   [1]

_____

_____

_____

11   Compare and contrast the three types of muscles.   [2]

_____

_____

_____

Focus on the NYS Learning Standards

Lesson 21 Respiratory and Circulatory Systems

LE 1.2d	During respiration, cells use oxygen to release the energy stored in food. The respiratory system supplies oxygen and removes carbon dioxide (gas exchange).
LE 1.2f	The circulatory system moves substances to and from cells, where they are needed or produced, responding to changing demands.
LE 1.2a, LE 1.2b	

Oxygen and carbon dioxide are moved into and out of the body by the respiratory system and moved within the body by the circulatory system.

The **circulatory system** is a system made of organs that function in transporting materials around the body.

The **heart** is a muscle that pumps bloods through the body. The rate at which the heart beats is known as the **pulse rate**. The places in the body where the pulse rate can be felt and measured are known as **pulse points**. Two common pulse points are in the neck and wrists.

Blood is a fluid that is carried by the circulatory system and is made up of plasma, red blood cells, white blood cells, and platelets. *Plasma* is made mostly of water and carries carbon dioxide, food, and wastes. *Red blood cells* carry oxygen and pick up carbon dioxide and wastes. *White blood cells* fight infections and diseases. *Platelets* make blood clot.

Arteries, capillaries, and **veins** are the three types of blood vessels. Arteries carry blood away from the heart. The arteries branch into smaller blood vessels, and then into capillaries, where at the cell, gas exchange takes place. At the cell, capillaries pick up carbon dioxide and other wastes and transport the wastes through veins to the heart. The heart pumps blood to the lungs, where the gas exchange takes place in the alveoli.

RESPIRATORY SYSTEM

The **respiratory system** is a system made of structures and organs that function in moving oxygen and carbon dioxide in and out of the body.

Cells needs oxygen for **cellular respiration**, in which food is broken down to release energy. They release carbon dioxide in the process. Too much carbon dioxide in the body can be dangerous.

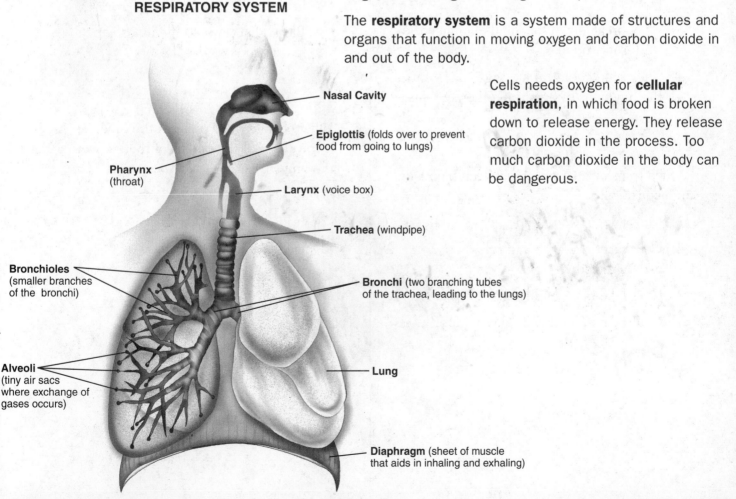

- **Nasal Cavity**
- **Epiglottis** (folds over to prevent food from going to lungs)
- **Pharynx** (throat)
- **Larynx** (voice box)
- **Trachea** (windpipe)
- **Bronchioles** (smaller branches of the bronchi)
- **Bronchi** (two branching tubes of the trachea, leading to the lungs)
- **Alveoli** (tiny air sacs where exchange of gases occurs)
- **Lung**
- **Diaphragm** (sheet of muscle that aids in inhaling and exhaling)

NYS Test Practice

Directions (1–8): Decide which choice is the best answer. Circle the number of the answer you have chosen.

1 In which organ is carbon dioxide transferred from blood to air that will be expelled by the body?

  (1) brain

  (2) liver

  (3) heart

  (4) lung

2 In what way do the respiratory and circulatory systems interact?

  (1) They increase and decrease the temperature of the body in a feedback loop.

  (2) They move carbon dioxide and oxygen into and out of the body and throughout the body.

  (3) They break down food and eliminate the wastes it produces.

  (4) They send chemical messages that control the functions of organs in other systems.

3 Which transfer takes place between blood and individual cells?

  (1) Cells take in water and release food.

  (2) Cells take in oxygen and release carbon dioxide.

  (3) Cells take in air and release nutrients.

  (4) Cells take in food and release water.

4 The role of the heart in the circulatory system is to

  (1) destroy platelets

  (2) produce red blood cells

  (3) force blood through the body

  (4) remove carbon dioxide

5 How is blood that flows from the heart to the lungs different from blood that flows from the heart to other parts of the body?

  (1) Blood that flows to the lungs moves slowly.

  (2) Blood that flows to the lungs carries food and nutrients.

  (3) Blood that flows to the lungs is poor in oxygen.

  (4) Blood that flows to the lungs is rich in oxygen.

6 What changes take place in the blood as it travels to all the organs of the body other than the lungs?

  (1) It picks up oxygen.

  (2) It loses red blood cells.

  (3) It loses plasma.

  (4) It loses oxygen.

7   Which is the best explanation for why regular aerobic exercise benefits the body?

(1) Exercise brings more oxygen into the body.

(2) Exercise strengthens the heart muscle.

(3) Exercise decreases the number of alveoli.

(4) Over time, exercise constricts blood vessels.

8   Which part of the blood fights infection and disease?

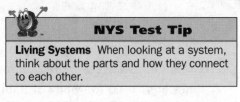

NYS Test Tip

Living Systems When looking at a system, think about the parts and how they connect to each other.

(1) red blood cells

(2) plasma

(3) platelets

(4) white blood cells

Directions (9–11): Record your answers on the lines provided below each question.

9   How is an artery like a vein? How are they different?   [2]

_____

_____

10   During what process is food broken down in the presence of oxygen?   [1]

_____

11   The table shows the target pulse rate during exercise for people of different ages.

Age	Target Pulse Rate per Minute
20	120–170
30	114–162
40	108–153
50	102–145
60	96–136
70	90–128

What conclusion about pulse rate can you reach based on the data in the table?   [1]

_____

Focus on the NYS Learning Standards

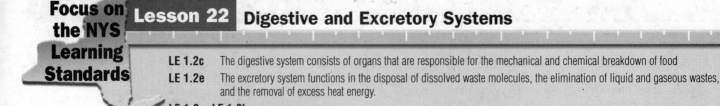

Lesson 22   Digestive and Excretory Systems

LE 1.2c	The digestive system consists of organs that are responsible for the mechanical and chemical breakdown of food
LE 1.2e	The excretory system functions in the disposal of dissolved waste molecules, the elimination of liquid and gaseous wastes, and the removal of excess heat energy.

LE 1.2a, LE 1.2b

The digestive system breaks down food into usable forms, and the excretory system functions to rid the body of liquid and gaseous wastes.

Mechanical digestion is the breaking down of food into smaller pieces by chewing and by the movements of the stomach.

Chemical digestion is the process that chemically changes food into molecules, called *nutrients*, that can be transported by blood and absorbed by cells.

The **digestive system** is a system made of organs that function in breaking food down into usable forms. The organs of the digestive system include the *mouth* (mechanical and chemical digestion), *pharynx* (throat), *esophagus* (tube to stomach), *stomach* (mechanical and chemical digestion), *liver* (produces bile, a digestive fluid), *pancreas gland* (enzymes and hormones secreted), *small intestine* (site of most chemical digestion and nutrient absorption), *large intestine* (water is absorbed; undigested material moves to the rectum), and *rectum* (feces is expelled).

Enzymes are chemicals that speed up chemical reactions involved in digestion.

The **excretory system** is a system made of organs that function in eliminating liquid and gaseous wastes from the body. The excretory system includes the *lungs, skin,* and *kidneys.* The lungs remove carbon dioxide from the body. The skin releases water, salt, and heat through sweating. The kidneys are the main organs of excretion and they filter the blood, removing excess water, dissolved salts, and other wastes.

Nutrients are chemical substances found in foods needed for growth, energy, and carrying out life processes. Nutrients include carbohydrates (starches and sugars), fats, proteins, vitamins, and minerals.

THE DIGESTIVE SYSTEM

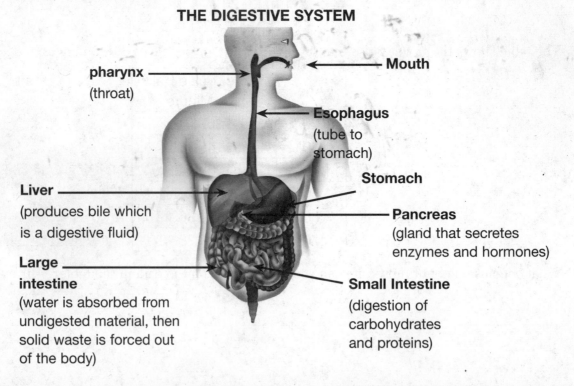

pharynx (throat)

Mouth

Esophagus (tube to stomach)

Stomach

Pancreas (gland that secretes enzymes and hormones)

Liver (produces bile which is a digestive fluid)

Large intestine (water is absorbed from undigested material, then solid waste is forced out of the body)

Small Intestine (digestion of carbohydrates and proteins)

NYS Test Practice

Directions (1–8): Decide which choice is the best answer. Circle the number of the answer you have chosen.

1   Which organ is a part of the excretory system?

   (1) skin

   (2) large intestine

   (3) esophagus

   (4) heart

2   Chemical digestion breaks food into

   (1) smaller pieces

   (2) molecules

   (3) salt

   (4) enzymes

3   Enzymes are *not* found in the large intestine. What can you conclude?

   (1) The large intestine does not carry out mechanical digestion.

   (2) The large intestine does not carry out chemical digestion.

   (3) The large intestine is not an organ.

   (4) Blood does not absorb minerals or water from the large intestine.

4   Which nutrient begins to be digested in the mouth?

   (1) carbohydrates

   (2) fats

   (3) proteins

   (4) vitamins and minerals

Base your answer to question 5 on the information below and on your knowledge of science.

Digestive Enzymes

Enzyme	Effect
ptyalin	breaks down starch
pepsin	breaks down protein
trypsin, lipase, and amylase	breaks down protein, starch, and fats
sucrase, maltase	breaks down fats, simpler proteins, and complex sugars

5   If your body stopped producing pepsin, what would be the most likely result?

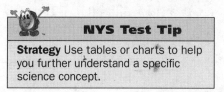

NYS Test Tip

Strategy Use tables or charts to help you further understand a specific science concept.

   (1) You would be totally unable to eat fats.

   (2) Your body would not produce bile.

   (3) It would take your body longer to digest all foods.

   (4) It would take your body longer to digest proteins.

6   What would happen if someone's kidneys stopped functioning?

   (1) The other two excretory organs, the lungs and the skin, would take over.

   (2) The blood would fill up with toxic wastes.

   (3) The blood would bypass the kidneys.

   (4) The person would urinate more often.

7 Which digestive organ is the site of most nutrient absorption?

(1) small intestine

(2) large intestine

(3) esophagus

(4) stomach

8 The role of the excretory system is to

(1) carry oxygen to the cells of the body

(2) break food into smaller components

(3) eliminate liquid and gaseous wastes

(4) make food that cells can use

Directions (9–10):Record your answers on the lines provided below each question.

9 How does sweating help the human body to stay healthy? [1]

_____

_____

_____

10 What two types of digestion take place in the mouth? [2]

NYS Test Tip

Living Systems Know what each system does as well as how it interacts with other systems.

_____

_____

_____

Lesson 23 The Endocrine System

LE 1.2h   The nervous and endocrine systems interact to control and coordinate the body's responses to changes in the environment, and to regulate growth, development, and reproduction.

LE 1.2a, ICT 4.1

Understand the parts and function of the endocrine system.

The **endocrine system** is responsible for regulating mood, controlling growth and development, and regulating tissue function, as well as taking part in reproductive processes. Whereas spontaneous processes are controlled by the nervous system, slow processes that occur over time, such as cell growth, are controlled by the endocrine system.

Hormones are chemical messengers in the endocrine system that transfer information from one set of cells to another. Many different hormones can circulate in the blood at any given time, but each one affects a specific type of cell that responds to its message. These cells, known as *target cells,* have receptors that latch onto only specific hormones. When a hormone reaches its target cell, it locks onto the cell's specific receptors and transmits chemical instructions to the cell.

Hormones are produced by glands. A **gland** is a group of cells that secretes chemicals. Some types of glands release their secretions in specific areas. For example, sweat glands release secretions in the skin and salivary glands release secretions in the mouth. Endocrine glands, however, release hormones directly into the bloodstream. The hormones are then transported by blood to cells in other parts of the body.

The major glands of the endocrine system are the hypothalamus, pituitary, thyroid, parathyroids, adrenals, pineal body, and the reproductive glands. The pancreas also secretes hormones even though it is also associated with the digestive system.

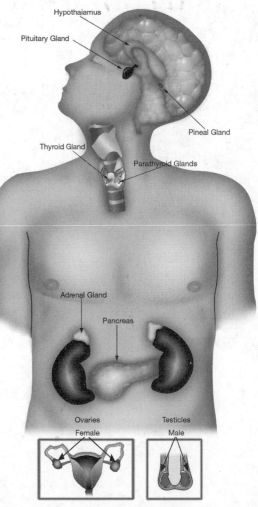

Once a gland secretes a hormone, the chemical messenger travels through the bloodstream to target cells that can receive its message. Along the way, special proteins bind to some of the hormones. The proteins control the amount of hormone that is available to affect the target cells.

Hormone levels are controlled by *feedback mechanisms.* When hormone levels reach a certain level, any further secretion is controlled by mechanisms that maintain that level of hormone in the blood. For example, suppose the thyroid gland has secreted enough thyroid hormones into the blood. The pituitary gland senses the level and adjusts its release of thyrotropin, which is the hormone that stimulates the thyroid gland to produce thyroid hormones. In this way, homeostasis is maintained in the body.

Directions (1–7): Decide which choice is the best answer. Circle the number of the answer you have chosen.

1 The hormones in an endocrine system can be likened to a

(1) receiver

(2) recycler

(3) messenger

(4) provider

2 The main structures of the endocrine system are

(1) glands

(2) blood cells

(3) bones

(4) neurons

3 An organ that is part of the digestive system and the endocrine system is the

(1) heart

(2) small intestine

(3) kidney

(4) pancreas

4 The substances secreted by endocrine glands are called

(1) proteins

(2) hormones

(3) cells

(4) receptors

5 Where are glands located in the body?

(1) They are spread throughout.

(2) They are located in the brain.

(3) They are attached to nerve cells.

(4) They float through the bloodstream.

6 The endocrine system is mainly responsible for

(1) providing energy

(2) regulating processes

(3) removing waste

(4) transporting materials

7 How are the nervous and endocrine systems similar?

(1) Both depend on the activity of glands.

(2) Both transmit electrical messages.

(3) Both respond immediately to stimuli.

(4) Both coordinate body activities.

Directions (8–9): Record your answers on the lines provided below each question.

8   What is the main role of the endocrine system?   [1]

_____

_____

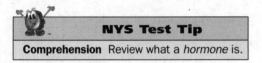

NYS Test Tip

Comprehension Review what a *hormone* is.

9   How do feedback mechanisms affect the endocrine system?   [2]

_____

_____

_____

_____

Focus on the NYS Learning Standards

Lesson 24 **The Reproductive System**

LE 1.2i   The male and female reproductive systems are responsible for producing sex cells necessary for the production of offspring.
LE 1.2a, LE 4.1c, LE 4.2a, LE 4.2b, LE 4.3a, LE 4.3b, ICT 4.1

Understand the role of the male and female reproductive systems.

Reproduction is the process through which an organism makes offspring similar to itself. Humans take part in sexual reproduction, in which male and female sex cells unite during **fertilization.** The male sex cell is the **sperm** and the female sex cell is the **egg.** The sperm and egg each carry one half of the genetic information for the new individual.

The **male reproductive system** is responsible for producing sperm and delivering it to the female reproductive system.

The **testicles,** or *testes*, produce and store millions of sperm cells. The testicles are also part of the endocrine system because they produce hormones, such as *testosterone.* This hormone is involved in development as boys grow into men.

The **vas deferens** transports semen, which is a fluid that contains sperm. The **epididymis** is a set of coiled tubes that connects to the vas deferens. The epididymis and the testicles are located in a pouch of skin, known as the **scrotum,** which is located outside of the pelvis. The size of the scrotum can change in order to maintain a proper temperature for the sperm.

The **urethra** is a channel that carries the semen to the outside of the body through the **penis.**

The **female reproductive system** is responsible for producing eggs and supporting the development of a fertilized egg.

The **vagina** is a muscular tube that extends to the opening of the uterus. The vagina is where sperm enters the female reproductive system. It is also the pathway through which a baby passes during birth. For this reason, it is also known as the *birth canal.*

The **uterus** has a thick lining and muscular walls. Two **fallopian tubes,** or *oviducts*, connect the uterus to the ovaries. The **ovaries** produce and store eggs. Each month, a mature egg is released from an ovary into a fallopian tube in a process known as **ovulation.** The ovaries are also part of the endocrine system because they produce hormones, such as *estrogen* and *progesterone*. These help a girl develop into a woman and prepare a woman's body for the development of a baby.

If the egg is fertilized, it will become implanted in the wall of the uterus. There it will grow and develop. If the egg is not fertilized, it will break down and be released through the vagina.

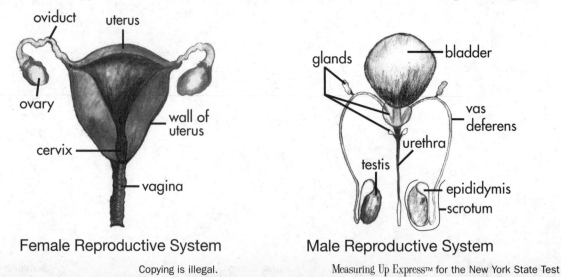

Female Reproductive System   Male Reproductive System

NYS Test Practice

Directions (1–7): Decide which choice is the best answer. Circle the number of the answer you have chosen.

1 The sex cells produced by the female reproductive system are

(1) eggs

(2) sperm

(3) ovaries

(4) hormones

2 What happens during fertilization?

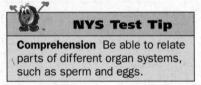

NYS Test Tip

Comprehension Be able to relate parts of different organ systems, such as sperm and eggs.

(1) A male produces testosterone.

(2) A baby is born.

(3) A sperm unites with an egg.

(4) The vas deferens becomes blocked.

3 Where does a fertilized egg grow and develop?

(1) scrotum

(2) vagina

(3) ovary

(4) uterus

4 Which is a female reproductive hormone?

(1) testosterone

(2) estrogen

(3) insulin

(4) thyroid

5 One function of the male reproductive system is to

(1) remove wastes from the body

(2) deliver oxygen to cells

(3) regulate hormone levels in the blood

(4) deliver sperm to the female reproductive system

6 About how often does ovulation occur?

(1) every day

(2) once a week

(3) once a month

(4) one a year

7 To what stimulus does the scrotum respond by changing size?

(1) motion

(2) temperature

(3) water level

(4) time of day

Directions (8–9): Record your answers on the lines provided below each question.

8   Trace the path of an egg after it is released from an ovary.   [1]

_____

_____

_____

9   How is the genetic information in sperm and egg cells different from other cells? Why?   [2]

_____

_____

_____

Lesson 25 Health and Nutrition

LE 5.2a Food provides molecules that serve as fuel and building material for all organisms.
LE 5.2b Foods contain a variety of substances, which include carbohydrates, fats, vitamins, proteins, minerals, and water. Each substance is vital to the survival of the organism.
LE 1.2a, LE 1.2b, LE 5.2c, LE 5.2d, LE 5.2e

Recognize that foods contain materials that the body needs to survive and grow.

Metabolism is the sum of all chemical reactions in the body. Certain factors can influence metabolism, including hormones, exercise, diet, and aging.

In order for the chemical reactions of the body to proceed, the cells need nutrients. Nutrients are provided by foods. The digestive system breaks down foods and releases the nutrients for the cells to use.

Foods contain several different types of nutrients. **Carbohydrates** are sugars, starches, and cellulose that provide the body with energy. Simple carbohydrates are found in fruits, dairy products, and some refined foods. They are digested quickly and give the body a surge of energy. Complex carbohydrates are found in such foods as vegetables, whole grain breads, and brown rice. They are digested more slowly by the body and supply energy over a longer period of time. When carbohydrates are digested, they are broken down into simple sugar called glucose.

Foods also contain fats. **Fats** and oils are found in meat, dairy, and eggs as well as butter, margarine, and shortening. Fat is important in the body because it is a component in cell membranes, it stores energy, and it lubricates body surfaces. Too much fat, however, can lead to heart illness and obesity.

Vitamins are substances necessary in small amounts to sustain life. They must be obtained from food because either the body does not produce them, or it produces them in amounts that are too small. Different vitamins help the body in specific ways. Vitamin A, for example, helps maintain the health of eyes and skin. The B vitamins help the body use energy and make red blood cells. Vitamin C keeps body tissues healthy, and helps protect the body from illness. Vitamin D helps the body absorb the calcium it needs to maintain strong bones and teeth.

Proteins are substances necessary for building many structures in the body, such as muscles and organs. They are involved in tissue growth and repair, and they create and signal hormones. Proteins are found in foods such as eggs, meat, and dairy, as well as grains, legumes, nuts, and seeds.

Water makes up about 70 percent of the human body. It is necessary for many chemical reactions in the body to proceed. It might be considered the most important nutrient because a person cannot survive for very long without water.

The amount of energy in foods is measured in **Calories.** The number of Calories in each type of food varies as does the number of Calories needed by each person. To maintain homeostasis, a person must take in the minimum daily amount of each type of nutrient. The proper amount depends on age, size, gender, and the amount of physical activity the person performs each day.

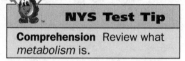

Directions (1–7): Decide which choice is the best answer. Circle the number of the answer you have chosen.

1   The sum of all chemical reactions in the body is

> **NYS Test Tip**
>
> **Comprehension** Review what *metabolism* is.

 (1) metabolism

 (2) digestion

 (3) respiration

 (4) excretion

2   A nutritionist is studying the energy content in different foods. She should measure the energy content of food in

 (1) servings

 (2) grams

 (3) Calories

 (4) pounds

3   Which body system breaks down food to release the nutrients that cells need?

 (1) endocrine system

 (2) digestive system

 (3) circulatory system

 (4) excretory system

4   If a human body is likened to a car, food is most like

 (1) the outside frame

 (2) the exhaust it gives off

 (3) the fuel it uses

 (4) the tires

5   All of the following are examples of carbohydrates except

 (1) sugars

 (2) starches

 (3) oils

 (4) cellulose

6   What is one way that proteins are needed by the body?

 (1) They act as a building material.

 (2) They break down vitamins.

 (3) They release energy from foods.

 (4) They store energy.

7   Which food is the greatest source of fat?

 (1) fruit

 (2) bread

 (3) brown rice

 (4) butter

Directions (8–9): Record your answers on the lines provided below each question.

8   Why does a person need to take in vitamins through foods each day?   [1]

_____

_____

9   How might the minimum daily intake vary with the amount of physical activity?   [1]

_____

_____

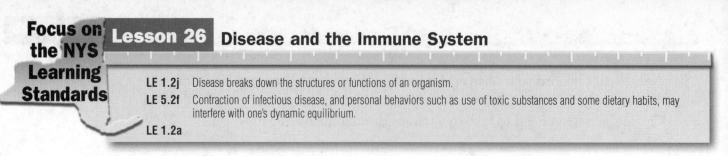

Focus on the NYS Learning Standards

Lesson 26 Disease and the Immune System

LE 1.2j   Disease breaks down the structures or functions of an organism.
LE 5.2f   Contraction of infectious disease, and personal behaviors such as use of toxic substances and some dietary habits, may interfere with one's dynamic equilibrium.
LE 1.2a

Know how the body protects itself from disease, as well as how personal actions may interfere with the immune system.

A **disease** is any disorder of the body that prevents it from functioning properly. An *infectious disease* is one that can be spread from one person to another. It is spread by bacteria, viruses, fungi, or parasites. A **pathogen** is an organism that causes disease. Some pathogens destroy cells in the body. Others release chemicals that interfere with normal body processes. A *noninfectious disease* cannot be spread from one person to another.

The **immune system** is the body system that protects the body from infectious disease. The first line of defense of the immune system includes the surfaces of the skin, breathing passages, mouth, and stomach. These barriers trap and kill most pathogens that come in contact with the body.

If pathogens manage to enter the body, they release chemicals that trigger an **inflammatory response.** Fluids and white blood cells enter tissues from nearby blood vessels. White blood cells known as phagocytes engulf pathogens and destroy them.

If the pathogen infection is severe enough, it then triggers an **immune response.** White blood cells known as lymphocytes are involved in the immune response. T lymphocytes, or T cells, identify the **antigens** on the pathogen. B lymphocytes, or B cells, then produce **antibodies** that bind with that specific antigen. Some antibodies make pathogens clump together. Others prevent pathogens from destroying cells, and still others make it easier for phagocytes to destroy pathogens.

Antibodies	B cells	T cells
proteins that bind to pathogens and mark them for destruction by macrophages	make antibodies; memory B cells remember how to make antibodies for specific pathogens	puncture infected cells; coordinate immune response

A person's health can suffer because of personal behaviors. For example, a person might not take in enough vitamins or minerals. A deficiency of vitamin D, for example, means that a person will not be able to absorb enough calcium. This may lead to a disease called *rickets*. A lack of vitamin C may lead to *scurvy*, which is a disease that involves bleeding gums and swollen joints. A lack of iron can lead to *anemia*.

In some cases, a damaged or weakened organ may lead to sickness. *Cirrhosis* occurs when a person consumes too much alcohol, thereby damaging liver cells. If a person's poor diet leads to clogged arteries, the heart may not get enough blood. People can decrease their risk of disease by maintaining a healthy lifestyle and avoiding poor habits.

Measuring Up Express™ for the New York State Test

NYS Test Practice

Directions (1–7): Decide which choice is the best answer. Circle the number of the answer you have chosen.

1   The main function of the immune system is to

(1) produce new blood cells

(2) protect the body from infectious disease

(3) prevent a person from an unhealthy lifestyle

(4) remove toxins from the blood

2   How does a disease affect an organism?

(1) It breaks down the structures of the organism.

(2) It causes the organism to shrink in size.

(3) It prevents the organism from using energy.

(4) It increases the person's metabolism.

3   An example of an infectious disease is

(1) diabetes

(2) allergies

(3) heart disease

(4) tuberculosis

4   What is the role of phagocytes in the immune system?

(1) to produce antibodies

(2) to recognize antigens on pathogens

(3) to engulf and destroy pathogens

(4) to create a barrier so pathogens cannot enter the body

5   Antibodies affect pathogens by

(1) engulfing and digesting them

(2) binding with their antigens

(3) preventing them from entering the body

(4) producing white blood cells

6   A person increases the risk of disease by

(1) taking drugs

(2) taking vitamins daily

(3) exercising regularly

(4) drinking a lot of water

7   Drinking alcohol excessively can lead to the direct breakdown of the

(1) lungs

(2) brain

(3) kidney

(4) liver

Directions (8–9): Record your answers on the lines provided below each question.

8 How is an infectious disease different from a noninfectious disease? [1]

_____

_____

_____

9 How do T cells and B cells work together to destroy pathogens? [1]

_____

_____

 Measuring Up Express™ for the New York State Test

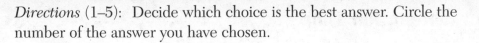

Directions (1–5): Decide which choice is the best answer. Circle the number of the answer you have chosen.

1 How might the circulatory system be directly affected by a breakdown in the skeletal system?

(1) Blood cells would not be produced.

(2) Oxygen could not be transferred to blood.

(3) Wastes could not be removed by blood.

(4) Blood could not move through the body.

2 Blood is oxygen rich when it travels to the heart from the

(1) brain   (3) lungs

(2) liver   (4) kidneys

3 Which organ of the human body produces cells that contain half the genetic information of all other body cells?

(1) ovary   (3) brain

(2) uterus   (4) kidney

4 How would the body be affected if the walls of the small intestine became thick and rubbery?

(1) Nutrients would not be able to enter the bloodstream.

(2) Wastes could not be removed from the body.

(3) Oxygen could not be delivered to cells.

(4) The activities of organs could not be regulated.

5 If the kidneys stop working, the body will

(1) have a slower metabolism

(2) lose oxygen to the air

(3) retain excess fluid

(4) be unable to absorb nutrients

Directions (6): Record your answer on the lines provided below the question.

6 A doctor tells a patient that her daily intake of fat should be less than 30 percent of the total calories. There are 9 calories in each gram of fat. Explain how to find the limit of fat in grams for a person on a 2,000-calorie diet. [2]

_____

_____

_____

Higher-Order Performance Task

Reaction Time

Task:

You are going to investigate the reaction time of your nervous system to an external stimulus.

Materials:
- 30-cm ruler
- pens of different colors
- graph paper

Directions:

1. Sit in a chair with your arm resting on a desk. Your wrist should hang off the edge of the desk.

2. Have a partner hold a ruler just above your hand with the 0-mark on the ruler closest to your fingers.

3. When your partner lets go of the ruler, try to catch it between your thumb and forefinger as quickly as you can.

4. In Data Table 1, record the marking on the ruler where your fingers caught it for Partner 1's Trial 1. Then repeat two more times.

Data Table 1

Marking On Ruler (cm)

	Trial 1	Trial 2	Trial 3
Partner 1			
Partner 2			

5. Change places with your partner and repeat Steps 1 through 4.

6. Your reaction time is the length of time it took for your eyes to send a message to your brain that the ruler was falling, and then for your brain to send a message directing your fingers to catch it. Compare each measurement you recorded with the reaction time indicated on the chart. Round each measurement to the nearest 5 centimeters. Record the reaction time in Data Table 2.

Reaction Time

Distance on Ruler (cm)	Reaction Time (s)
5	0.10
10	0.14
15	0.18
20	0.20
25	0.23
30	0.25

Data Table 2

Reaction Time (seconds)

	Trial 1	Trial 2	Trial 3
Partner 1			
Partner 2			

7. Draw a graph to record your results. Write the times from the reaction time chart along the y-axis. Write "Trial 1," "Trial 2," and "Trial 3" across the x-axis. In one color, make a mark at the reaction times for each trial for Partner 1. Draw a bar from the x-axis to each mark. Next to each bar for Partner 1, create a bar for Partner 2 in a different color using the data from Partner 2.

8. Did the reaction times change from Trial 1 to Trial 3? How can you tell?

_____

_____

9. Did the reaction time differ between the two partners? How can you tell?

_____

_____

10. Describe how you might adjust the procedure to look for relationships between reaction time and a body characteristic, such as age, height, or participation in sports.

_____

_____

_____

_____

11. With your teacher's approval, conduct your revised experiment. Share your results with the class.

12. When you have finished, put all the materials back the way you found them.

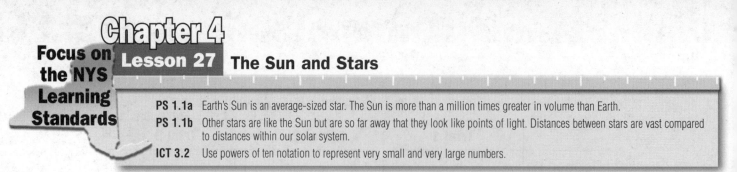

Chapter 4

Focus on the NYS Learning Standards

Lesson 27 The Sun and Stars

PS 1.1a Earth's Sun is an average-sized star. The Sun is more than a million times greater in volume than Earth.

PS 1.1b Other stars are like the Sun but are so far away that they look like points of light. Distances between stars are vast compared to distances within our solar system.

ICT 3.2 Use powers of ten notation to represent very small and very large numbers.

Understand how stars form and how they differ from one another.

A **star** is a glowing ball of hot gas. Stars form when clouds of dust and gas collapse under the force of gravity. The immense pressure created by gravity causes fusion reactions to begin, in which hydrogen atoms join together to form heavier helium atoms. This process creates huge amounts of energy, part of which is radiated away as visible light. The Sun, on which Earth depends for energy, is just one of billions of stars in the universe.

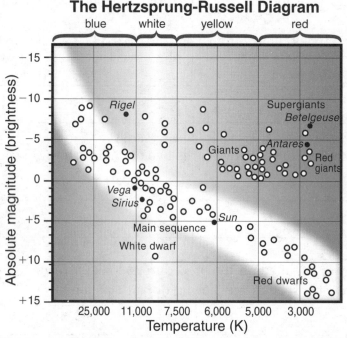

The **Hertzsprung-Russell diagram** organizes stars according to their temperature and brightness. According to the diagram, the Sun is an average star in terms of temperature and brightness. It is also average in terms of size when compared with other stars. When compared with Earth, however, the Sun is a million times greater in volume than Earth.

To an observer on Earth, the Sun appears to be the largest star in the sky. The reason is that the Sun is closer to Earth than any other star. Other stars are so far away from Earth that they look like small points of light. If all stars were at the same distance from Earth, it would become obvious that many stars are much larger than the Sun.

To describe the vast distances between objects in space, scientists use a unit of distance known as the **light-year.** One light-year is the distance that light can travel in one year. Because nothing is known to travel faster than the speed of light, one light-year is a great distance. Light travels 300,000 kilometers per second, which means that it covers 9.5 trillion kilometers in one year. The closest star to the Sun is about 4 light-years away.

Scientists also use **scientific notation** to describe very large numbers. In scientific notation, a base number is described to a power of 10. That means that 300,000 kilometers per second would become 3.0×10^6 kilometers per second.

NYS Test Practice

Directions (1–7): Decide which choice is the best answer. Circle the number of the answer you have chosen.

1   The unit that is best for expressing distances between stars is the

(1) angstrom

(2) meter

(3) light-year

(4) degree

2   When compared with other stars in the universe, the Sun is

(1) average in size

(2) larger the most

(3) smaller than most

(4) the largest star there is

3   When compared with the volume of Earth, the Sun's volume is about

(1) the same

(2) a million times smaller

(3) twice as great

(4) a million times greater

4   Why does the Sun look larger than other star?

(1) Its volume is greater than other stars.

(2) It shines more brightly than other stars.

(3) It is closer to Earth than other stars.

(4) It is a different color than other stars.

5   The next closest star to the Sun is 4 light-years away. About how far away is this star from the Sun?

(1) 10 trillion kilometers

(2) 20 trillion kilometers

(3) 30 trillion kilometers

(4) 40 trillion kilometers

6   When compared with distance between planets in the solar system, distances between stars are

(1) about the same

(2) much larger

(3) a little smaller

(4) much smaller

7   An astronomer finds the distance between two stars to be 25,000,000,000,000 kilometers. How is this number written in scientific notation?

(1) 2.5×10^{13} km

(2) 25×10^{13} km

(3) 2.5×10^{12} km

(4) 25×13 km

Directions (8–10): Record your answers on the lines provided below each question.

8   A student is making a model showing the Sun, Earth, and another star.

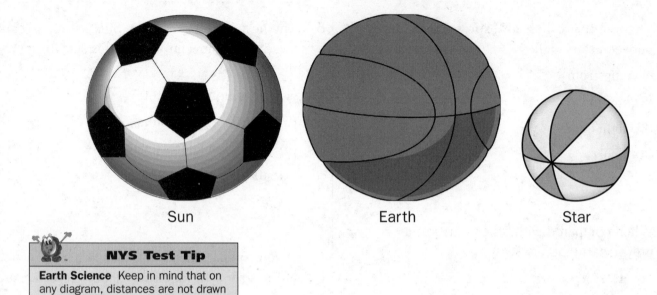

Sun   Earth   Star

NYS Test Tip

Earth Science Keep in mind that on any diagram, distances are not drawn to scale unless it says that they are.

What are two shortcomings of the model?   [1]

_____

_____

_____

_____

9   Explain *two* similarities between stars.   [1]

_____

_____

10 How are stars different?   [1]

_____

_____

Focus on the NYS Learning Standards

Lesson 28 Earth's Motion

PS 1.1h	The apparent motions of the Sun, Moon, planets, and stars across the sky can be explained by Earth's rotation and revolution.
PS 1.1i	The tilt of Earth's axis of rotation and the revolution of Earth around the Sun cause seasons on Earth. The length of daylight varies depending on latitude and season.
PS 1.1e, ICT 5.2	

Explain how Earth's regular rotation causes night and day, and how Earth's tilt and revolution cause seasons.

An **axis** is the imaginary line passing through a planet's poles, around which the planet rotates.

Rotation is the turning of an object on its axis. Earth rotates on its axis much like a top spins. However, Earth's axis is slightly tilted when compared with the direction to the Sun. Earth rotates once every 24 hours, so one rotation is equal to one day.

Revolution is the movement of an object in a path around another body. It takes about 365.26 days for one revolution of Earth around the Sun.

An **orbit** is the elliptical path a body takes as it travels around another body in space.

A **solstice** occurs when the Sun's direct rays point to one of the tropics.

The **summer solstice** occurs in the Northern Hemisphere when the Sun's direct rays point directly at the Tropic of Cancer, a latitude line north of the equator. The Sun passes through the summer solstice on or around June 21. On this day, the Northern Hemisphere has its longest period of daylight and its shortest night. This marks the first day of summer. Because more direct radiation is striking the Northern Hemisphere, it experiences warm weather from the solstice through the next couple of months. The opposite occurs in the Southern Hemisphere.

The **winter solstice** occurs in the Northern Hemisphere when the Sun's direct rays point directly at the Tropic of Capricorn, a latitude line south of the equator. The Sun passes through the winter solstice on or around December 21. On this day, the Northern Hemisphere has its longest night and its shortest period of daylight. This marks the first day of winter. Because less direct radiation is striking the Northern Hemisphere, it experiences cold weather from the winter solstice through the next couple of months. The opposite occurs in the Southern Hemisphere.

An **equinox** occurs when the Sun's direct rays point to the equator. During an equinox, neither pole leans toward the Sun. An equinox occurs twice a year. The *vernal* or spring equinox occurs at noon around March 21 and marks the first day of spring. The *autumnal* equinox occurs at noon around September 23 and marks the first day of autumn.

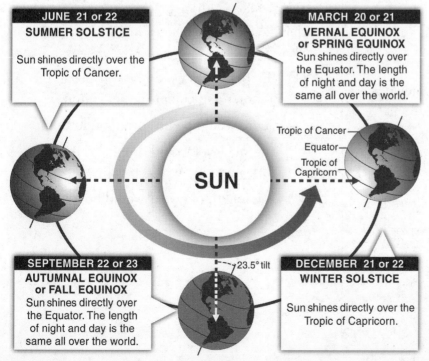

JUNE 21 or 22
SUMMER SOLSTICE
Sun shines directly over the Tropic of Cancer.

MARCH 20 or 21
VERNAL EQUINOX or SPRING EQUINOX
Sun shines directly over the Equator. The length of night and day is the same all over the world.

SUN

Tropic of Cancer
Equator
Tropic of Capricorn

23.5° tilt

SEPTEMBER 22 or 23
AUTUMNAL EQUINOX or FALL EQUINOX
Sun shines directly over the Equator. The length of night and day is the same all over the world.

DECEMBER 21 or 22
WINTER SOLSTICE
Sun shines directly over the Tropic of Capricorn.

NYS Test Practice   *Directions* (1–7): Decide which choice is the best answer. Circle the number of the answer you have chosen.

1   One reason that Earth has seasons is that it

(1) rotates on its axis

(2) revolves around the Sun

(3) is shaped like a sphere

(4) has a Moon

2   If Earth were not tilted on its axis, but rotated as shown,

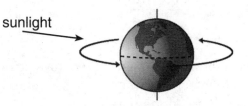

sunlight

(1) the number of hours in a day would decrease

(2) there would be no North or South Pole

(3) the seasons would be hotter in summer and colder in winter.

(4) the length of day and night would always be the same

3   What would be the most significant change if Earth did not rotate, but still revolved?

(1) One half of Earth would always have nighttime and the other half would always have daytime.

(2) The tilt of Earth's axis would be altered.

(3) The polar caps would increase in size.

(4) Each place on Earth would have 6 months of daytime followed by 6 months of nighttime.

4   Look at the diagram below.

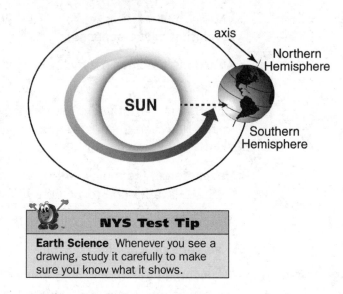

NYS Test Tip

Earth Science Whenever you see a drawing, study it carefully to make sure you know what it shows.

Which season does the diagram show?

(1) summer in the Northern Hemisphere

(2) autumn in the Northern Hemisphere

(3) winter in the Northern Hemisphere

(4) winter in the Southern Hemisphere

5   If Earth were tilted at an angle greater than 23.5°, what changes might there be in New York?

(1) Temperatures would be warmer in the summer and colder in the winter.

(2) There would be no spring or autumn.

(3) The sea level would drop, and the New York shoreline would be larger.

(4) The length of a year would be longer.

6   Examine the diagram below.

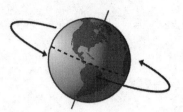

The diagram illustrates

(1) Earth's orbit

(2) Earth's rotation

(3) Earth's revolution

(4) Earth's ascension

7   Why does the position of the Sun appear to change in the sky?

(1) The Sun moves up and down throughout the day.

(2) The Sun moves out of the solar system and then returns.

(3) The Sun appears to move as Earth moves relative to the Sun.

(4) Earth tilts toward the Sun during the day and away from the Sun at night.

Directions (8–9): Record your answers on the lines provided below each question.

8   Describe where the North Pole tilts during winter and summer in the Northern Hemisphere.   [2]

_____

_____

_____

9   Spring is the season that occurs between winter and summer. How does the length of day and night compare in spring?   [2]

_____

_____

Lesson 29 **Movements of the Moon**

PS 1.1e   Most objects in the solar system have a regular and predictable motion. These motions explain such phenomena as a day, a year, phases of the Moon, eclipses, tides, meteor showers, and comets.

PS 1.1g   Moons are seen by reflected light. Our Moon orbits Earth, while Earth orbits the Sun. The Moon's phases as observed from Earth are the result of seeing different portions of the lighted area of the Moon's surface. The phases repeat in a cyclic pattern in about one month.

PS 1.1h   The apparent motions of the Sun, Moon, planets, and stars across the sky can be explained by Earth's rotation and revolution.

Understand the effects of the movements of the Moon.

Just as Earth revolves around the Sun, the Moon revolves around Earth. The Moon takes about 28 days to make one revolution around Earth. The length of the Moon's revolution is the same as its rotation. As a result, the same side of the Moon always faces Earth.

The Moon does not produce its own light. One half of the Moon is always lit by the light of the Sun. Observers on Earth see light that is reflected by the Moon.

As the Moon revolves around Earth, observers on Earth see different portions of the lit half of the Moon. The various appearances of the Moon are called the **phases of the Moon.** The phases of the Moon result from the changing relationship among the Moon, Earth, and the Sun. As the moon passes from new to full, people say that the moon is "waxing" because it looks larger. As the moon passes from full to new, it is said to be "waning."

Lunar Cycle

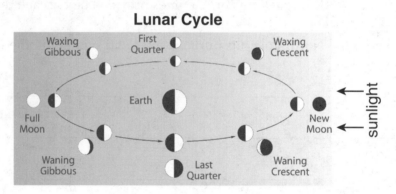

The Moon's motion also causes tides. The **tides** are changes in the levels of Earth's oceans caused by the pull of gravity from the Moon and Sun. As the Moon revolves around Earth, it creates high tides on the side of Earth facing the Moon as well as the opposite side of Earth. It creates low tides on the sides of Earth perpendicular to the Moon.

The Sun also exerts a gravitational force on Earth's oceans. The Sun's pull can add to or take away from the effects of the Moon. **Spring tides** occur during the New Moon and Full Moon phases, when the tidal bulges from the Moon and Sun add together. **Neap tides** occur during the first quarter and last quarter phases of the Moon, when the Moon and Sun are at right angles to each other.

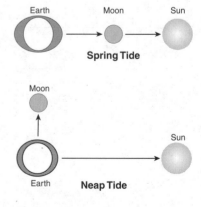

An *eclipse* occurs when an object in the path of the Sun's light casts a shadow. A **solar eclipse** happens when a New Moon passes directly between the Sun and Earth. During a solar eclipse, a shadow of the Moon forms on parts of Earth.

A **lunar eclipse** happens when the Full Moon moves through the shadow of Earth. During a lunar eclipse, Earth blocks some or all of the Sun's light causing the Moon to darken.

Measuring Up Express™ for the New York State Test

NYS Test Practice

Directions (1–6): Decide which choice is the best answer. Circle the number of the answer you have chosen.

1 What is one effect of the Moon's 28-day rotation as it makes one revolution around Earth?

(1) The phases of the Moon change more quickly than they would otherwise.

(2) The tides are not as strong as they would be otherwise.

(3) The same side of the Moon is always facing Earth.

(4) Solar eclipses can block the entire Sun.

2 Which phase of the Moon occurs when the Moon is between the Sun and Earth?

(1) full

(2) first quarter

(3) waxing gibbous

(4) new

3 Approximately how long does it take the Moon to transition from a New Moon to a Full Moon and back to a New Moon?

(1) 1 day

(2) 1 week

(3) 1 month

(4) 1 year

4 Examine the diagram.

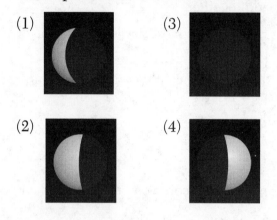

Which phase of the Moon will occur next?

(1)

(3)

(2)

(4)

5 Which of these events on Earth is directly related to the motion of the Moon?

(1) ocean tides

(2) day and night

(3) seasons

(4) years

6   Why are high tides higher than normal during a spring tide?

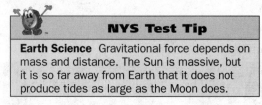

NYS Test Tip

Earth Science   Gravitational force depends on mass and distance. The Sun is massive, but it is so far away from Earth that it does not produce tides as large as the Moon does.

(1)   The Moon is closest to Earth at this time of the month.

(2)   The gravitational pulls of the Moon and Sun add together.

(3)   Earth moves most slowly at this time of the year.

(4)   The oceans begin flow slightly because Earth tilts.

Directions (7–8):   Record your answers on the lines provided below each question.

7   What is the difference between a waxing Moon and a waning Moon?   [2]

_____

_____

_____

8   How is it possible for the Moon, which is smaller than Earth, to block light from the Sun during a solar eclipse?   [2]

_____

_____

_____

Lesson 30 The Solar System

PS 1.1c The Sun and the planets that revolve around it are the major bodies in the solar system. Other members include comets, moons, and asteroids. Earth's orbit is nearly circular.

PS 1.1e Most objects in the solar system have a regular and predictable motion. These motions explain such phenomena as a day, a year, phases of the Moon, eclipses, tides, meteor showers, and comets.

PS 1.1d, PS 1.1j, ICT 5.2

Trace the motion of objects in the solar system, and know that their motion is governed by gravity.

The **solar system** includes the Sun, all the planets, and their moons. It also includes smaller objects, such as dwarf planets, asteroids, and comets.

All objects in the solar system are held by the gravitational pull of the Sun. **Gravity** is the force of attraction between any pair of objects in the universe. Because the mass of the Sun is so great, its gravitational pull is strong enough to keep planets and other objects in orbit around it.

A **planet** is a large, ball-shaped object that revolves around the Sun. All of the planets are nearly spherical in shape. The path a planet follows as it revolves is known as its **orbit**. The orbit of a planet is nearly circular. A more precise description is as a circle that is slightly stretched, or an **ellipse**. The length of time it takes for a planet to complete one revolution determines one year on that planet.

The four planets closest to the Sun are the **inner planets**. The inner planets are Mercury, Venus, Earth, and Mars. These planets are rocky, dense, and smaller than the outer planets.

The four planets farthest away from the Sun are the **outer planets**. The outer planets are Jupiter, Saturn, Uranus, and Neptune. The outer planets are made mostly of gases.

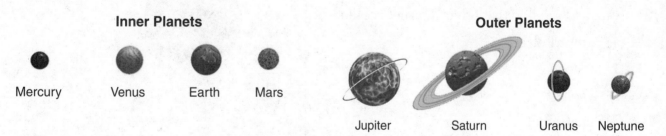

Inner Planets

Mercury   Venus   Earth   Mars

Outer Planets

Jupiter   Saturn   Uranus   Neptune

A **moon** is a natural object that orbits a planet. Earth has one moon, but other planets have more than one moon or no moons at all.

A **dwarf planet** is an object that has enough mass that it forms a sphere. A dwarf planet is not a moon, but is not as massive as a planet. Pluto, once considered to be a planet, was renamed as a dwarf planet called a *plutoid*.

An **asteroid** is a rock or large boulder that orbits the Sun. Most are located in the asteroid belt between Mars and Jupiter.

Comets are chunks of frozen gases, ice, and dust. They are often described as dirty snowballs. As a comet approaches the Sun, some of the frozen gases evaporate and form a bright tail that is visible from Earth.

Directions (1–8): Decide which choice is the best answer. Circle the number of the answer you have chosen.

1 Of those listed, which is the largest spherical object that revolves around the Sun in an elliptical orbit?

(1) asteroid

(2) comet

(3) planet

(4) moon

2 The force responsible for holding the planets in their orbits around the Sun is due to

(1) gravity

(2) electricity

(3) magnetism

(4) temperature

3 A natural satellite that orbits a planet is called

(1) a dwarf planet

(2) a moon

(3) a comet

(4) an asteroid

4 Which object most closely resembles the shape of a planet in the solar system?

(1)

(2)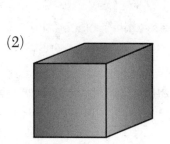

(3)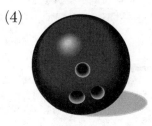

(4)

5 The inner planets in order beginning with the planet closest to the Sun are

(1) Mercury, Venus, Earth, Mars

(2) Earth, Venus, Mars, Mercury

(3) Mars, Earth, Venus, Mercury

(4) Venus, Mercury, Mars, Earth

6   The length of one year on a planet is most directly related to its

   (1) diameter

   (2) revolution

   (3) rotation

   (4) temperature

7   An astronomer observes an object with a tail passing near the Sun. The object is most likely

   (1) an asteroid

   (2) a dwarf planet

   (3) a moon

   (4) a comet

8   Eris and Ceres are two dwarf planets in the solar system. What must be true about these objects?

   (1) They revolve around larger planets.

   (2) They have at least one moon.

   (3) They are nearly spherical in shape.

   (4) They evaporate near the Sun.

Directions (9–10): Record your answers on the lines provided below each question.

9   How is the orbit of a moon different from the orbit of a planet?   [1]

_____

_____

10 The length of one year on Earth is 365 days. The length of one year on Mercury is about 2 Earth-years. What does this tell you about Mercury's orbit?   [1]

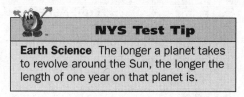

NYS Test Tip

Earth Science The longer a planet takes to revolve around the Sun, the longer the length of one year on that planet is.

_____

_____

Focus on the NYS Learning Standards

Lesson 31 **Latitude and Longitude**

PS 1.1f The latitude/longitude coordinate system and our system of time are based on celestial observations.

Understand the geographical and celestial coordinate systems.

The most common way to locate points on the surface of Earth is using **latitude** and **longitude**. These coordinate values are measured in degrees. They represent angular distances from the center of Earth. Any location on Earth can be described precisely by giving its latitude and longitude.

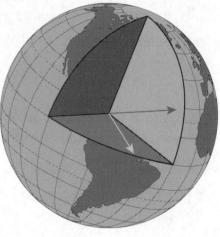

The **equator** is an imaginary line around the center of Earth. It is an equal distance from both poles. The latitude measurement describing the equator is 0 degrees. The equator is the starting point for measuring latitude.

A line, such as the equator, connecting points with the same latitude is known as a **line of latitude.** All lines of latitude are parallel to the equator, and are sometimes known as **parallels.** Lines of latitude are equally spaced. There are 90 degrees between the equator and the North Pole and 90 degrees between the equator and the South Pole. Latitudes north of the equator are generally given positive values and latitudes south of the equator are given negative values.

Lines of longitude run perpendicular to lines of latitude. They are also known as **meridians.** There is no obvious starting point for lines of longitude as there is for latitude. By international agreement, the line of longitude running through Greenwich, England is currently given the value of 0 degrees. It is known as the **prime meridian.** There are 180 degrees of longitude east of the Prime Meridian and 180 degrees of longitude west of the Prime Meridian.

The lines of latitude and longitude on a map are geographical coordinates. To describe positions of stars or planets, scientists can also use celestial coordinates. The lines correlating to lines of latitude are known as *declination* and the lines correlating to longitude are known as right *ascension*.

Everyone along the same line of longitude observes the same time. For example, all people along the same line of longitude observe sunrise at the same time. Everyone on the same line of latitude observes the same part of the sky. Observers at different latitudes see different parts of the sky, or they see the same objects in the sky but at different altitudes.

Celestial Sphere

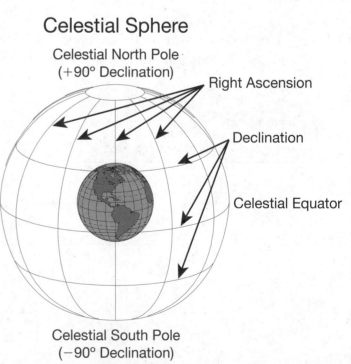

Celestial North Pole
(+90° Declination)

Right Ascension

Declination

Celestial Equator

Celestial South Pole
(−90° Declination)

NYS Test Practice

Directions (1–5): Decide which choice is the best answer. Circle the number of the answer you have chosen.

Base your answers to questions 1 through 3 on the diagram below and on your knowledge of science.

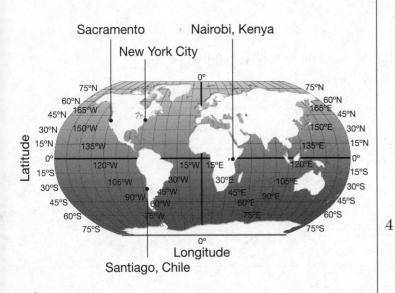

1 What line of latitude is closest to New York City, New York?

(1) 10° N

(2) 40° N

(3) 60° N

(4) 90° N

2 What line of longitude is closest to Sacramento, California?

(1) 45° W

(2) 90° W

(3) 150° W

(4) 180° W

3 Which city is closest to the equator?

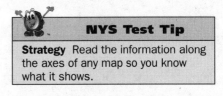

NYS Test Tip

Strategy Read the information along the axes of any map so you know what it shows.

(1) New York City, New York

(2) Sacramento, California

(3) Santiago, Chile

(4) Nairobi, Kenya

4 Why might observations of objects in the sky change throughout the day?

(1) Earth rotates on its axis.

(2) Earth revolves around the Sun.

(3) Lines of longitude shift on Earth over time.

(4) Earth's poles shift during a day.

5 A researcher is standing at a location with a latitude of 90 degrees. The researcher looks directly upward to the sky and observes a star named Polaris. How will Polaris appear to move during the next 24 hours?

(1) It will move up and down.

(2) It will move in a curve toward the equator.

(3) It will spin in a circle.

(4) It will move in a horizontal line.

Directions (6–9): Record your answers on the lines provided below each question.

6   Why are lines of latitude called parallels?   [1]

_____

_____

7   What does Greenwich, England have to do with finding your location on a map?   [1]

_____

_____

8   Where do all lines of longitude meet?   [1]

_____

_____

9   Scientists often use compasses to relate direction to location on a map. Describe a compass and list the cardinal directions that can be determined using the magnetic compass shown.   [2]

_____

_____

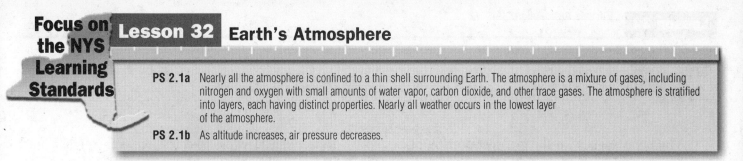

PS 2.1a Nearly all the atmosphere is confined to a thin shell surrounding Earth. The atmosphere is a mixture of gases, including nitrogen and oxygen with small amounts of water vapor, carbon dioxide, and other trace gases. The atmosphere is stratified into layers, each having distinct properties. Nearly all weather occurs in the lowest layer of the atmosphere.

PS 2.1b As altitude increases, air pressure decreases.

Identify the characteristics of Earth's atmosphere.

The **atmosphere** is a thin shell of gases surrounding Earth. The atmosphere is a mixture of gases, made up mostly of nitrogen and oxygen. It also contains small amounts of other gases, including water vapor, carbon dioxide, argon, and other trace gases.

Gaseous composition
of dry air

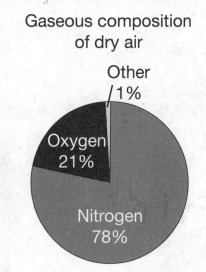

The atmosphere is described by layers with distinct properties. The layer closest to Earth is the **troposphere.** Nearly all weather occurs in this layer.

The next layer is the **stratosphere.** This layer contains the ozone layer. Weather balloons travel in this layer of the atmosphere.

Above the stratosphere is the **mesosphere.** Temperatures in this layer become colder as altitude increases.

The fourth layer of the atmosphere is the **thermosphere.** The air in this layer becomes very thin and temperature increases with altitude due to energy from the Sun.

The **exosphere** is the outermost layer of the atmosphere. Air particles are very widely spaced in this layer. There is no real limit to this layer because beyond it lies outer space.

Air pressure is the force of air particles over a given area. Another way to think of air pressure is as the weight of air above a point. As altitude in the atmosphere increases, air pressure decreases.

Exosphere

Troposphere

Mesosphere

Thermosphere

Stratosphere

Directions (1–8): Decide which choice is the best answer. Circle the number of the answer you have chosen.

1 Which gas makes up the greatest portion of the atmosphere?

   (1) oxygen

   (2) carbon dioxide

   (3) nitrogen

   (4) water vapor

2 The ozone layer protects and insulates Earth from some of the Sun's harmful radiation. In which layer of the atmosphere is this found?

   (1) troposphere

   (2) stratosphere

   (3) mesosphere

   (4) thermosphere

3 The layer of the atmosphere in which nearly all weather occurs is the

   (1) troposphere

   (2) stratosphere

   (3) mesosphere

   (4) thermosphere

4 What happens to air pressure as a climber ascends Mount Everest?

   (1) Air pressure stays the same.

   (2) Air pressure increases.

   (3) Air pressure decreases.

   (4) Air pressure increases and then decreases.

Base your answers to questions 5 through 7 on the table below. The table shows the altitude at which each layer of the atmosphere begins and ends.

Layer	Altitude (km)
Troposphere	0-15
Stratosphere	15-50
Mesosphere	50-85
Thermosphere	85-600

5 Which is the thickest layer of the atmosphere?

   (1) troposphere

   (2) stratosphere

   (3) mesosphere

   (4) thermosphere

6 A communications satellite orbits Earth at an altitude of 242 kilometers. In what layer of the atmosphere is the satellite located?

   (1) troposphere

   (2) stratosphere

   (3) mesosphere

   (4) thermosphere

   Measuring Up Express™ for the New York State Test

7   A weather balloon can reach an altitude of 27.4 kilometers before it bursts. In what layer of the atmosphere will the weather balloon burst?

(1) troposphere

(2) stratosphere

(3) mesosphere

(4) thermosphere

8   Which layer of the atmosphere has the greatest air pressure?

(1) troposphere

(2) stratosphere

(3) mesosphere

(4) thermosphere

Directions (9–10):   Record your answers on the lines provided below each question.

9   What is Earth's atmosphere?   [1]

_____

_____

10   Why does pressure decrease with altitude?   [1]

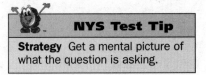

NYS Test Tip

Strategy Get a mental picture of what the question is asking.

_____

_____

_____

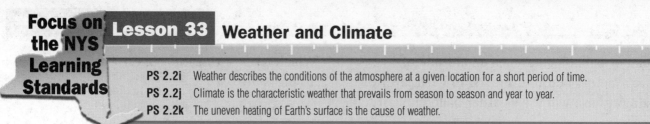

Lesson 33 Weather and Climate

PS 2.2i Weather describes the conditions of the atmosphere at a given location for a short period of time.
PS 2.2j Climate is the characteristic weather that prevails from season to season and year to year.
PS 2.2k The uneven heating of Earth's surface is the cause of weather.

Differentiate between weather and climate.

Weather describes the conditions of the atmosphere at a certain place for short periods, such as hours or days. Characteristics of weather include air temperature, air pressure, wind speed, humidity, and precipitation.

Air **temperature** is a measure of how warm or cold the air is. A **thermometer** is used to measure air temperature.

Air pressure is a measure of the force per unit area of the particles of air. A **barometer** is used to measure air pressure.

Wind speed is a measure of how fast air is moving. An **anemometer** is used to measure wind speed.

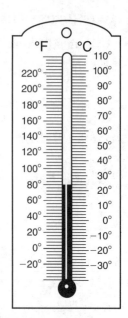

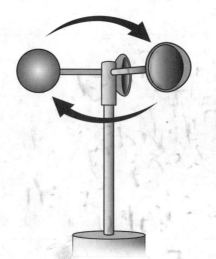

Wind is caused by the uneven heating of Earth's atmosphere. When an area of the atmosphere is heated by the Sun, it becomes warmer than surrounding areas. As air warms, its particles spread apart so its pressure decreases. The air pressure of a warmer region will be lower than the air pressure of a colder region. Air flows from areas of higher pressure to areas of lower pressure. The movement of air is wind.

The uneven heating of the atmosphere also leads to precipitation. When liquid water on Earth's surface absorbs energy from the Sun, it changes into water vapor in the atmosphere. When water vapor in the atmosphere loses energy, it changes into droplets of liquid water. Tiny droplets can combine and grow into larger drops. When they become heavy enough, the drops can fall back down to Earth's surface.

Precipitation is water that falls to Earth's surface as rain, sleet, hail, or snow. A **rain gauge** is used to measure the amount of rain that has fallen. A ruler is used to measure the amount of snow.

Climate describes the long-term weather patterns in a region. Despite short-term changes, the climate in a region prevails from season to season and year to year. For example, a temperate climate has moderate rainfall with distinct warm and cool seasons.

     Measuring Up Express™ for the New York State Test

NYS Test Practice

Directions (1–6): Decide which choice is the best answer. Circle the number of the answer you have chosen.

Base your answers to questions 1 through 3 on the table below and on your knowledge of science.

Climate	Average Precipitation (cm)	Average Temperature (°C)
Tropical moist (rainforest)	175–250	27
Dry tropical (desert)	0.25	above 16
Tundra	18	−8
Dry mid-latitude (grassland)	81	31

1   What conditions best describe the climate of a tropical rainforest?

(1) cool temperatures, little precipitation

(2) cool temperatures, plenty of precipitation

(3) hot temperatures, little precipitation

(4) warm temperatures, plenty of precipitation

2   The climate in a region is described as dry with less than one inch of rainfall a year. The average annual temperature is above 18°C (64°F). The region is most likely

(1) a desert

(2) a tundra

(3) a temperate forest

(4) a tropical rainforest

3   What characteristic do desert and tundra climates have in common?

(1) low temperatures

(2) little precipitation

(3) location

(4) wildlife

4   Energy from the Sun causes liquid water to become water vapor. What happens when that water vapor cools?

(1) It falls to Earth as precipitation.

(2) It changes back into liquid water.

(3) It seeps into the ground.

(4) It changes into a gas.

5   Which description gives the weather conditions in a location?

(1) It has wet and dry seasons every year.

(2) It receives about 42 cm of rain each year.

(3) It is a desert.

(4) It is snowing.

6   A scientist provided a description of the weather and climate in Albany, New York. How are the two descriptions different?

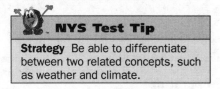

NYS Test Tip

Strategy Be able to differentiate between two related concepts, such as weather and climate.

(1)   Weather describes precipitation, whereas climate describes temperature conditions.

(2)   Weather describes conditions at a specific point in time, whereas climate describes long-term conditions.

(3)   Weather describes hazardous conditions, whereas climate describes pleasant conditions.

(4)   Weather describes conditions over land, whereas climate describes conditions over water.

Directions (7–8): Record your answers on the lines provided below each question.

7   What information does a weather report provide about a region?   [1]

_____

_____

8   If you know the climate of a region, what information do you know about the region?   [1]

_____

_____

Focus on the NYS Learning Standards

Lesson 34 Weather Systems and Changes

PS 2.2l	Air masses form when air remains nearly stationary over a large section of Earth's surface and takes on the conditions of temperature and humidity from that location. Weather conditions at a location are determined primarily by temperature, humidity, and pressure of air masses over that location.
PS 2.2m	Most local weather condition changes are caused by movement of air masses.

PS 2.2n, PS 2.2o, PS 2.2p, PS 2.2q, PS 2.2r, IS 3.2, ICT 3.1

Understand how weather systems develop and change and how they can be described.

An **air mass** is a body of air that remains over part of Earth's surface for a period of time and takes on the temperature and humidity of that area. The weather in an area depends on the characteristics of the air mass above it.

Once formed, air masses can move. Their movement is generally determined by **prevailing winds** and air currents in the atmosphere. Most local weather condition changes are caused by movements of air masses. Weather systems generally move from west to east across the United States.

A **front** forms when air masses of different temperatures meet. A **cold front** forms when a mass of cold air meets warm air and forces it upward. A **warm front** forms when a warm air mass meets a cold air mass, and the warm air rises above it.

A region of the atmosphere with higher pressure than the surrounding area is known as an **area of high pressure** (H). Air tends to spiral outward from the center of area of high pressure, causing the air to sink, warm, and absorb moisture. High-pressure systems generally bring fair weather.

A region of the atmosphere with lower pressure than the surrounding area is known as an **area of low pressure** (L). Air tends to spiral inward toward the center of an area of low pressure. This rising air often causes cloudy and rainy weather.

Weather can become hazardous occasionally. Hazardous weather conditions include thunderstorms, tornadoes, hurricanes, ice storms, and blizzards.

Hazardous weather	Description
Thunderstorm	Intense rainfall, with thunder, lighting, and high winds
Tornado	Violent swirling air with winds up to 500 km/h
Hurricane	Severe thunderstorms and high winds over a large area
Ice storm	Heavy rainfall in freezing temperatures that cause ice to form on structures
Blizzard	Intense snowstorm with high, cold winds

Substances in the atmosphere can all affect weather conditions. They enter the atmosphere through natural processes and human activities. These substances include dust from volcanic eruptions along with **greenhouse gases,** such as carbon dioxide and methane. Greenhouse gases are often released during the combustion of fossil fuels.

NYS Test Practice

Directions (1–7): Decide which choice is the best answer. Circle the number of the answer you have chosen.

1   The diagram shows a change in weather conditions.

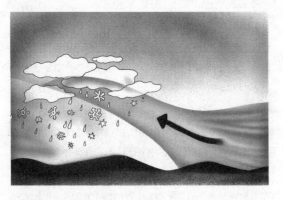

What change is occurring in the diagram?

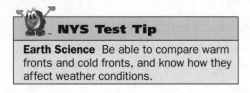

NYS Test Tip

Earth Science Be able to compare warm fronts and cold fronts, and know how they affect weather conditions.

(1) A warm front forms as a warm air mass encounters a cold air mass.

(2) Warm air causes clouds to form that produce a thunderstorm.

(3) A high pressure area causes clear weather to develop.

(4) A cold front forms as cold air moves over warm air.

2   A weather forecaster records areas of high pressure using a barometer. The weather conditions near the area of high pressure most likely involve

(1) tornadoes

(2) thunderstorms

(3) clear skies

(4) light rain or snow

3   The diagram shows the pattern of prevailing winds on Earth.

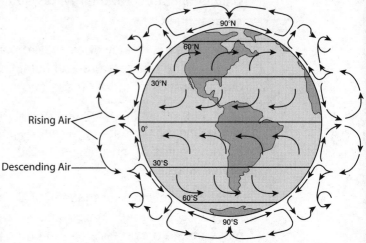

In which direction do prevailing winds blow air masses toward New York?

(1) southward from Canada

(2) eastward from Ohio

(3) northward from Florida

(4) westward from the Atlantic Ocean

4   Which type of hazardous weather is associated with high winds and heavy snow that makes it difficult to see when driving?

(1) tornado

(2) thunderstorm

(3) ice storm

(4) blizzard

5 How does a front form in the atmosphere?

(1) Water drops in clouds lose energy and freeze.

(2) Particles of air become warm and spread apart.

(3) Two air masses at different temperatures meet.

(4) High winds spiral around a single point.

6 Most local weather condition changes are caused by

(1) the movement of air masses

(2) volcanic eruptions

(3) greenhouse gases

(4) ocean currents

7 Which process will release greenhouse gases into the atmosphere?

(1) burning coal

(2) planting trees

(3) photosynthesis

(4) precipitation

Directions (8–9): Record your answers on the lines provided below each question.

8 How does an air mass form?   [1]

_____

_____

_____

9 What causes an air mass to move?   [1]

_____

_____

Focus on the NYS Learning Standards

Lesson 35   Earth's Hydrosphere

PS 2.1d   The majority of the lithosphere is covered by a relatively thin layer of water called the hydrosphere.

PS 2.1j   Water circulates through the atmosphere, lithosphere, and hydrosphere in what is known as the water cycle.

Understand how water moves through the environment to make up Earth's hydrosphere.

The thin layer of water on or near Earth is known as the **hydrosphere**. Water cycles through the hydrosphere, as well as Earth's land (lithosphere) and air (atmosphere) in the **water cycle**.

In the water cycle, liquid water on Earth evaporates into **water vapor** in the air. Water vapor in the air cools and condenses into drops of liquid water. When the drops become heavy enough, they fall to Earth as **precipitation**.

A **watershed** is an area of land from which water drains into a particular body of water, such as a river or stream. Freshwater typically enters a watershed as either rainfall or snowmelt.

Surface water includes water that flows or remains on the surface of Earth, such as lakes, streams, ponds, and wetlands. Surface water is replenished by precipitation.

Runoff is water that flows across land into a body of water. Runoff may move into streams, rivers, lakes, estuaries, or oceans. As it runs across Earth's surface, some water soaks into the ground and is taken up from the soil by plants and other organisms.

Groundwater is water below Earth's surface that fills the spaces between materials such as sand, soil, or gravel. Groundwater makes up only a tiny fraction of the total amount of water on Earth. However, groundwater is the most important source of freshwater for humans, agriculture, and industrial purposes.

The **water table** is the upper limit of groundwater. In some areas, the water table is just below Earth's surface. In other areas, the water table is so far below the surface that people must dig deep wells to reach the groundwater. When too much water is used or when there is a drought, the water table will drop. Then deeper wells need to be dug.

A **wetland** is an area of land that is under water for part or all of the year. Wetlands include marshes, swamps, and bogs. Marshes and swamps can have fresh or salty water, depending on the source of the water that floods the land. For example, a *salt marsh* is an area that is flooded by ocean water at high tide.

Oceans cover nearly three-quarters of Earth's surface. This means that the majority of the lithosphere is covered by water.

The diagrams show various features of Earth's water systems.

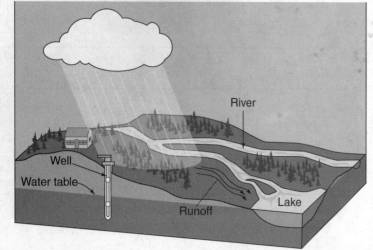

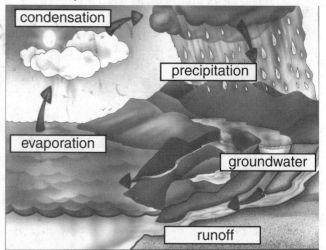

NYS Test Practice

Directions (1–8): Decide which choice is the best answer. Circle the number of the answer you have chosen.

Base your answers to questions 1 through 4 on the diagram below and on your knowledge of science.

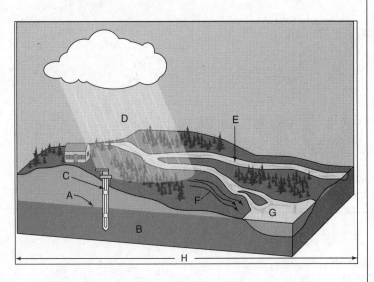

1 Which feature in the diagram represents surface water?

(1) D, E, and G

(2) B, E, and G

(3) Only E and G

(4) Only D and G

2 Feature H represents

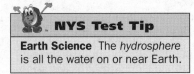

NYS Test Tip

Earth Science The *hydrosphere* is all the water on or near Earth.

(1) the water table

(2) groundwater

(3) a wetland

(4) a watershed

3 Features such as the one labeled "C" are used when

(1) the water table is far below the surface

(2) there is very little water in the watershed

(3) there is a need for uncontaminated water

(4) there is no source of surface water in the watershed

4 If the water level in Feature G goes down, what will also happen?

(1) A wetland will form.

(2) The well water will be unsafe to use.

(3) There will be more groundwater.

(4) The water table will go down.

5 Which statement is true?

(1) A freshwater marsh may become salty during a high tide.

(2) A wetland must remain underwater all the time.

(3) A salt marsh floods during a high tide.

(4) One type of wetland is a stream.

6 The process through which water in an ocean becomes water vapor in the air is

(1) runoff

(2) precipitation

(3) condensation

(4) evaporation

7   Precipitation that does not become surface water can become

    (1)   groundwater

    (2)   precipitation

    (3)   condensation

    (4)   evaporation

8   About what fraction of Earth's land is *not* covered by water?

    (1) $\frac{1}{2}$

    (2) $\frac{1}{3}$

    (3) $\frac{1}{4}$

    (4) $\frac{1}{10}$

Directions (9–10): Record your answers on the lines provided below each question.

9   What is the hydrosphere?   [1]

_____

10   How does water flow through the water cycle?   [1]

_____

_____

_____

Focus on the NYS Learning Standards

Lesson 36 Earth's Lithosphere

PS 2.1c The rock at Earth's surface forms a nearly continuous shell around Earth called the lithosphere.
PS 2.1e Rocks are composed of minerals. Only a few rock-forming minerals make up most of the rocks of Earth. Minerals are identified on the basis of physical properties such as streak, hardness, and reaction to acid.
PS 2.1f

Identify Earth's lithosphere and describe the rocks of which it is composed.

The outermost layer of the solid part of Earth is called the **lithosphere.** The lithosphere forms a nearly continuous shell around Earth.

The lithosphere is made up of rock. A **rock** is a collection of minerals that are packed tightly together. **Minerals** are solid materials that occur naturally and have a definite structure and set chemical composition.

A huge variety of minerals are found on Earth. Minerals are identified on the basis of physical properties, such as hardness, luster, streak, cleavage, and effervescence.

Hardness measures a mineral's ability to resist scratching. The Mohs' Hardness Scale is used to quantify the hardness of a mineral sample. The sample's hardness is the same as the softest mineral that can scratch it. On this scale, talc is the softest mineral and diamond is the hardest.

Luster describes the way a mineral reflects light. **Streak** is the color of the powder made when a mineral is scratched on a porcelain plate. A mineral's streak is not always the same as the mineral's color. Streak is useful because most minerals can occur in several different colors. **Cleavage** is the tendency of a mineral to break cleanly along certain lines. Not all minerals display cleavage—some break into rough, jagged pieces. **Effervescence** is the fizzing that occurs when certain minerals react with acid and give off gas bubbles. The chart describes the properties of several common minerals.

Properties of Some Common Minerals

Mineral	Color	Hardness	Luster	Streak	Cleavage or Fracture	Effervesces with Acid
Calcite	Clear, white	3	Glassy	White	Cleavage	Yes
Halite	White or clear	2.5	Glassy	White	Cleavage	No
Hematite	Red to black	6	Dull, earthy	Red	Fracture	No
Gold	Yellow	2.5	Metallic	Yellow	Fracture	No
Gypsum	White	2	Pearly	White	Cleavage	No
Pyrite	Yellow	6	Metallic	Black	Fracture	No
Quartz	White, brown, pink, clear	7	Glassy	White	Fracture	No

Some rocks also contain fossils. A **fossil** is a remnant from an organism that lived a long time ago. A fossil could be a part of the organism, such as bones or teeth; it can be an impression of an organism, such as a leaf print; or it can be something left behind by the organism, such as a nest.

NYS Test Practice

Directions (1–7): Decide which choice is the best answer. Circle the number of the answer you have chosen.

Base your answers to questions 1 and 2 on the chart below and on your knowledge of science.

Mohs' Hardness Scale

Hardness	Mineral	Can Be Scratched By:
1	Talc	
2	Gypsum	A fingernail
3	Calcite	A penny
4	Fluorite	
5	Apatite	A knife blade
6	Orthoclase	
7	Quartz	A steel file
8	Topaz	
9	Corundum	
10	Diamond	

1   An unknown mineral sample can be scratched by a knife blade but not by a fingernail. The mineral might be

(1) diamond

(2) quartz

(3) calcite

(4) topaz

2   A sample of silver can scratch gypsum and can be scratched by fluorite. What might be the hardness of silver on Mohs' scale of hardness?

(1) 1.8

(2) 2.7

(3) 4.1

(4) 5.6

3   Which term would help define what Earth's lithosphere is?

(1) water

(2) air

(3) living things

(4) land

4   A student found a mineral that does not break cleanly, has a black streak, and has a hardness of 3. Which mineral could the student have?

Mineral Identification Chart

Fracture Cleavage	Streak	Hardness	Luster	Mineral Name
cleavage in one direction	yellow or brown	5 - 5.5	submetallic	GOETHITE
cleavage sometimes indistinct	black	1	metallic or submetallic	GRAPHITE
fracture	black	3	metallic	BORNITE
cleavage in 3 directions At 90°	lead - gray	3	metallic	GALENA
fracture	reddish	6	metallic or submetallic	HEMATITE

(1) galena

(2) bornite

(3) goethite

(4) graphite

5 A student found a mineral crystal outside his house. Which would *not* be a useful way for him to collect data to identify the mineral?

(1) look at it under a microscope

(2) rub it against a known mineral

(3) check its acid reaction

(4) measure its temperature

6 What can scientists learn about by studying fossils found in rocks?

(1) past climates and environments

(2) the types of minerals in the rock

(3) how the rock will change in the future

(4) the number of different minerals that exist

7 A student finds that a sample of rock effervesces when mixed with acid. Which mineral might the student be studying?

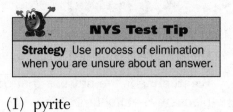

NYS Test Tip

Strategy Use process of elimination when you are unsure about an answer.

(1) pyrite

(2) quartz

(3) calcite

(4) gold

Directions (8–9): Record your answers on the lines provided below each question.

8 You have a sample of an unknown mineral that can be scratched by quartz, but not by orthoclase. How can you determine the range of its hardness? [1]

_____

_____

_____

9 How are the rocks in Earth's lithosphere related to minerals? [1]

_____

PS 2.1g The dynamic processes that wear away Earth's surface include weathering and erosion.

PS 2.1h The process of weathering breaks down rocks to form sediment. Soil consists of sediment, organic material, water, and air.

PS 2.1i Erosion is the transport of sediment. Gravity is the driving force behind erosion. Gravity can act directly or through agents such as moving water, wind, and glaciers.

Understand the dynamic processes of weathering and erosion.

Weathering is the process that occurs when rocks are slowly broken down into smaller pieces by natural processes. Weathering activities are divided into two categories: mechanical and chemical.

Mechanical weathering breaks rocks apart by physical means without changing the composition of the rock. For example, gravity can cause a rock to fall and split, or water can freeze and expand the cracks in rocks in a process known as *frost action*.

Chemical weathering changes the chemical composition of rock, such as when acid rain reacts with minerals or when oxidation occurs, forming rust.

The small pieces of rock produced by weathering are called **sediments.**

Erosion is the movement of sediment from one place to another by wind, flowing water, ice, or gravity.

Deposition occurs when sediment is dropped and it no longer moves. Over time, deposition creates new landforms, such as glacial moraines, dunes, beaches, floodplains, and deltas. A *glacial moraine* forms when sediment and rocks pushed by an advancing glacier are deposited as the glacier melts and retreats.

A **dune** is a mound of sand deposited by wind erosion.

A **glacier** is a huge mass of slowly moving ice. Glaciers carve valleys and push or break rocks.

When bedrock weathers, it begins to form soil. **Soil** contains sediment along with water, air, and organic materials. Organic materials come from living things.

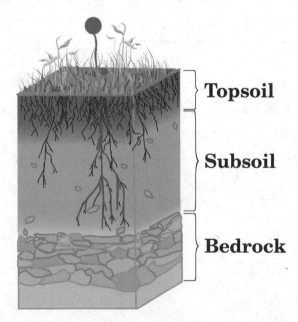

Topsoil

Subsoil

Bedrock

NYS Test Practice *Directions* (1–8): Decide which choice is the best answer. Circle the number of the answer you have chosen.

1   What process breaks down rock into smaller pieces?

   (1) erosion

   (2) deposition

   (3) weathering

   (4) condensation

2   The process that carries weathered sediment to new locations is

   (1) erosion

   (2) deposition

   (3) moraine

   (4) precipitation

3   A jetty was built along the Long Island coastline. What is the main purpose of the jetty?

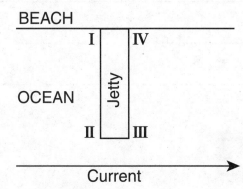

   (1) to create a place for people to fish

   (2) to prevent large waves from reaching the shoreline

   (3) to slow beach erosion at point IV and create a point for sand deposition at point I

   (4) to help increase the current moving from point II to point III

4   Which is an example of chemical weathering?

   (1) frost action

   (2) formation of rust

   (3) sediments grinding against each other

   (4) waves crashing against the shore

5   Animals such as sheep and cows are considered to be agents of erosion. How might they cause erosion?

   1) They make soft rocks dissolve.

   (2) They get in the way of runoff.

   (3) They remove plants that protect the ground.

   (4) They drink up all the water in an area.

6   The driving force behind erosion is the

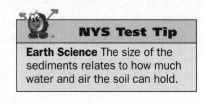

NYS Test Tip

Earth Science The size of the sediments relates to how much water and air the soil can hold.

   (1) growth of plants

   (2) evaporation of water

   (3) formation of soil

   (4) force of gravity

7   Suppose you run into this large pile of jagged rocks at the bottom of a mountain. What agent of erosion is most likely responsible for the rock pile?

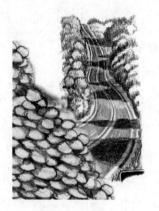

(1) waves

(2) moving water

(3) gravity

(4) wind

8   A builder wants to know if the land on which she is building a house is at risk for a sinkhole. What would be the most important thing to consider?

(1) if the rock beneath it is soft

(2) the distance to the nearest river

(3) how much wind the area gets

(4) if the rock contains iron

Directions (9–10): Record your answers on the lines provided below each question.

9   In what type of climate does chemical weathering generally happen most quickly? Why? [2]

_____

_____

_____

10 How are the processes of weathering and erosion related? [2]

_____

_____

_____

     Measuring Up Express™ for the New York State Test

Lesson 38 Earth's Interior

PS 2.2a The interior of Earth is hot. Heat flow and movement of material within Earth cause sections of Earth's crust to move. This may result in earthquakes, volcanic eruption, and the creation of mountains and ocean basins.

PS 2.2b Analysis of earthquake wave data (vibrational disturbances) leads to the conclusion that there are layers within Earth. These layers - the crust, mantle, outer core, and inner core - have distinct properties.

Describe the interior of Earth and how scientists came to understand it.

Earth's interior is divided into layers. The layers can be described by temperature, density, depth beneath Earth's surface, and the materials of which they are composed.

The **core** is Earth's innermost layer. It begins about 2,900 kilometers beneath Earth's surface. The core is very dense. Scientists think it is made mostly of the element iron and may also contain nickel. The core's temperature is about 5,000°C to 6,000°C, which is close to the temperature at the surface of the Sun.

The deepest part of the core is the **inner core.** Scientists believe the inner core is probably solid because the materials above it put huge amounts of pressure on it. The **outer core** is liquid.

The **mantle** surrounds the core. Most of Earth's mass is made up of the mantle. It is less dense than the core, and is made of rocks that contain the elements silicon, oxygen, iron, and magnesium. The mantle is cooler than the core, but still very hot. The surface of the mantle is about 1,200°C. The hottest material in the mantle rises up from the bottom, cools, and then sinks back down. The rising, cooling, and sinking occurs in a cycle that keeps repeating. The movement of materials in this way is known as a **convection current.**

The outside layer of Earth is the **crust.** The crust is Earth's shell and the part you walk on every day. It is made of light rocks and soil. It is the least dense and coolest layer of Earth. The crust is also the thinnest layer of Earth. On land, the crust is about 75 kilometers thick. Under the oceans, it is only about 8 kilometers thick. The most common elements in the crust are silicon and oxygen.

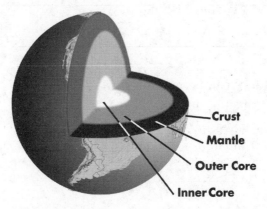

- Crust
- Mantle
- Outer Core
- Inner Core

Because of the tremendous depth and high temperatures, scientists cannot observe Earth's interior directly. What they believe about Earth's interior was learned by analyzing earthquake data. An earthquake occurs when parts of Earth's crust shift, or move. When this happens, waves of energy travel in all directions from the source of the earthquake. Three different types of waves, known as seismic waves, are produced. Scientists record these waves at different locations on Earth. By studying how the waves were changed as they traveled away from an earthquake, scientists were able to develop a model of Earth's interior.

NYS Test Practice

Directions (1–7): Decide which choice is the best answer. Circle the number of the answer you have chosen.

1 Generally, how does Earth's temperature change between the crust and the core?

(1) The temperature increases from crust to core.

(2) The temperature increases, but then cools off at the core.

(3) The temperature decreases from crust to core.

(4) The temperature stays the same throughout.

2 The thinnest layer of Earth is the

(1) inner core   (3) mantle

(2) outer core   (4) crust

3 Given what you know about the layers of Earth, which element is probably the least dense?

(1) nickel   (3) oxygen

(2) iron   (4) magnesium

4 The density of a substance can be measured in grams per cubic centimeter, or g/cm^3. The density of the mantle is about 3.3 to 5.7 g/cm^3. Which is a reasonable estimate for the density of the crust?

(1) 15.0 g/cm^3 (3) 7.2 g/cm^3

(2) 12.5 g/cm^3 (4) 2.7 g/cm^3

5 Which layer of Earth is believed to consist of liquid iron?

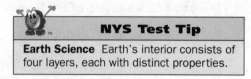

NYS Test Tip

Earth Science Earth's interior consists of four layers, each with distinct properties.

(1) inner core

(2) outer core

(3) mantle

(4) crust

6 Radiators create convection currents of air, much like the ones formed in the mantle. When hot air leaves a radiator, it rises to the top of a room. Based on what you know about Earth's interior, what happens to the air next?

(1) It heats up and sinks.

(2) It heats up and stays at the top.

(3) It cools off and sinks.

(4) It cools off and stays at the top.

7 Scientists have developed a model of Earth's interior based on data mainly from

(1) earthquakes

(2) volcanoes

(3) rock slides

(4) air masses

Directions (8–9): Record your answers on the lines provided below each question.

8   Why do scientists believe Earth's inner core is solid?   [1]

_____

_____

9   How do currents form in the mantle?   [2]

_____

_____

_____

Lesson 39 The Rock Cycle

PS 2.2g	Rocks are classified according to their method of formation. The three classes of rocks are sedimentary, metamorphic, and igneous. Most rocks show characteristics that give clues to their formation conditions.
PS 2.2h	The rock cycle model shows how types of rock or rock material may be transformed from one type of rock to another.
ICT 1.4	Describe how the output from one part of a system (which can include material, energy, or information) can become the input to other parts.
ICT 5.2	Observe patterns of change in trends or cycles and make predictions on what might happen in the future.

Learn about the rock cycle and how rocks and minerals form.

Minerals are naturally occurring solids that have a definite structure and chemical composition. There are many types of minerals found on Earth. Minerals can be identified using properties such as hardness, luster, the way a mineral breaks, and whether it reacts with acid.

Rocks are groups of minerals packed tightly together. Rocks vary depending on the kind of minerals they contain and how they were formed. There are three main groups of rocks:

• **Igneous rock** forms when magma cools and hardens. When the magma cools slowly, the rocks have a coarse texture. Fast cooling makes smooth-textured rocks. Granite, obsidian, basalt, and pumice are all igneous rocks.

• **Metamorphic rock** forms when heat and pressure change the form and chemical makeup of a rock. In a mineral, small crystals may grow larger. Or, the chemical makeup of the mineral may change. Earth's tectonic system creates metamorphic rocks by the immense pressure of plates pressing against each other. Examples of metamorphic rocks include marble, quartzite, gneiss, and slate.

• Most **sedimentary rock** forms from pieces of other rocks that have been broken apart and cemented together. The pieces are called *sediments*. Sediments are formed through **weathering** and carried from one place to another by **erosion**. The sediment settles by a process of *deposition*. They are compressed by layers of rock above. The pressure is so intense that it cements the sediments together. Many sedimentary rocks contain fossils. Examples of sedimentary rocks include coal, sandstone, limestone, and shale.

The **rock cycle**, shown in the diagram, describes the interactions that change rock from one form to another.

Any type of rock can be weathered and produce sediments or be changed by metamorphic processes. For example, when igneous rock is exposed to crashing waves, the water breaks the rock into sediment. Over time, the sediment compresses together and becomes sedimentary rock.

Under intense heat and high pressure, that sedimentary rock can be changed into metamorphic rock. Beneath Earth's surface, metamorphic rock can then melt into magma. During a volcanic eruption, magma is released onto Earth's surface where it cools to form igneous rock. Use the diagram to trace the different processes and changes that occur during the rock cycle.

The Rock Cycle

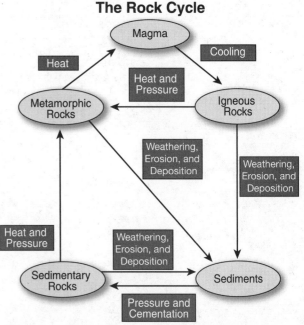

Directions (1–6): Decide which choice is the best answer. Circle the number of the answer you have chosen.

1 What is a role of Earth's water system in the formation of rocks?

(1) It supplies the magma to make igneous rocks.

(2) It applies pressure to and changes existing rocks.

(3) It weathers existing rocks and transports sediment.

(4) It changes the nature of minerals.

2 What kind of rock will most likely form when a continental plate slides over an oceanic plate?

(1) obsidian

(2) sandstone

(3) shale

(4) gneiss

3 Which sample has several layers of different colors and contains tiny seashells?

NYS Test Tip

Earth Science If a question asks about rock layers, it is probably referring to sedimentary rock. These rocks have layers because they form from small pieces of rock deposited over time.

(1) an igneous rock

(2) a sedimentary rock

(3) magma

(4) a metamorphic rock

4 Which list shows the correct order of events in the formation of a sedimentary rock?

(1) weathering, erosion, deposition, cementation

(2) weathering, cementation, erosion, deposition

(3) erosion, cementation, deposition, weathering

(4) cementation, weathering, transportation, erosion

5 Igneous and sedimentary rock can change into metamorphic rock as a result of

(1) the cooling of magma

(2) deposition and cementation

(3) pressure and cementation

(4) heat and pressure

6 A scientist is studying an unknown rock sample that has layers that look like they have been folded. It also has very large crystals. Which type of sample is the scientist studying?

(1) an igneous rock

(2) a sedimentary rock

(3) magma

(4) a metamorphic rock

Directions (7–9): Record your answers on the lines provided below each question.

7 Describe the process through which sandstone forms. [1]

_____

_____

_____

_____

8 What *three* processes change solid rock into layers of sediment? [2]

(1)_____

(2)_____

(3)_____

9 How does the rate at which magma cools affect the characteristics of the rock it forms? [1]

_____

_____

_____

Lesson 40 Plate Tectonics

PS 2.2d	Continents fitting together like puzzle parts and fossil correlations provided initial evidence that continents were once together.
PS 2.2e	The Theory of Plate Tectonics explains how the "solid" lithosphere consists of a series of plates that "float" on the partially molten section of the mantle. Convection cells within the mantle may be the driving force for the movement of the plates.
PS 2.2f	Plates may collide, move apart, or slide past one another. Most volcanic activity and mountain building occur at the boundaries of these plates, often resulting in earthquakes.
PS 2.2a, PS 2.2c, ICT 5.2	

Understand how plate tectonics explains many of Earth's features.

According to the **Theory of Plate Tectonics,** the outer part of Earth is divided into several distinct segments, called *plates*, that move. The outer layer of Earth that is made up of these plates is called the **lithosphere**. The lithosphere extends 50 to 100 kilometers down from Earth's surface.

The **asthenosphere** is the slowly-flowing layer of rock under the lithosphere. The asthenosphere is made of high-temperature rock that flows extremely slowly. The plates of the lithosphere float along on top of the flowing asthenosphere. Over the last several million years, Earth's continents have been slowly shifting location as they ride on the moving plates.

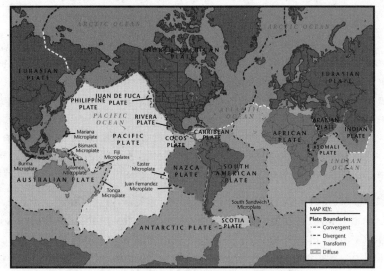

Map of Earth's Tectonic Plates

At a plate boundary, plates might be moving toward each other, moving away from each other, or sliding past each other. Boundaries where plates move toward one another are known as **convergent plate boundaries.**

Where plates push against each other, they can compress the lithosphere into folds like wrinkles in a rug. Earth's folded mountain belts such as the Appalachian Mountains formed because of plates pushing against each other over millions of years. The pressure that comes from the plates pushing together often creates metamorphic rocks within the mountain belts.

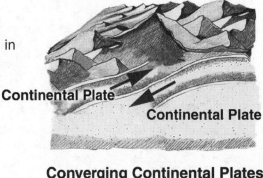

Converging Continental Plates
Mountains Formed

Another feature caused by converging plates is an **oceanic trench.** This is a deep place in the ocean floor where the edge of one plate plunges beneath another plate. Trenches can reach depths of up to 11 kilometers. Near oceanic trenches, islands sometimes form when melted material from the submerged plate rises back up and erupts out of volcanoes on the seafloor. The melted material cools and gradually piles up to form land masses that rise out of the water. The Tonga Islands in the western Pacific are an example of islands formed by this process.

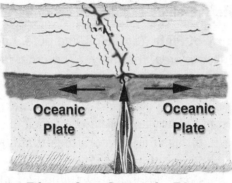

Diverging Oceanic Plates
Mid-ocean Ridge Formed

Divergent boundaries are places where plates are moving away from one another. Most of Earth's oceans have divergent plate boundaries running down their centers. Where the plates pull apart from each other, magma wells up and creates new igneous rocks at the edges of the plates, causing the lithosphere to grow. Earth's longest mountain chain, the mid-ocean ridge, was made out of this new igneous rock. The mid-ocean ridge is a tall chain of mountains that runs through the center of Earth's oceans. The island of Iceland is a part of that ridge that rises above the surface of the ocean.

Transform plate boundaries occur where plates slide past each other. Each plate moves slowly in the opposite direction. The zone between the plates is known as a **fault.** Most transform faults are located on the ocean floor, but some cut through continents. The San Andreas fault, for example, is a transform plate boundary in California. The two plates moving along this fault have been moving at a rate of about 5 centimeters per year relative to one another for about 10 million years.

NYS Test Practice *Directions* (1–7): Decide which choice is the best answer. Circle the number of the answer you have chosen.

1 At a convergent plate boundary,

   (1) plates pull away from each other

   (2) plates move toward each other

   (3) the lithosphere grows

   (4) stresses pull rocks apart

2 What type of rock forms at a plate boundary when magma wells up and hardens?

   (1) sedimentary

   (2) metamorphic

   (3) igneous

   (4) folded

3 Many metamorphic rocks are found along the southwestern border of Mexico. What is a likely reason for this?

   (1) The lithosphere is very thick there.

   (2) The asthenosphere is hottest there.

   (3) There is a convergent plate boundary there.

   (4) There is no magma generated there.

4 Which discovery provides evidence to support the Theory of Plate Tectonics?

   (1) Both South America and Africa have large rivers.

   (2) Both South America and Africa are inhabited by both plants and animals.

   (3) The climate in parts of South America are similar to the climate in parts of Africa.

   (4) The same fossils were found in South America and Africa.

5 The diagram shows a divergent plate boundary. At which point should the age of the lithosphere be the youngest?

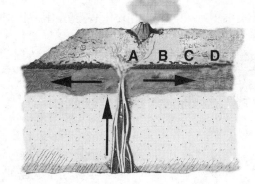

   (1) point A

   (2) point B

   (3) point C

   (4) point D

6 What is the driving force for the movement of Earth's plates?

(1) convection cells

(2) heavy winds

(3) earthquakes

(4) ocean waves

7 A scientist observes a section of folded rock. This observation suggests

(1) long periods of cold temperatures

(2) communities of large animals

(3) crustal movement in the past

(4) large supplies of groundwater

Directions (8–9): Record your answers on the lines provided below each question.

8 What type of plate boundary creates an oceanic trench? Why? [2]

_____

_____

_____

9 What is the relationship between the lithosphere and the asthenosphere? [1]

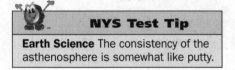

NYS Test Tip

Earth Science The consistency of the asthenosphere is somewhat like putty.

_____

Focus on the NYS Learning Standards

Lesson 41 Earthquakes and Volcanoes

PS 2.2a	The interior of Earth is hot. Heat flow and movement of material within Earth cause sections of Earth's crust to move. This may result in earthquakes, volcanic eruption, and the creation of mountains and ocean basins.
PS 2.2f	Plates may collide, move apart, or slide past one another. Most volcanic activity and mountain building occur at the boundaries of these plates, often resulting in earthquakes.

Understand how plate tectonics relates to earthquakes and volcanoes.

Lithospheric plates float on top of the asthenosphere. As a result, plates can move toward each other at **convergent boundaries,** away from each other at **divergent boundaries,** and past each other at **transform boundaries.**

At a convergent boundary, rocks may break and release tremendous amounts of energy. The result is an **earthquake.** An earthquake begins deep below Earth's surface, but the energy quickly travels as waves to the surface.

Another event that can occur at a convergent boundary is that one plate gets pushed down under the other. The plate can partially melt deep inside Earth. The melted material creates magma, which may rise to the surface and be released through a **volcano.** A volcano is an opening at Earth's surface where materials from Earth's interior can be released. Mount St. Helens in Washington is an example of such a volcano.

Volcanoes are also common near the converging plates of an oceanic trench. Islands sometimes form when melted material from the submerged plate rises back up and erupts from volcanoes on the seafloor. The melted material cools and gradually piles up to form land masses that rise out of the water. The Tonga Islands in the western Pacific are an example of islands that formed by this process.

Active volcanoes are also active at divergent boundaries, but they are mostly concealed under seawater. Earthquakes happen at divergent plate boundaries as well, when rocks in the lithosphere get pulled apart, snap, and release energy.

When plates slide past one another at a transform boundary, neither plate is destroyed and no magma is formed. As a result, volcanoes are not common at transform boundaries. Earthquakes, however, are very common at this type of boundary. During an earthquake, the energy built up as the plates grind past one another is released all at once. The energy travels as waves from the source. One of the strongest earthquakes in the United States occurred as a result of a shift along the San Andreas fault in California in 1906.

NYS Test Practice

Directions (1–7): Decide which choice is the best answer. Circle the number of the answer you have chosen.

Base your answers to questions 1 through 3 on the diagram below and on your knowledge.

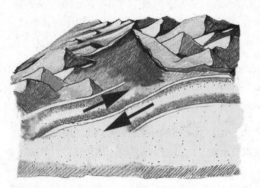

1 What might happen to the plate on the bottom if it is submerged deep enough?

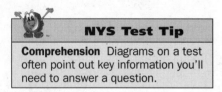

NYS Test Tip

Comprehension Diagrams on a test often point out key information you'll need to answer a question.

(1) It will form a volcanic island.

(2) It will melt to form magma.

(3) It will form a mountain.

(4) It will form a trench.

2 If the rocks break apart and release energy, the collision between the plates will produce

(1) an earthquake

(2) a volcano

(3) an island

(4) a mountain

3 How do sections of Earth's crust move?

(1) They float on the oceans that cover much of Earth's surface.

(2) They are pulled by the gravitational force of the Moon.

(3) They are pushed by strong winds as Earth rotates.

(4) They are carried by convection currents beneath the surface.

4 Which type of plate boundary is most likely to produce earthquakes, but not volcanoes?

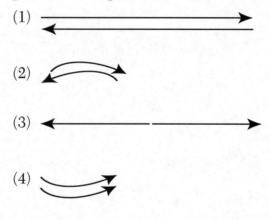

5 The energy from an earthquake is carried to the surface

(1) by rocks that are lifted to the surface

(2) by waves that travel through rock

(3) by magma that flows downward

(4) by plates that move over time

6 The process shown in the diagram is most often associated with

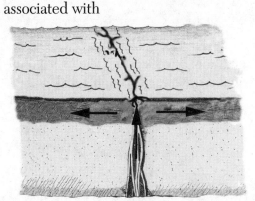

(1) volcanoes, but not earthquakes

(2) earthquakes, but not volcanoes

(3) both earthquakes and volcanoes

(4) neither earthquakes nor volcanoes

7 Why are volcanoes common along divergent boundaries?

(1) Magma is pushed upward as one plate pushes another upward.

(2) Magma forms when a plate is submerged under another.

(3) Magma cools as plates slide past one another.

(4) Magma rises as plates are pulled apart.

Directions (8): Record your answer on the lines provided below the question.

8. Each triangle on the map shows the location of a volcano that is currently active. Use the map to relate volcanoes to plate tectonics. [2]

_____

_____

Directions (1–3): Decide which choice is the best answer. Circle the number of the answer you have chosen.

1 What would be the effect on New York if Earth's tilt were to decrease?

(1) The weather would become rainier.

(2) The nights would become much longer than the days.

(3) The climate would become warmer.

(4) The temperature changes between the seasons would become greater.

2 One way that the movement of Earth's plates contributes to the rock cycle is by

(1) weathering rock into small sediments over time

(2) lifting rocks upward to form tall mountains

(3) moving rocks from one location to another over time

(4) submerging plates into Earth's mantle where they melt into magma

3 The diagram shows seismic waves from an earthquake traveling through Earth.

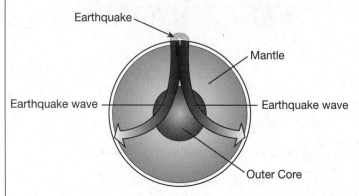

What conclusions might scientists reach based on the data that led to the diagram?

(1) Earth's core has the same density as the mantle.

(2) Earth's core is denser than the mantle.

(3) Earth's core is less dense than the mantle.

(4) Earth's core has no density.

Directions (4): Record your answer on the lines provided below the question.

4 Why is the Sun said to "rise" in the east and "set" in the west? [2]

_____

_____

_____

_____

Higher-Order Performance Task
Effects of the Sun's Angle

Task:

You are going to investigate how the angle at which light strikes a surface affects its temperature.

Materials:

- 3 lamps that can be angled
- 3 identical plastic containers
- sand or soil
- 3 thermometers

Directions:

1. Fill the plastic containers with the same amount of sand. You can tell by comparing the level of sand in each container.

2. Insert a thermometer into the center of each container of sand.

3. Place the first lamp directly over the first container of sand. Arrange the other lamps as shown.

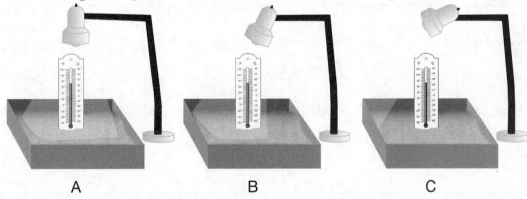

A   B   C

4. Make a data table similar to the one shown so that you can record the measurement on each thermometer every two minutes for 20 minutes.

Time (min)	Temperature (°F)		
	Container A	Container B	Container C
2			
4			
6			
8			

5. Turn on all three lamps. Observe the temperature and record your results.

6. Create a line graph of your results. Plot temperature on the *y*-axis and time on the *x*-axis. Draw the line for each container in a different color.

7. Which container had the greatest final temperature?

   _____

8. Which container showed the least increase in temperature?

   _____

9. Write a conclusion that relates the angle of the light to the change in temperature.

   _____

   _____

10. Based on your experiment, explain why temperatures at the equator are warmer than at the poles.

    _____

    _____

    _____

    _____

11. Relate the experiment to temperature changes that occur from one season to another in New York.

    _____

    _____

    _____

    _____

12. Relate the experiment to temperature changes that occur near the equator.

    _____

    _____

13. When you have finished, put all the materials back the way you found them.

PS 3.3a   All matter is made up of atoms. Atoms are far too small to see with a light microscope.

PS 3.3b   Atoms and molecules are perpetually in motion. The greater the temperature, the greater the motion.

PS 3.3c   Atoms may join together in well-defined molecules or may be arranged in regular geometric patterns.

PS 3.3e   The atoms of any one element are different from the atoms of other elements.

You can describe matter in terms of atoms and molecules.

Matter is anything that has mass and occupies space. All matter is made up of particles that are too small to see with a light microscope.

An **atom** is the building block of matter. Atoms are made up of smaller particles, known as *subatomic particles*. These include protons, neutrons, and electrons.

Protons have a positive electric charge and **neutrons** have no charge. Protons and neutrons are located in the center, or **nucleus**, of an atom. An **electron** is a very small particle with a negative charge found outside the nucleus.

As you add electrons, protons, and neutrons, the size and mass of the atom increase. In their stable state atoms are neutral, in that they have the same number of positive protons as they do negative electrons.

An **element** is a substance that cannot be broken down into simpler substances. All atoms in an element are the same. The atoms from one element are different from the atoms of any other element. Each element has a different number of protons in its atoms. Aluminum (Al), carbon (C), and oxygen (O), are examples of elements. The letters in parentheses show the symbol for each element.

A **molecule** is a particle that is made up of two or more atoms joined together. A molecule can have atoms that are alike, such as oxygen (O_2), or different, such as water (H_2O). Atoms and molecules are always in motion.

A **compound** is formed when the atoms of two or more elements combine to form a new substance. The ratio of the different atoms in a compound is always the same. Sugar is a compound of carbon, oxygen, and hydrogen. In some compounds, atoms are arranged in regular geometric patterns.

Unlike molecules and compounds, a **mixture** is formed when two or more elements combine but do not form a new substance. A mixture can be separated into the original substances by physical processes.

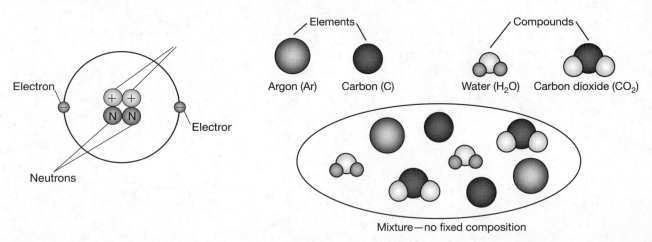

Electron   Electror   Neutrons

Elements   Argon (Ar)   Carbon (C)

Compounds   Water (H_2O)   Carbon dioxide (CO_2)

Mixture—no fixed composition

   *Directions* (1–7): Decide which choice is the best answer. Circle the number of the answer you have chosen.

1   Which statement about the diagrams shown below is true?

HYDROGEN MOLECULE

WATER MOLECULE

O   Oxygen atom

H   Hydrogen atom

(1) All matter is made up of compounds.

(2) All matter is made up of atoms.

(3) All matter is made up of mixtures.

(4) All atoms are the same.

2   The atoms in a molecule are

(1) always alike

(2) always different from each other

(3) sometimes alike and sometimes different

(4) broken down into compounds by chemical reactions

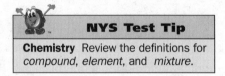

NYS Test Tip

Chemistry Review the definitions for *compound*, *element*, and *mixture*.

3   A subatomic particle that has an electric charge of zero is

(1) an electron

(2) a neutron

(3) a proton

(4) a nucleus

4   When humans exhale, they release a gas called carbon dioxide (CO_2). CO_2 is

(1) an atom

(2) an element

(3) a mixture

(4) a molecule

5   The table below shows information about a carbon atom.

number of protons	number of neutrons	charge on atom
6	7	0

How many electrons are in the carbon atom?

(1) 1

(2) 6

(3) 7

(4) 13

6   The diagram shows one model of the atom.

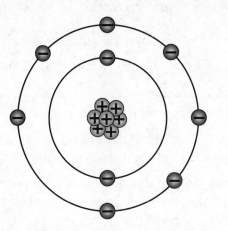

What aspect of the atom cannot be shown by this type of model?

(1) Atoms vary from one element to another.

(2) Atoms are electrically neutral.

(3) Atoms are made up of smaller particles.

(4) Atoms are in constant motion.

7   Why can't you see atoms with a light microscope?

(1) They are invisible.

(2) They are too small to see.

(3) They do not exist on Earth.

(4) They are destroyed by light.

Directions (8–9): Record your answers on the lines provided below each question.

8   What part of an atom makes up most of its mass?   [1]

_____

9   How are the atoms of one element different from another?   [1]

_____

Lesson 43 **Properties of Elements**

PS 3.2d   Substances are often placed in categories if they react in similar ways. Examples include metals, nonmetals, and noble gases.

PS 3.3f   There are more than 100 elements. Elements combine in a multitude of ways to produce compounds that account for all living and nonliving substances. Few elements are found in their pure form.

PS 3.3g   The periodic table is one useful model for classifying elements. The periodic table can be used to predict properties of elements (metals, nonmetals, noble gases).

Identify how elements are organized and classified according to their properties.

The **atomic number** of an element is the number of protons in the nucleus of its atoms. The **mass number** is the number of protons and neutrons in the nucleus of an atom.

The **periodic table** is an arrangement of elements in a table according to their atomic numbers and physical properties. More than 100 known elements are organized in the periodic table. You can find the periodic table in the back of this book.

A **group** is a set of elements in one column in the periodic table. Elements in the same group have similar properties because they have the same number of valence electrons. **Valence electrons** are the outermost electrons in an atom. Elements with the same valence number tend to react in similar ways. Elements combine in many different ways, and few elements are found uncombined in nature. A **period** is a row of the periodic table.

A **chemical symbol** is an abbreviation of the name of an element.

Isotopes of an element contain the same number of protons but different numbers of neutrons. The **average atomic mass** of an element is the average mass of the mixture of isotopes of the element.

Metals are elements characterized by a shiny surface, the ability to be easily shaped, and high conductivity of electricity and heat. The **alkali metals** (group 1, except for hydrogen) are metals with only one valence electron. These metals are highly reactive and are found in nature only in compounds. The **alkaline earth metals** (group 2) are metals with two valence electrons. These metals are slightly less reactive than the alkali and they are harder. The **transition metals** (groups 3 through 12) are elements that have valance electrons at two different energy levels. These are much less reactive than the alkali and the alkaline metals.

Nonmetals are elements characterized by a brittle nature, little or no luster, and poor conductivity of electricity and heat. Highly reactive nonmetals are in group 17, called the *halogens*. They have seven valence numbers and easily react with elements with one valence number (group 1).

Semimetals, also called *metalloids*, are elements that share some properties of metals and some of nonmetals. These elements lie on either side of the bold zigzag line in the periodic table. The elements to the left of the zigzag line are metals and those on the right are nonmetals.

Inert gas, also called **noble gas** (group 18), is a category of elements that contain helium, neon, argon, krypton, xenon, and radon. All have eight valance electrons, except for helium, which has two. These elements do not to react easily, if at all, with other elements.

Oxygen Atom
2 e⁻ first energy level
6 e⁻ second energy level

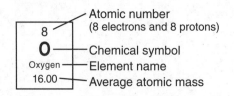

NYS Test Practice

Directions (1–8): Decide which choice is the best answer. Circle the number of the answer you have chosen.

1   Most of the elements in the periodic table are

(1) highly reactive metals

(2) highly reactive nonmetals

(3) less reactive metals

(4) nonreactive nonmetals

2   Magnesium, an alkaline earth metal, is in column 2 of the periodic table. Why would it react in a similar manner to other elements in this column?

(1) It has the same number of neutrons but a different number of electrons as other elements in the column.

(2) It has the same atomic number as other elements in the column.

(3) It has the same average atomic mass as other elements in the column.

(4) It has the same number of valence electrons as other elements in the column.

3   Which element shares similar properties with the element carbon (C)? You may refer to a Periodic Table.

(1) boron (B)

(2) nitrogen (N)

(3) aluminum (Al)

(4) silicon (Si)

4   A student reads about a substance with the following properties. The substance is brittle, is a poor conductor of heat and electricity, is black in color, and has a low melting point. What is this substance?

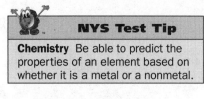

NYS Test Tip

Chemistry Be able to predict the properties of an element based on whether it is a metal or a nonmetal.

(1) It is a metallic solid.

(2) It is a nonmetallic solid.

(3) It is a gas.

(4) It is a liquid.

5   Why don't noble gases react with other elements?

(1) They do not contain electrons.

(2) They have a full set of valence electrons.

(3) They do not exist in nature.

(4) They are colorless.

6   The atomic number of oxygen (O) is 8. The mass number of one of its isotopes is 18. How many neutrons are in the isotope?

(1) 6

(2) 8

(3) 10

(4) 26

7   Which is a noble gas?

    (1)   xenon

    (2)   hydrogen

    (3)   potassium

    (4)   silicon

8   Which of these elements would you expect to be a good conductor of heat and electricity?

    (1)   neon

    (2)   titanium

    (3)   carbon

    (4)   iodine

Directions (9–10): Record your answers on the lines provided below each question.

9   Why are the halogens highly reactive?   [1]

_____

10   There are a few more than 100 known elements, yet there are millions of different compounds in nature. How can this be true?   [1]

_____

Lesson 44 States of Matter

PS 3.1c The motion of particles helps to explain the phases (states) of matter as well as changes from one phase to another. The phase in which matter exists depends on the attractive forces among its particles.

PS 3.3b Atoms and molecules are perpetually in motion. The greater the temperature, the greater the motion.

PS 3.1d, PS 3.1e, PS 3.1f

Relate the motion of particles of matter to its state.

According to the **kinetic theory of matter,** the particles that make up matter are in constant motion. Matter can exist in different states, depending on the motion of its particles.

Matter is **solid** when it has a definite volume and shape. Particles of matter in the solid state do not experience much motion. Instead, particles vibrate in somewhat fixed positions. A block of ice is water in the solid state. A solid can't be forced into a space smaller than its volume.

Matter is **liquid** when it has a definite volume and takes the shape of its container. Particles of matter in the liquid state have greater motion than in the solid state. They are free to move past one another. Tap water is in the liquid state. A liquid also can't normally be squeezed into a container smaller than its volume.

Matter is a **gas** when it has no definite volume or shape. The particles of a gas move at high speeds in all directions. Gases can expand and contract to fill the space they are in. Gases can also be compressed into a smaller space. Water that evaporates from puddles becomes water vapor, which is invisible water in the gas state. Propane is a gas that is pumped into a metal container.

There is a fourth state of matter known as plasma. **Plasma** is a state of matter that consists of a gaslike mixture of charged particles. Plasma is the most common form of matter in the universe because it makes up the Sun and stars.

solid   liquid   gas

When matter is heated, its particles move faster and farther apart. When matter is cooled, its particles move more slowly and remain closer together. At a certain point, matter can change from one state to another.

When a solid is heated, the motion of its particles increases. When they break out of their fixed positions, the solid changes into a liquid. This process is known as **melting**. The temperature at which a substance changes from a solid to a liquid is the **melting point** of that substance.

If heat is added to a liquid, the motion of its particles increases. When the motion becomes so great that the particles escape the liquid, the substance changes into a gas. This process is known as **boiling**. The temperature at which a substance changes from a liquid to a gas is the **boiling point** of that substance. A change from the liquid state to the gas state at temperatures less than the boiling point is known as **evaporation**.

If a gas is cooled, the motion of its particles decreases. When the motion becomes slow enough, the gas changes into a liquid in a process known as **condensation**. If the resulting liquid is cooled further, its particles move even more slowly. The liquid changes into a solid in a process known as **freezing**.

Directions (1–8): Decide which choice is the best answer. Circle the number of the answer you have chosen.

1   The diagram shows matter in two states.

What difference between solids and liquids is shown?

(1) Solids have a definite shape, but liquids do not.

(2) Liquids have a definite shape, but solids do not.

(3) Liquids have a definite volume, but solids do not.

(4) Solids have a definite volume, but liquids do not.

2   What change of state occurs when water vapor in the atmosphere cools?

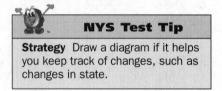

NYS Test Tip

Strategy Draw a diagram if it helps you keep track of changes, such as changes in state.

(1) liquid to solid

(2) liquid to gas

(3) gas to liquid

(4) solid to gas

3   A sample of matter that has a definite volume but not a definite shape is a

(1) solid

(2) liquid

(3) gas

(4) plasma

4   In which sample do the particles of matter have the least amount of motion?

(1) a cup of warm water

(2) a pan of hot oil

(3) a pitcher of lemonade

(4) a frozen popsicle

5   Which is the most common state of matter in the universe?

(1) the gas state, because the atmosphere is made up of gas

(2) the solid state, because the universe is so cold that everything is frozen

(3) the plasma state, because most of the mass in the universe is found in the stars

(4) the liquid state, because water vapor is invisible and is found everywhere

6   A sample of liquid water freezes into ice. How is the ice different from the liquid water?

(1) The ice is made of different particles than the liquid.

(2) The particles in the ice experience less motion than the particles in the liquid.

(3) The particles in the ice are at a higher temperature than the particles in the liquid.

(4) The particles in the ice are charged whereas the particles in the liquid are not.

7   When compared with the particles in a sample of a gas, the same particles in a liquid

(1) are larger

(2) move farther apart

(3) are heavier

(4) move more slowly

8   A student is observing a sample of matter in the liquid state. What must be true about the sample?

(1) It has a definite volume.

(2) It has a definite shape.

(3) It has both a definite volume and shape.

(4) It has neither a definite volume nor shape.

Directions (9–10):   Record your answers on the lines provided below each question.

9   What happens to the water molecules in a beaker as the water that is heated from 10°C to 90°C?   [1]

_____

10   In which state does matter take both the shape and volume of its container?   [1]

_____

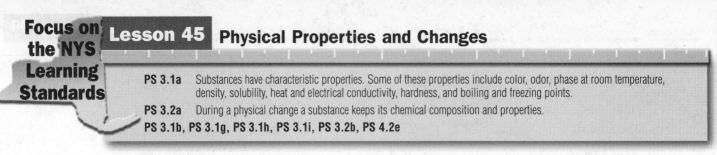

Focus on the NYS Learning Standards

Lesson 45 Physical Properties and Changes

PS 3.1a   Substances have characteristic properties. Some of these properties include color, odor, phase at room temperature, density, solubility, heat and electrical conductivity, hardness, and boiling and freezing points.

PS 3.2a   During a physical change a substance keeps its chemical composition and properties.

PS 3.1b, PS 3.1g, PS 3.1h, PS 3.1i, PS 3.2b, PS 4.2e

Understand that matter can be described by physical properties and can undergo physical changes.

A **physical property** is a characteristic that can be observed or measured without changing the identity of the substance. Physical properties include color, odor, state, density, solubility, hardness, and boiling and freezing points.

Solubility is the ability of a substance to dissolve in another substance. The substance that dissolves is called the **solute**. The substance that does the dissolving is called the **solvent**. Solubility is affected by the nature of the solute and solvent, the temperature, and pressure. The rate at which a solute dissolves can be affected by the size of the particles, stirring, temperature, and the amount of solute already dissolved.

Density is the ratio of mass to the volume of a substance. Another description of density is the amount of matter in a given amount of space. If two objects have the same volume but different masses, they have different densities. Most substances have a unique density.

Buoyancy is the upward force exerted on an object in a fluid. It is determined by the relative densities of the substances. A substance will float in a substance that is denser than itself. An object will sink if it is more dense than the fluid into which it is placed.

A **mixture** is a group of substances that keep their composition and can be separated by physical means. A fruit salad is an example of a mixture. Each item in the fruit salad is the same as it was before the fruits were mixed. Any particular fruit can be picked out of the salad. The physical properties of matter can be used to separate a mixture. Iron is magnetic, for example. It can be removed from a mixture of iron and sand with a magnet. Salt dissolves in water. It can be separated out of a mixture by dissolving it in water.

A **physical change** in matter occurs when the form or appearance of matter changes, but its composition stays the same. Tearing a sheet of paper in half, bending a piece of metal, and breaking a cracker in half are physical changes. Changes in state are also physical changes. When matter changes from one state to another, its composition does not change—only its form changes.

Directions (1–7): Decide which choice is the best answer. Circle the number of the answer you have chosen.

1 Like other metals, one physical property of copper is that it

(1) has a dull appearance

(2) can conduct electricity

(3) shatters easily

(4) prevents the flow of heat

2 The table lists the masses of four substances.

Substance	Mass (g)
Liquid A	2.5
Solid A	3.5
Liquid B	3.3
Solid B	5.5

NYS Test Tip

Chemistry A statement such as "lead is heavier than feathers" is incorrect because it does not specify the volume of lead or feathers. Only density combines both properties.

If the volumes of all the substances are the same, which statement describes what would happen if they were all placed in the same container?

(1) Liquid B would float on liquid A.

(2) Solid A would float in liquid A.

(3) Liquid B would be at the top of the container.

(4) Solid B would be at the bottom of the container.

3 Which is the result of buoyancy?

(1) An ice cube floats in water.

(2) A puddle of water evaporates.

(3) A raindrop falls from a cloud.

(4) Water sinks into spaces in soil.

4 A student is conducting an investigation to study solubility. The student adds a sugar cube to a beaker of water and measures how long it takes all of the sugar to dissolve. The student wants to repeat the procedure in such a way that the sugar dissolves more quickly. All of the following will increase the rate at which the sugar dissolves except

(1) stirring the mixture steadily

(2) raising the temperature of the water

(3) using water with sugar already dissolved in it

(4) using granulated sugar instead of a sugar cube

5 Which statement about the physical properties of oil and vinegar is supported by the picture?

(1) Vinegar is less dense than oil.

(2) Oil is less dense than vinegar.

(3) Vinegar is soluble in oil.

(4) Oil is soluble in vinegar.

6 Which action represents a physical change of a substance?

(1) a match burns

(2) fireworks explode

(3) a hammer breaks glass

(4) a cake bakes

7 An example of a physical change in matter occurs when

(1) water vapor condenses to form drops of liquid water

(2) a metal bike left outside forms rust

(3) a bunch of bananas turns from green to yellow

(4) a log burns into ashes in a campfire

Directions (8–10): Record your answers on the lines provided below each question.

8 A block of wood is added to a tub of water. What physical property of the water and wood determine the buoyancy of the wood? [1]

9 Four identical boxes are filled with four different substances. The mass of each box is shown.

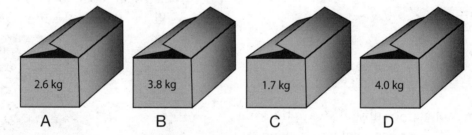

| 2.6 kg | 3.8 kg | 1.7 kg | 4.0 kg |
| A | B | C | D |

Which substance has the greatest density? How do you know? [2]

10 Name two physical properties of an ice cream cone. Then describe one physical change that might happen to the ice cream. [2]

Focus on the NYS Learning Standards

Lesson 46 Chemical Properties and Changes

PS 3.2c During a chemical change, substances react in characteristic ways to form new substances with different physical and chemical properties.

PS 3.2e The Law of Conservation of Mass states that during an ordinary chemical reaction matter cannot be created or destroyed.

PS 3.2d, PS 3.3d

Understand that matter can be described by chemical properties and can undergo chemical changes.

A **chemical property** describes a characteristic or behavior of a substance under specific conditions. Unlike a physical property, a chemical property can be observed only while matter is changing from one substance to another. The ability of a substance to change into one or more new substances is known as its *reactivity*. The ability to burn, rust, or tarnish are examples of chemical properties.

A **chemical change** occurs when a substance undergoes a change in its chemical and physical properties. Another way to describe a chemical change is as a **chemical reaction.** The substances that enter into a chemical reaction are the *reactants*. The substances that are yielded by a chemical reaction are known as the *products*. During a chemical reaction, one or more reactants change into one or more products.

The chemical and physical properties of the products are different from those of the reactants. For example, sodium reacts with chlorine to produce sodium chloride. Sodium is a soft, gray metal. Chlorine is a greenish-yellow gas. Together they form a white crystal that is safe to eat. A chemical equation, such as the one below, can be used to describe a chemical reaction.

$$Na \quad + \quad Cl \quad \rightarrow \quad NaCl$$

| Sodium | Chlorine | Sodium chloride |

Remember that the reactivity of atoms depends on the number of valence electrons it has. Atoms combine in order to obtain a full set of valence electrons. For most atoms, a full set of valence electrons is 8. Sodium has 1 valence electron and chlorine has 7. When they combine, sodium gives its one valence electron to chlorine. In this way, they both have a complete outer set of electrons. The way that elements are organized in the periodic table gives clues to their reactivity.

According to the **Law of Conservation of Mass,** the total mass of the reactants is equal to the total mass of the products. Matter can neither be created nor destroyed during a chemical reaction, so no mass is lost and no new mass is produced.

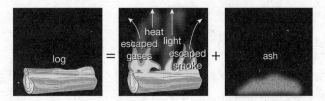

Wood burns when it combines with oxygen in the air. The mass of the products—the ash and escaped smoke and gases—is equal to the mass of the log and the oxygen it combined with as it burned.

NYS Test Practice

Directions (1–7): Decide which choice is the best answer. Circle the number of the answer you have chosen.

1 Which example describes a chemical property of a silver fork?

(1) It is shiny.

(2) It can bend.

(3) It can tarnish.

(4) It has a smooth texture.

2 The chemical composition of a piece of wood changes when

(1) it is sawed in half

(2) it is painted

(3) a nail is hammered into it

(4) it burns into ashes

3 Which change is an example of a chemical reaction?

(1) Dough bakes into cookies in an oven.

(2) Solid ice cream melts into a liquid.

(3) Metal is heated and bent into shape.

(4) A sugar cube is broken into granules.

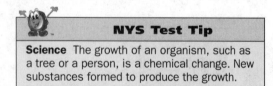

NYS Test Tip

Science The growth of an organism, such as a tree or a person, is a chemical change. New substances formed to produce the growth.

4 During photosynthesis, plants use the energy of sunlight to change carbon dioxide and water into sugar and oxygen. What is a product in this chemical reaction?

(1) sunlight (3) water

(2) sugar (4) carbon dioxide

5 What must be true about the masses of the substances involved in the chemical reaction below?

$AgNO_3$ + NaCl → AgCl + $NANO_3$
silver nitrate   sodium chloride   silver chloride   sodium nitrate

(1) The mass of silver nitrate is equal to the mass of sodium chloride.

(2) The mass of silver nitrate is equal to the mass of silver chloride.

(3) The mass of sodium chloride is equal to the mass of sodium nitrate.

(4) The mass of silver nitrate and sodium chloride equals the mass of silver chloride and sodium nitrate.

6 Which of these elements is considered to be unreactive?

(1) sodium (Na)

(2) calcium (Ca)

(3) argon (Ar)

(4) hydrogen (H)

7 What does the Law of Conservation of Mass suggest about chemical reactions?

(1) No matter is created or destroyed during a chemical reaction.

(2) The substances used in a chemical reaction should not be wasted.

(3) The reactants in a chemical react exist in limited supplies.

(4) The mass of the products is always greater than the mass of the reactants.

Directions (8–9): Record your answers on the lines provided below each question.

8   An iron tool with a mass of 350 g is left outside all winter. In the spring, the mass of the rusted tool is greater than 350 grams. Where did the added mass come from, and does it violate the Law of Conservation of Mass?   [1]

_____

_____

_____

9   What causes the alkaline earth metals, such as magnesium, to be more reactive than other elements, such as noble gases?   [2]

_____

_____

_____

Lesson 47 Energy Resources

PS 4.1a The Sun is a major source of energy for Earth. Other sources of energy include nuclear and geothermal energy.

PS 4.1b Fossil fuels contain stored solar energy and are considered nonrenewable resources.

You can trace the source of most energy on Earth to the Sun.

Plants living millions of years ago gathered energy from the Sun, just as plants do today. This energy remained in the plants or was passed on to animals. Many of these plants and animals were buried by sediments after they died. Over millions of years, heat and pressure below Earth's surface transformed these organisms into natural gas, petroleum, or coal. Coal, natural gas, and petroleum are **fossil fuels**—sources of energy made from the remains of these ancient plants and animals. Fossil fuels, therefore, contain solar energy stored millions of years ago.

Most of the energy used today comes from burning fossil fuels. Fossil fuels have many advantages. For one thing, they are a concentrated energy source. That means that when you burn a small volume of a fossil fuel, it can provide a large amount of energy. Also, a large, efficient system is in place to obtain and distribute fossil fuels around the world. Finally, they are relatively inexpensive.

However, there are many disadvantages to using fossil fuels as sources of energy. Burning fossil fuels leads to air pollution: for example, pollutants from car emissions can cause a dirty haze in the air called *smog*, and pollutants from coal plants can cause acid rain. Coal mining and oil drilling can destroy habitats. Also, underground mining can be dangerous for workers, and oil pipelines and tanker ships have caused major oil spills.

Finally, because fossil fuels take millions of years to form, they are nonrenewable. A **nonrenewable resource** is any resource that cannot be replaced as quickly as it is used. This means that, eventually, Earth will run out of fossil fuels.

One alternative to fossil fuels is nuclear energy. Nuclear energy is generated by splitting the nucleus of an atom, often uranium, into two smaller nuclei through the process of nuclear fission. This releases some of the stored energy inside the nucleus. In a nuclear power plant, this energy is converted to electrical energy. However, nuclear energy is also nonrenewable— there is only a limited supply of uranium on Earth. In addition, the waste from nuclear power plants is radioactive for thousands of years.

Other alternatives to fossil fuels are renewable. A **renewable resource** is a resource that can be replaced as quickly as humans use it. Solar, water, wind, biomass, and geothermal power sources are considered renewable.

Many renewable energy sources can be gathered directly from the natural environment. Solar energy shines on solar cells, which convert this energy to electrical energy. Blowing wind turns wind turbines, to convert mechanical energy to electrical energy. Moving water turns turbines in a dam, also converting mechanical energy to electrical energy. Even heated geothermal water below Earth's surface can be used to generate steam, which turns turbines to produce electrical energy.

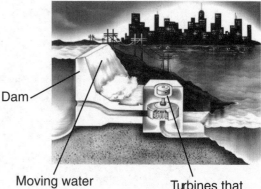

Dam

Moving water

Turbines that make electricity

Trees, grasses, and other plants can be grown to produce biomass energy. These crops can be burned to produce electrical energy. They can also be processed into oils that can be used in cars or furnaces.

NYS Test Practice

Directions (1–7): Decide which choice is the best answer. Circle the number of the answer you have chosen.

1 Why might coal be considered a more efficient source of energy than biomass?

  (1) Coal is a more concentrated energy source.

  (2) Coal is nonpolluting.

  (3) Biomass grows very slowly.

  (4) Biomass is only available in windy areas.

2 Which of these energy resources is renewable?

  (1) coal

  (2) natural gas

  (3) biomass

  (4) petroleum

3 What is one disadvantage of using natural gas?

NYS Test Tip

Strategy It may help to create a chart showing the advantages and disadvantages of different energy resources.

  (1) Natural gas makes radioactive waste.

  (2) Natural gas cannot be created as quickly as it is used.

  (3) Pollution from burning natural gas can cause acid rain.

  (4) Natural gas is not a very concentrated source of energy.

4 Which renewable energy source converts steam to electrical energy?

  (1) geothermal

  (2) solar

  (3) water

  (4) wind

5 Which type of energy produces waste that is dangerous for many years to come?

  (1) geothermal

  (2) nuclear

  (3) solar

  (4) wind

6 What was the original source of the energy stored in fossil fuels?

  (1) the Sun

  (2) wind

  (3) soil

  (4) ocean waves

7 To utilize geothermal energy, a scientist would need to look

  (1) in the sky

  (2) underground

  (3) to space

  (4) beneath the ocean's surface

Directions (8–9): Record your answers on the lines provided below each question.

8   Why are fossil fuels the most commonly used type of energy?   [2]

_____

_____

9   How can coal contain stored solar energy?   [2]

_____

_____

_____

Lesson 48   Energy Forms and Transformations

PS 4.1d   Different forms of energy include heat, light, electrical, mechanical, sound, nuclear, and chemical. Energy is transformed in many ways.

PS 4.1e   Energy can be considered to be either kinetic energy, which is the energy of motion, or potential energy, which depends on relative position.

PS 4.5a   Energy cannot be created or destroyed, but only changed from one form into another.

PS 4.1c, PS 4.5b

Identify the various forms of energy, and recognize how energy transforms.

Most activities in everyday life involve energy. **Energy** is the ability to do work or cause change.

There are two general types of energy: kinetic energy and potential energy. **Kinetic energy** is energy of motion, as in the motion of falling water. The greater the mass and velocity of the moving object, the more kinetic energy it has. **Potential energy** is stored energy that depends on the relationship of objects with respect to one another. For example, lifting a wrecking ball gives it potential energy. Releasing the ball changes the potential energy to kinetic energy that can knock down a wall.

Energy also exists in different forms. Forms of energy include thermal, light, electrical, mechanical, sound, nuclear, and chemical.

Thermal energy is the energy of moving particles in a sample of matter. The faster the particles of matter move, the more thermal energy the substance has. Thermal energy can be transferred from a warmer object to a cooler object as **heat**.

Light energy is energy made up of electromagnetic waves. It is sometimes called *radiant energy*. The **electromagnetic spectrum** contains all wavelengths of electromagnetic energy.

Electrical energy is energy produced by moving electrons. These moving electrons make up an *electric current,* which travels through wires from a power plant to a house or apartment. You can use this energy by plugging an electrical appliance into a wall outlet—the electric current causes the appliance to work. Electrical energy can be measured in units of energy called *joules*.

Mechanical energy is energy produced when work is done on an object. When you go bowling, the mechanical energy in the bowling ball knocks down the pins. Mechanical energy involves the movement of an object.

Sound energy is energy produced by an object's vibrations. This vibration travels outwards in all directions as a wave, and when the wave reaches your ears, you hear the vibration as a sound. Because it involves motion, sound energy is generally considered a form of mechanical energy.

Nuclear energy is the potential energy stored in the center, or nucleus, of an atom. This energy is released during changes to an atom's nucleus. The Sun releases nuclear energy by joining small hydrogen nuclei together to form a helium nucleus. This reaction is called *fusion*. Power plants produce nuclear energy using *fission*—the splitting of nuclei in atoms of a radioactive element, such as uranium. Both fusion and fission release large amounts of energy from atoms. Power plants often convert nuclear energy to electrical energy.

Chemical energy is the potential energy stored in bonds between a compound's atoms. This energy is released when the molecule is broken down. For example, when you eat a sandwich, your stomach and intestines break down compounds in the sandwich. This allows the chemical energy from the food to be used by your cells to power your body.

Energy can change, or **transform**, from one form to another. A lamp transforms electrical energy into light energy. A solar cell transforms light energy into electrical energy. When you run, you transform chemical energy into mechanical energy.

Some processes involve several transformations of energy. Consider a flashlight. Chemical energy is stored in the battery. This energy is transformed into electrical energy. The electrical energy is carried to the light bulb. There it is transformed into light energy that you can see.

The energy transformations related to fossil fuels, such as coal, are even more complex. Recall that coal was formed over millions of years. Ancient plants conducted photosynthesis, during which they transformed the light energy of the Sun into chemical energy stored in food. When the plants died, any stored chemical energy was trapped in their tissues. The plants became buried under layers of soil and water. Over millions of years, heat and high pressure changed the plants into coal. The chemical energy from the plants became stored in the coal.

Today, that coal is burned in many power plants. When it is burned, the chemical energy is transformed into thermal energy and radiant energy (light). The thermal energy is transferred to water as heat. The water is heated until it boils and forms steam. The steam is then forced through pipes to the turbine. A *turbine* is like a large fan with blades. When the turbine turns, it runs an electric generator. The generator produces electricity. In this way, the mechanical energy of the steam is transformed into electrical energy.

chemical → thermal → mechanical → electrical
energy   energy   energy   energy

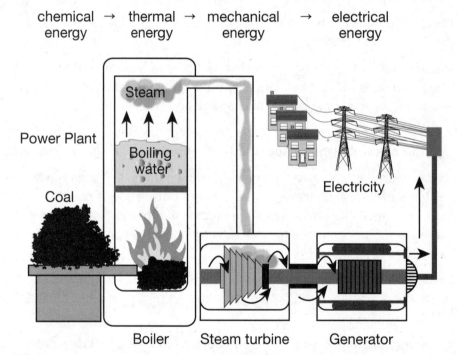

Most power plants involve a turbine that turns an electrical generator. The difference is the source of energy that turns the turbine. Some electrical power plants use the mechanical energy of flowing water or wind. Others use the nuclear energy released when atoms are split apart.

In an energy transformation, no new energy is created. No energy is destroyed. These observations are known as the **Law of Conservation of Energy**. The total amount of energy is the same before and after a transformation.

That does not mean that energy transformations are completely efficient. Some useful energy is always turned to thermal energy. This energy is transferred to the surroundings as heat. Useful energy is any energy that is able to do work. The heat energy is not used to do work so it is said to be lost.

Think about a light bulb. When you flip the switch, the bulb lights up as electrical energy is transformed into radiant energy. Some electrical energy is transformed into heat and is lost to the atmosphere. This is why a light bulb becomes hot when it is on. No energy is destroyed, but not all of the energy is transformed into the light that you want to use.

 Measuring Up Express™ for the New York State Test

NYS Test Practice

Directions (1–7): Decide which choice is the best answer. Circle the number of the answer you have chosen.

1   What energy transformation takes place when firewood is burned to boil water?

(1) Chemical energy changes to thermal energy.

(2) Chemical energy changes to electrical energy.

(3) Kinetic energy changes to potential energy.

(4) Nuclear energy changes to chemical energy.

2   The reaction below shows cellular respiration.

oxygen + glucose → carbon dioxide + water + energy

$$6O_2 + C_6H_{12}O_6 \rightarrow 6CO_2 + 6H_2O + \text{energy}$$

What is true about this reaction?

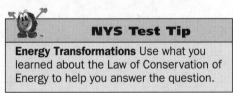

NYS Test Tip

Energy Transformations Use what you learned about the Law of Conservation of Energy to help you answer the question.

(1) The chemical energy in glucose was destroyed.

(2) Energy was lost because carbon dioxide and water are not energy.

(3) Chemical energy was converted into other forms of energy.

(4) Light energy changed into gases and water, and chemical energy was destroyed.

3   Which statement is true about an object at rest?

(1) It may have kinetic energy.

(2) It may have potential energy.

(3) It has both kinetic and potential energy.

(4) It has neither kinetic nor potential energy.

4   What is true about the potential and kinetic energy of water after it has fallen halfway down a waterfall?

(1) The potential energy of the water is greater than the kinetic energy.

(2) The kinetic energy of the water is greater than the potential energy.

(3) The potential energy and kinetic energy of the water are equal.

(4) The kinetic energy cancels out the potential energy.

5   In the engine of a car, chemical energy in gasoline is transformed into mechanical energy to move the car. However, the amount of chemical energy converted does *not* equal the amount of mechanical energy produced. What happened to the remaining energy?

(1) Most of it was destroyed in the process of transformation.

(2) Most of it was transformed to electrical energy and stored in the battery.

(3) Most of it was transformed to heat energy and released into the environment.

(4) Most of it was transformed into sound energy and released into the environment.

6   During an earthquake,

(1) kinetic energy changes to potential energy

(2) kinetic energy changes to chemical energy

(3) potential energy changes to kinetic energy

(4) potential energy changes to chemical energy

7   The energy stored in the bonds that hold matter together is

(1) chemical energy

(2) nuclear energy

(3) electrical energy

(4) electromagnetic energy

Directions (8–9): Record your answers on the lines provided below each question.

8   How do the kinetic and potential energy of a leaf change as it falls from a branch to the ground?   [1]

_____

_____

_____

9   What form of energy is produced in every transformation?   [1]

_____

Focus on the NYS Learning Standards

Lesson 49 Heat

PS 4.2a   Heat moves in predictable ways, flowing from warmer objects to cooler ones, until both reach the same temperature.
PS 4.2b   Heat can be transferred through matter by the collisions of atoms and/or molecules (conduction) or through space (radiation). In a liquid or gas, currents will facilitate the transfer of heat (convection).
PS 4.2c, PS 4.2d

You can describe the ways that heat is transferred and how a change in heat affects matter.

Anything in motion has kinetic energy. Particles of matter are in constant motion so they have kinetic energy. They also have potential energy. The total energy of the particles in a sample of matter is **thermal energy**.

Temperature is a measure of the average kinetic energy of the particles that make up a substance. Temperature is measured with a thermometer.

Thermal energy that flows from an object at a higher temperature to an object at a lower temperature is known as **heat**. When heat is transferred to or from a substance, the temperature of the substance may change. Generally, the temperature rises when heat is transferred to matter. The temperature falls when heat is transferred from matter.

This is not true when a heat transfer causes a substance to change its state. Remember that solids melt and liquids boil when they are heated. That means that heat is transferred to the substances. As heat energy is transferred to a substance, its temperature generally rises. At the melting and boiling point, however, the temperature does not change even though the substances are absorbing heat. The additional energy acts to break the attractive forces between the particles and does not result in a change in temperature. The same is true when substances condense and freeze. The loss of energy during these changes in state affects the attractive forces between particles and does not result in a temperature change.

Most substances expand as they are heated. On the contrary, most substances contract when cold. Metal bridges, for example, are designed with joints that allow the metal to expand in hot weather and contract in cold weather. Water is an exception to this rule. Water expands when it freezes.

Heat is transferred by conduction, convection, and radiation.

Conduction is the transfer of heat from direct contact between particles. Heat is transferred from a stove to the bottom of a pot by conduction.

Convection is the transfer of heat energy by the movement of currents within a fluid. A **convection current** is the circular flow created by convection. After conduction heats the bottom of the pot, the heated water at the bottom of the pot rises. It displaces the cooler water at the top of the pot, which sinks down toward the bottom. There, the cooler water heats up and rises in turn. This cycle makes the water in the pot move in a circular motion, or a current. This circular motion of heated water causes the water throughout the pot to heat up. Convection currents occur in air too.

Radiation is the transfer of energy by electromagnetic waves. You notice that if you hold out your hand to the pot and stove, your hand will get warmer, even if you don't actually touch the hot objects. This is because electromagnetic waves transfer heat from the pot and stove to your hand.

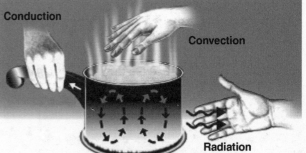

Conduction

Convection

Radiation

Directions (1–8): Decide which choice is the best answer. Circle the number of the answer you have chosen.

1 Sometimes you see dew, which are droplets of water, on grass in the morning. It is formed when water vapor in the air

(1) absorbs heat

(2) loses heat

(3) changes into a different substance

(4) expands

2 A glass of ice cubes and water is −5°C. Heat is transferred from the air to the ice water. What happens to the temperature of ice water?

(1) The temperature increases until it reaches 0°C.

(2) The temperature decreases until it reaches −10°C.

(3) The temperature decreases then increases.

(4) The temperature remains the same.

3 Which term describes the process of transferring heat by direct contact?

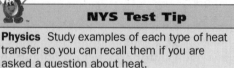

NYS Test Tip

Physics Study examples of each type of heat transfer so you can recall them if you are asked a question about heat.

(1) conduction

(2) convection current

(3) convection

(4) radiation

4 What happens to cooler liquid as hot liquid rises inside the same container?

(1) It evaporates into a gas.

(2) It warms up by conduction.

(3) It sinks down in the container.

(4) It rises to the top of the container.

5 A student sets up the beakers shown.

Beaker A   Beaker B

What will happen if the two beakers are left near one another?

(1) Heat will flow from Beaker B to Beaker A until they reach the same temperature.

(2) Heat will flow from Beaker A to Beaker B until they reach the same temperature.

(3) Heat will flow back and forth between the beakers until both are at 72°C.

(4) Heat will not flow from one beaker to the other.

6 A heater at floor level heats a room using

   (1) thermal expansion   (3) conduction

   (2) radiation   (4) convection

7 What happens to most substances, such as metals, when they are heated?

   (1) They expand.

   (2) They contract.

   (3) They float.

   (4) They flow.

8 During which change of state is energy released?

   (1) melting

   (2) boiling

   (3) evaporation

   (4) condensation

Directions (9–10): Record your answers on the lines provided below each question.

9 How is radiation different from conduction and convection? [1]

_____

10 How can you predict the direction of heat flow between two objects? [1]

_____

Lesson 50 Energy and Chemical Reactions

PS 4.3a In chemical reactions, energy is transferred into or out of a system. Light, electricity, or mechanical motion may be involved in such transfers in addition to heat.

PS 4.5a Energy cannot be created or destroyed, but only changed from one form into another.

PS 3.3d, PS 4.5b

Recognize that energy is either absorbed or released during every chemical reaction.

Chemical energy is the energy stored in the bonds that hold matter together. During a chemical reaction, chemical bonds between atoms of the reactants are broken and new bonds are formed in the products. Breaking and forming chemical bonds involve energy. That energy may be in the form of heat, light, electricity, or even mechanical energy.

The energy required to start a chemical reaction is known as **activation energy.** Particles of matter must combine with energy greater than or equal to the activation energy in order to react.

The rate of a chemical reaction can be increased by increasing the number of particles that collide with the energy they need to react. Increasing the temperature, for example, increases the average kinetic energy of the particles. Increasing the surface area of the reactants also increases the number of opportunities for collisions between particles. A **catalyst** is a substance that lowers the activation energy required for a chemical reaction. That means that more particles will collide with enough energy to react. The catalyst is not used up during the reaction, so it does not become a reactant.

An **exothermic reaction** is a chemical reaction in which energy is released. The total energy of the products is less than the total energy of the reactants.

An **endothermic reaction** is a chemical reaction in which energy is absorbed. The total energy of the products is greater than the total energy of the reactants.

The **Law of Conservation of Energy** states that energy is neither created nor destroyed during a chemical reaction. Even though the energy of the reactants may be different from the energy of the products, the total amount of the entire system is conserved. The system includes the reactants, products, and the environment in which they are located.

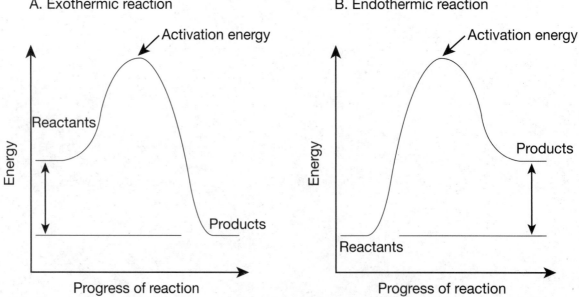

A. Exothermic reaction   B. Endothermic reaction

Directions (1–6): Decide which choice is the best answer. Circle the number of the answer you have chosen.

1   The graph shows the change in energy during the chemical reaction for cellular respiration.

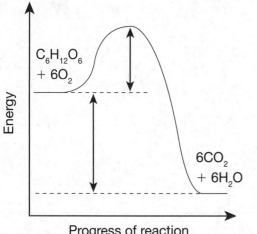

Based on the graph, you can conclude that during this chemical reaction

(1) energy is given off

(2) energy is absorbed

(3) energy is destroyed

(4) energy is created

2   An enzyme is a substance that reduces the activation energy for a chemical reaction. How will lowering the activation energy affect the chemical reaction?

(1) It will prevent it from happening.

(2) It will speed up the reaction.

(3) It will change the reactants.

(4) It will slow down the reaction.

3   During a chemical reaction, one form of energy is transformed into another. What must be true about the transformation of energy?

(1) Some energy is created in the products.

(2) Some of the energy of the reactants is destroyed.

(3) The energy of the reactants is exactly equal to the energy of the products.

(4) Some energy is transformed into heat that is released into the system.

4   Which equation represents an endothermic reaction?

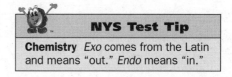

NYS Test Tip

Chemistry *Exo* comes from the Latin and means "out." *Endo* means "in."

(1) A + B + energy $\rightarrow$ C + D + energy

(2) A + B $\rightarrow$ C + D + energy

(3) A + B + energy $\rightarrow$ C + D

(4) A + B $\rightarrow$ C + D

5   Which is an endothermic process?

(1) cooking an egg

(2) burning a candle

(3) exploding fireworks

(4) making ice cubes

6 When baking soda reacts with water, the reaction is exothermic. What happens to the energy between the reactants and products?

(1) It is created, causing the products to have more energy than the reactants.

(2) It is destroyed, causing the products to have less energy than the reactants.

(3) It is released into the system, raising the temperature slightly

(4) It is absorbed by the system, lowering its temperature slightly.

Directions (7–8): Record your answers on the lines provided below each question.

7 Why is energy involved in chemical reactions? [1]

_____

_____

8 The equations below describe two chemical equations.

$$2KClO_3 + Heat \rightarrow 2KCl + 3O_2$$

$$2SO_2 + O_2 \rightarrow 2SO_3 + Heat$$

How are these two chemical reactions different in terms of energy? [2]

_____

_____

 Measuring Up Express™ for the New York State Test

Lesson 51 Electromagnetic and Sound Waves

PS 4.4a Different forms of electromagnetic energy have different wavelengths.

PS 4.4b Light passes through some materials, sometimes refracting in the process. Materials absorb and reflect light, and may transmit light. To see an object, light from that object, emitted by or reflected from it, must enter the eye.

PS 4.4c Vibrations in materials set up wave-like disturbances that spread away from the source. Sound waves are an example. Vibrational waves move at different speeds in different materials. Sound cannot travel in a vacuum.

Demonstrate an understanding of the electromagnetic energy and sound waves.

A **wave** can transmit energy through matter and space. Examples include water waves, sound waves, and light waves.

A **transverse wave** has vibrations perpendicular to the direction in which the wave moves. Transverse waves can be modeled by flipping a rope up and down. Transverse waves are described by high points called *crests* and low points called *troughs*. Electromagnetic waves are transverse waves made up of vibrating electric and magnetic fields.

In a **longitudinal wave,** the particles vibrate parallel to the direction in which the wave is traveling. Longitudinal waves are made up of *compressions* (where particles are close together) and *rarefactions* (where particles are farther apart). These compressions and rarefactions transfer energy much as a coiled spring would when pulled and released.

Light energy is transferred by electromagnetic waves. **Electromagnetic waves** are waves produced by the motion of electrically charged particles. Electromagnetic waves are often called **electromagnetic radiation** because they radiate from the particles. All electromagnetic waves travel at the same speed through a vacuum—300,000 km/s. (This speed is also called the *speed of light.*)

Wavelength is the distance between a point on a wave and an identical point on the next wave. For example, one wavelength might be measured from the crest of one wave to the next or from a compression on one wave to a compression on the next wave. The shorter the wavelength, the more energy radiation it has.

Frequency is the number of waves that pass a place in a given amount of time. Frequency is expressed in hertz (Hz). One hertz is the same as one wave per second.

The **electromagnetic spectrum** organizes electromagnetic waves according to wavelength.

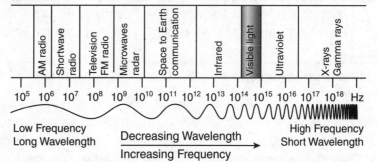

Radio waves have long wavelengths and low frequencies. Each frequency for AM, FM, and shortwave radios is a different station. Radio waves are used in radios, televisions, cell phones, radar, microwaves, GPS, and many computers. **Infrared radiation** has a wavelength slightly longer than visible light. The Sun (and anything warm) is constantly emitting infrared radiation, and Earth absorbs it and turns the energy into molecular motion, or thermal energy. **Visible radiation** or *light* is the only part of the electromagnetic spectrum you can see. It is made up of the colors of the spectrum. **Ultraviolet radiation,** commonly called *UV rays,* can kill healthy skin cells and cause sunburns, and overexposure can cause skin cancer. But UV rays also enable your skin to produce vitamin D. UV lamps are used in hospitals to sterilize surgical instruments. Ozone found in Earth's upper atmosphere protects us by blocking most of the Sun's UV radiation.

Although visible light makes up only a small portion of the electromagnetic spectrum, it makes it possible to see objects. The wavelength of light determines its color. The colors of the spectrum in order of decreasing wavelengths are red, orange, yellow, green, blue, indigo, and violet. White light is made up of all of the wavelengths of visible light. When light strikes an object, it can be transmitted, absorbed, or reflected. If the light is **transmitted**, it passes through the object, such as a window. If the light is **reflected**, it bounces back from the surface. If the light is **absorbed**, it is not reflected or transmitted by the object.

The color of an object is the wavelength of light that is reflected back to the eye. When matter absorbs all the light, the matter will appear as black. When matter absorbs all the wavelengths of color except those of red, for example, which is reflected, you will see that object as red.

If light is transmitted through an object, it can be refracted. **Refraction** is the bending of light when it strikes a surface at an angle. A **prism** is a triangular glass that refracts the light twice, once when it enters the prism and again when it leaves the prism and enters the air. Because the shorter wavelengths of light are refracted more than the longer wavelengths, violet is bent the most. As a result, different colors (*spectrum*) are separated when they emerge from the prism.

Light is reflected from a mirror and refracted by a lens. The table describes the type of image formed by different types of mirrors and lenses.

Shape	Type of Mirror or Lens	Type of Image Formed
⊱	A *concave mirror* is a polished surface that is curved inward.	inverted, real images Size of image: smaller, larger, or the same size as the original object
⊰	A *convex mirror* is curved outward.	upright, virtual images Size of image: smaller than the original object
◇	A *convex lens* is thicker in the middle than at the edges.	inverted, real images Size of image: smaller, larger, or the same size as the original object
)(	A *concave lens* is thinner in the middle than at the edges.	upright, virtual images Size of image: smaller than the original object

Mirrors create images by reflection and lenses create images by refraction.

Like light, sound travels as a wave. However, sound travels as a longitudinal wave. A sound wave is produced when an object vibrates. The vibration causes nearby particles of matter to vibrate as well. The vibration is transferred. Unlike light waves, sound waves cannot travel in a vacuum. They need matter in which to travel. Sound waves travel the fastest through solids, less fast through liquids, and the slowest through gases.

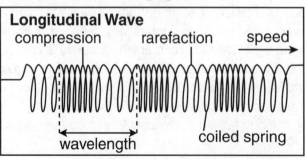

Copying is illegal. Measuring Up Express™ for the New York State Test

NYS Test Practice   *Directions* (1–8): Decide which choice is the best answer. Circle the number of the answer you have chosen.

1   Which kind of waves cannot travel through the vacuum of space?

(1) visible light

(2) sound waves

(3) x-rays

(4) ultraviolet radiation

2   Which form of energy does not come directly from the Sun to Earth?

(1) visible light

(2) infrared waves

(3) sound waves

(4) microwaves

3   If a type of electromagnetic wave has a very short wavelength, what else must be true about it?

(1) It has a lot of energy.

(2) It doesn't have much energy.

(3) It is a radio wave.

(4) Its frequency is decreasing.

4   Electromagnetic waves with short wavelengths and high frequencies can penetrate human body cells. Examples of these types of waves include

(1) television and radio signals

(2) infrared and microwaves

(3) ultraviolet and microwaves

(4) x-rays and gamma rays

5   The wave behavior shown in the image below is an example of

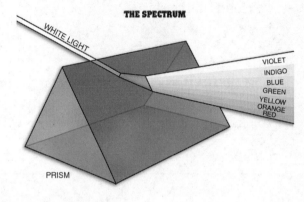

(1) reflection

(2) refraction

(3) diffraction

(4) interference

6   Light from a flashlight strikes the silvery surface of a DVD and bounces back. This is an example of

(1) diffraction

(2) diffusion

(3) reflection

(4) interference

7   Which statement about sound energy is true?

(1) It travels as moving electrons.

(2) It does not need matter to travel.

(3) It travels as electromagnetic waves.

(4) It travels as vibrations through matter.

8   Through which of these materials would a
    sound wave travel at the greatest speed?

    (1) helium in a balloon

    (2) a metal railroad track

    (3) water in a swimming pool

    (4) clouds in the sky

Directions (9–10):Record your answers on the lines provided below each question.

9   Explain how a lemon can appear yellow when white light strikes it.   [1]

_____

_____

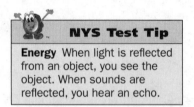

NYS Test Tip

Energy When light is reflected
from an object, you see the
object. When sounds are
reflected, you hear an echo.

10   How do compressions and rarefactions form in a sound wave?   [2]

_____

_____

PS 4.4e   Electrical circuits provide a means of transferring electrical energy.

PS 4.4f   Without touching them, material that has been electrically charged attracts uncharged material, and may either attract or repel other charged material.

PS 4.4g   Without direct contact, a magnet attracts certain materials and either attracts or repels other magnets. The attractive force of a magnet is greatest at its poles.

PS 4.4d

Demonstrate an understanding of electricity and magnetism.

Electrical energy is the energy of moving electric charges. It can be produced from a variety of energy sources and can be transformed into almost any other form of energy.

Static electricity is the build up of electric charges on an object. Without being in direct contact, electrically charged materials can exert forces on one another. Materials with like electric charges repel one another and materials with unlike electric charges attract one another.

An **electric current** is a flow of electric charges through matter. Electric currents can transfer electrical energy to power devices such as televisions, computers, and flashlights. The rate at which charges pass a given point in a given amount of time is called *current*. Current (*I*) is measured in the units of *amperes,* or amps (*A*).

Voltage is a measure of the potential energy per unit charge and is measured in the units of volts (*V*). You can think of voltage as an electric pressure that can produce a current. **Resistance** is the opposition to the flow of electric charge and is measured in *ohms* (Ω). Resistance can be thought of as electric friction. Voltage can be calculated in the following equation, which is known as Ohm's law:

$$voltage = current \times resistance, \text{ or } V = IR$$

Current flows in wires and in electric devices when the wires and devices are connected in a complete closed path called a **circuit**. A *series circuit* provides one path for electric current to flow through. In a *parallel circuit*, electric current has more than one path.

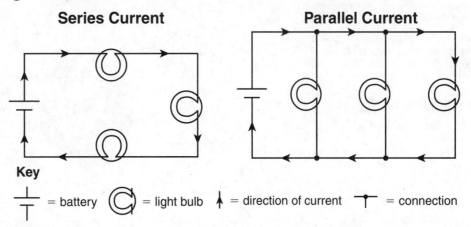

Series Current   **Parallel Current**

Key

$\dashv\vdash$ = battery $\mathbb{C}$ = light bulb $\uparrow$ = direction of current $\top$ = connection

A **magnet** is a material that attracts iron or materials containing iron. All magnets exert *magnetic forces* on other magnets and on objects containing certain metals such as iron, steel, cobalt, and nickel. The magnetic force of a magnet can attract or repel other magnets without being in direct contact. Magnetic forces are found in the area that surrounds each magnet called the *magnetic field.* The magnetic forces of a magnet are strongest at its two ends, or *magnetic poles.* All magnets have two poles, a north pole and a south pole. The opposite poles of magnets will attract each other, but the same poles will repel each other.

NYS Test Practice

Directions (1–7): Decide which choice is the best answer. Circle the number of the answer you have chosen.

1   Why isn't the light bulb in this circuit illuminated?

(1) The switch is open so electrical energy is not transferred to the bulb.

(2) The switch is open so the circuit is closed and electrical energy is transferred away from the bulb.

(3) The circuit is missing a power source.

(4) The circuit is missing a load.

2   A lamp, a radio, and an electric fan are connected in that order in a series circuit. All three devices are turned on. What will happen when you turn off the radio?

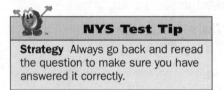

NYS Test Tip

Strategy Always go back and reread the question to make sure you have answered it correctly.

(1) The lamp will keep working, but the electric fan will not.

(2) The electric fan will keep working, but the lamp will not.

(3) The lamp and the electric fan will keep working.

(4) The lamp and the electric fan will stop working.

3   Which two objects will attract one another?

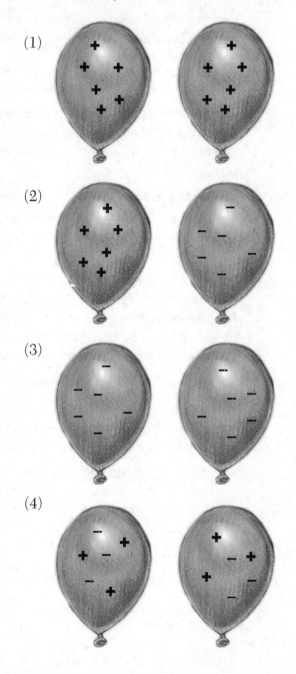

(1)

(2)

(3)

(4)

4   A source of electrical energy in many circuits is

(1) a wire   (3) a battery

(2) a lamp   (4) a switch

5 A student moves a magnet close to another magnet that is lying on a table.

What will happen to the magnet on the table?

(1) The magnet will move closer to the magnet in the student's hand and will stick to it.

(2) The magnet will move closer to the magnet in the student's hand but will not touch it.

(3) The magnet will move away from the magnet in the student's hand.

(4) The magnet will move neither closer to nor away from the magnet in the student's hand.

6 The magnetic forces of a bar magnet are strongest

(1) in the center

(2) at the ends

(3) in a magnetic field around it

(4) above or below it

7 Which statement about magnetic poles is true?

(1) Magnets have two poles: a north pole and a south pole.

(2) Magnets have two poles: either two north poles or two south poles.

(3) Magnets can have more than two poles, but must have one north pole and one south pole.

(4) Magnets can have less than two poles, but must have one north pole.

Directions (8–9): Record your answers on the lines provided below each question.

8 How is a series circuit like a parallel circuit? How are they different?   [2]

_____

_____

_____

9 Why aren't the electric force and magnetic force considered to be contact forces like the force of friction?   [1]

_____

_____

Directions (1–3): Decide which choice is the best answer. Circle the number of the answer you have chosen.

1   How does heating a sample of ice affect the water molecules?

   (1) It causes them to give up energy so the bonds between them become stronger.

   (2) It causes them to lose atoms so they become smaller and lighter.

   (3) It causes them to gain thermal energy so they move faster and farther apart.

   (4) It causes them to join together so they can exert greater pressure on their container.

2   Light entering the eye is refracted by the lens of the eye. This light forms a real image on the back of the eye that is interpreted by the brain. What kind of lens is the lens of the eye?

   (1) concave   (3) plane

   (2) convex   (4) diffracting

3   A pendulum is a mass on a string that swings back and forth as shown below.

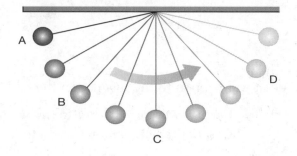

At which point is the potential energy of the ball greatest?

   (1) A   (3) C

   (2) B   (4) D

Directions (4):   Record your answer on the lines provided below the question.

4   Suppose you have a sample of aluminum and a sample of lead. Each sample has a volume of 5.0 cm³. Compare the samples in terms of mass. Explain your answer. [2]

Density of Substances at Room Temperature

Substance	Density (g/cm³)
Aluminum	2.70
Lead	11.35

Higher-Order Performance Task
Conservation of Mass in a Chemical Reaction

Task:

You will observe the conservation of mass in a chemical reaction and describe the effects of the chemical changes.

Materials:

- baking soda
- calcium chloride
- 2 large self-sealing bags
- universal indicator solution or water
- plastic film canister with lid (or a test tube with a cork)

- 2 plastic spoons
- balance
- 10 mL graduated cylinder

Directions:

1. Make a list of evidence that would indicate a chemical change has taken place.

_____

_____

2. Use one of the spoons to place one level spoonful of baking soda into a self-sealing bag. Use the other spoon to place two level spoonfuls of calcium chloride into the same bag.

3. Use the graduated cylinder to measure 5 mL of the universal indicator solution or water.

4. The baking soda, calcium chloride, and liquid are starting materials in the change that you will observe. Keep their properties in mind while performing the rest of the experiment.

5. Pour the liquid from the graduated cylinder into the film canister and place the lid securely on the canister. Place it in the self-sealing bag with the powders.

6. Squeeze all the excess air out of the bag and seal it. Then, without opening the bag, open the film canister.

7. Mix the liquid with the powders. Record your observations.

_____

_____

_____

_____

8. What did you observe that would indicate a chemical change?

_____

_____

9. Design an experiment to determine how the mass of the system changed during the reaction. Describe your procedure below.

_____

_____

_____

_____

10. After your instructor checks your procedure, perform your experiment. Make a data table in the space below to record your findings.

Data Table

11. Speculate why a change in mass or no change in mass occurred in your experiment.

_____

12. How was the plastic bag useful for determining the mass in your experiment?

_____

_____

_____

13. When you are finished, follow your teacher's instructions and put the materials where they belong. Dry any objects that are wet and wipe up any spills.

Chapter 6
Focus on the NYS Learning Standards
Lesson 53 The Motion of Objects

PS 5.1a	The motion of an object is always judged with respect to some other object or point. The idea of absolute motion or rest is misleading.
PS 5.1b	The motion of an object can be described by its position, direction of motion, and speed.

Understand how the motion of an object can be described and measured.

Motion is a change in an object's position relative to a specific reference point.

A **reference point** is an object or group of objects assumed to be at rest, or stationary. An object that is at rest when compared with one reference point may be in motion when compared with another. For example, a desk is at rest when compared with the floor beneath it. That same desk is in motion when compared with the Sun because the desk is on Earth, which constantly revolves around the Sun. No object can be considered at rest or in motion relative to every reference point.

Motion can be described by measuring how the position of an object changes over time relative to some reference point. The **speed** of an object is the change in the position of the object divided by the amount of time it took to change position.

$$\text{speed} = \frac{\text{distance}}{\text{time}}$$

Some common units of speeds are kilometers per hour (km/h), miles per hour (mi/h), and meters per second (m/s). The speed at any instant in an object's motion is known as *instantaneous speed*. More often, you know information about the overall motion of the object. In this case, you calculate the average speed.

Velocity is speed in a particular direction. It is measured in the same units as speed, but includes information about the object's direction as well. For example, a baseball might have a velocity of 90 mi/h east.

Motion can be represented by a line graph of distance versus time. The shape of the line gives information about how an object is moving. For example, a straight line that slopes upward shows constant speed for an object moving away from a reference point. A straight line that slopes downward shows constant speed for an object moving toward a reference point. A straight horizontal line shows that an object is not moving toward or away from a reference point.

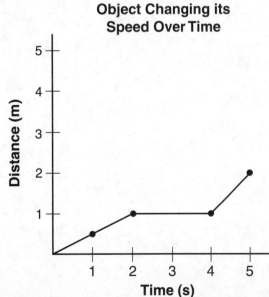

Object Changing its Speed Over Time

NYS Test Practice

Directions (1–6): Decide which choice is the best answer. Circle the number of the answer you have chosen.

Base your answers to questions 1 through 3 on the diagram below and on your knowledge of science.

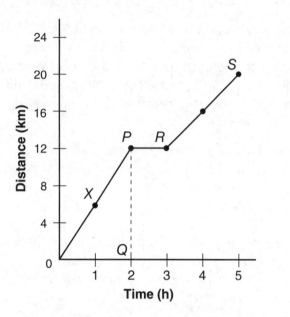

1 According to the graph, what was the total distance the object moved from the reference point?

(1) 12 km

(2) 16 km

(3) 20 km

(4) 24 km

2 During which period of time did the object stop moving?

(1) from hour 1 to hour 2

(2) from hour 2 to hour 3

(3) from hour 3 to hour 4

(4) from hour 4 to hour 5

3 What was the average speed of the object throughout its entire motion?

(1) 1 km/h   (3) 3 km/h

(2) 2 km/h   (4) 4 km/h

4 What is the average speed of a runner who finishes a 100–meter dash in 19.6 seconds?

NYS Test Tip

Strategy Always make sure you include the correct unit of measurement in your calculations.

(1) 0.196 m/s

(2) 5.1 m/s

(3) 80.4 m/s

(4) 119.6 m/s

5 A person sitting in a train is moving when compared with a train station. That same person is at rest when compared with

(1) the seats on the train

(2) the train tracks

(3) a building along the train tracks

(4) another train it is passing

6 Which is a measure of velocity?

(1) 4 kilometers

(2) 3 meters per second

(3) 1 mile per hour south

(4) 5 hours

Measuring Up Express™ for the New York State Test

Directions (7–8): Record your answers on the lines provided below each question.

7   How is velocity different from speed?   [1]

_____

_____

8   Two students described the same object as being at rest and in motion. How might they both be correct?   [1]

_____

_____

_____

PS 5.1c   An object's motion is the result of the combined effect of all forces acting on the object. A moving object that is not subjected to a force will continue to move at a constant speed in a straight line. An object at rest will remain at rest.

PS 5.1d   Force is directly related to an object's mass and acceleration. The greater the force, the greater the change in motion.

PS 5.1e   For every action there is an equal and opposite reaction.

PS 5.2d

Identify that forces acting on an object determine its motion.

A **force** is a push or a pull. Every force has a magnitude and a direction. The magnitude of force is measured in units called **newtons** (N). A force that causes an object with a mass of 1 kg to accelerate 1 m/s² is equivalent to 1 Newton.

All of the forces acting on an object combine to produce a **net force**. If the net force on an object experiencing forces is zero, the forces are said to be balanced. **Balanced forces** on an object do not change the motion of the object.

If there is a net force on an object, the forces are said to be unbalanced. **Unbalanced forces** on an object cause a change in the motion of the object. The objects can change direction, speed up, or slow down. In other words, an unbalanced force can cause an object to accelerate.

The acceleration depends on the magnitude of the force and the mass of the object. Force is equal to mass multiplied by acceleration ($F = ma$). Acceleration increases as the force on the object increases.

The **acceleration** of an object is the rate or change in velocity (a change in direction or a change in speed). If a race car goes from 0 m/s to 32 m/s in 4 seconds, its acceleration is 32 m/s divided by 4 s, or 8 m/s². Acceleration can be graphically represented as shown below left.

The motion of an object will not change unless an unbalanced force acts on it. An object at rest will remain at rest and an object in motion will remain in motion at constant speed in the same direction unless an unbalanced force acts on it. The tendency of an object at rest to remain at rest and the tendency of an object in motion to remain in motion at a constant velocity, unless a force acts on it is known as **inertia**. The more mass an object has, the more inertia it has.

Friction is the force between objects that works against their movement past each other. One force causes motion and the other force opposes motion. The force of friction depends on surface texture and strength with which the objects are squeezed together.

For every force exerted on an object, the object exerts an equal and opposite force. These are known as *action-reaction forces*.

240 N   180 N

The magnitude and direction of the net force on the rope is 60 N to the left. (240 N − 180 N = 60 N)

NYS Test Practice

Directions (1–10): Decide which choice is the best answer. Circle the number of the answer you have chosen.

1   If two students push a box with a force of 3 N each in the same direction, and there is no other unbalanced force on the box, what is the magnitude of the net force on the box?

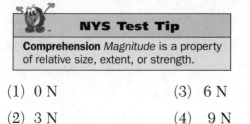

> **NYS Test Tip**
>
> **Comprehension** *Magnitude* is a property of relative size, extent, or strength.

   (1) 0 N   (3) 6 N

   (2) 3 N   (4) 9 N

2   If two students each push a box with a force of 3 N in opposite directions, and there is no other unbalanced force on the box, what is the magnitude of the net force exerted on the box?

   (1) 0 N   (3) 6 N

   (2) 3 N   (4) 12 N

3   A student pulls a bag with a force of 50 N. The force of friction between the bag and the floor is 15 N. What is the net force on the bag?

   (1) 15 N   (3) 50 N

   (2) 35 N   (4) 65 N

4   The box shown below has two forces acting on it. The arrows represent the size and direction of the forces. Which arrow best represents the net force on the box?

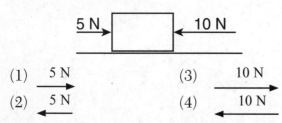

   (1)   5 N   (3)   10 N

   (2)   5 N   (4)   10 N

5   What must happen for an object to accelerate?

   (1) An unbalanced force must act on it.

   (2) A balanced force must act on it.

   (3) No forces must act on it.

   (4) Only one force can act on it.

6   Like friction, all forces are

   (1) a form of energy

   (2) a push or pull

   (3) anything with mass or volume

   (4) the mass in a given volume

7   An ice skater exerts a force of 10 N on the wall of the ice rink. What is the magnitude of the force the wall exerts on the skater?

   (1) 5 N

   (2) 10 N

   (3) 20 N

   (4) 50 N

8   A shopper exerts a constant force on a shopping cart. As the shopper adds groceries to the shopping cart, its acceleration

   (1) increases

   (2) decreases

   (3) stays the same

   (4) increases and then decreases

9 An acorn falls from a tree. How does the force of friction affect the acorn?

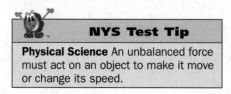

NYS Test Tip

Physical Science An unbalanced force must act on an object to make it move or change its speed.

(1) It pushes it horizontally.

(2) It pulls it downward.

(2) It opposes its downward motion.

(4) It squeezes it into a smaller space.

10 A rocket burns fuel to produce gases. The gases are expelled out of the bottom of the rocket. What causes the rocket to move forward?

(1) The gases are thinner than air, so the rocket rises.

(2) The gases heat the air around the rocket, making it thinner.

(3) The air exerts an equal and opposite force on the rocket.

(4) The gases exert an equal and opposite force on the rocket.

Directions (11–12):   Record your answers on the lines provided below each question.

11 How is it possible that an object can have forces acting on it, but it does not accelerate?   [1]

_____

12 How is the acceleration of an object related to the force exerted on it and its mass?   [2]

_____

_____

Focus on the NYS Learning Standards

Lesson 55 | Universal Forces

PS 5.2a	Every object exerts gravitational force on every other object. Gravitational force depends on how much mass the objects have and on how far apart they are. Gravity is one of the forces acting on orbiting objects and projectiles.
PS 5.2b	Electric currents and magnets can exert a force on each other.

Recognize the universal forces and how they affect matter.

Scientists have identified four fundamental forces, or **universal forces.**

One of the universal forces is **gravity.** Gravity is an attractive force that exists between any two masses in the universe. It is the weakest of the universal forces, but it can act over infinite distance.

The magnitude of the gravitational force depends on the masses and the distance between them. The gravitational force increases as mass increases and decreases as distance increases. The gravitational force can be calculated using the equation:

$$F_G = \frac{G\, m_1 m_2}{r^2}$$

In this equation, m_1 represents one of the masses and m_2 represents the other. The r in the denominator represents the distance between the objects as measured from their centers. The letter G represents the universal gravitational constant.

The gravitational force is responsible for holding the solar system together. This force was responsible for causing stars and planets to form. Near a large object, such as a planet, the gravitational force pulls objects downward. Earth, for example, pulls objects toward its center.

The **electromagnetic force** is another universal force. This force arises from the relationship between electric current and magnetism. An electric current in a wire creates a magnetic field around the wire. In fact, if the wire carrying the current is coiled around an iron core, an **electromagnet** is formed.

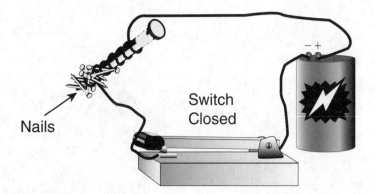

Nails

Switch Closed

Just as electricity gives rise to magnetism, magnetism can produce an electric current. A changing magnetic field can generate an electric current in a circuit. This is known as **electromagnetic induction.** This phenomenon is used in many electric generators. Like the gravitational force, the combined electromagnetic force can act over great distances. This is the strongest of the four universal forces.

The remaining universal forces are the nuclear **strong force** and the nuclear **weak force.** These forces act over extremely small distances. The strong force, for example, acts over a distance about equal to the diameter of the nucleus of a medium-size atom. The weak force acts over a distance shorter than the diameter of a proton. These forces are involved in holding the nucleus of an atom together and in determining changes that can occur to an atomic nucleus.

Directions (1–7): Decide which choice is the best answer. Circle the number of the answer you have chosen.

1   How does gravity affect any pair of objects?

> **NYS Test Tip**
>
> **Physical Science** Gravity causes objects in the universe to speed up, slow down, or change direction.

(1) It pushes them apart.

(2) It pulls them together.

(3) It moves them past each other.

(4) It gives them an electric charge.

2   Which factors affect the magnitude of the gravitational force between two objects?

(1) mass and distance

(2) distance and temperature

(3) volume and mass

(4) size and location

3   Why does the Sun exert a greater gravitational force on Mars than Earth does?

(1) The Sun is hotter than Earth is.

(2) The Sun is farther away from Mars than Earth is.

(3) The Sun has more mass than Earth has.

(4) The Sun contains more gases than Earth does.

4   As the distance between two objects increases, the gravitational force between them

(1) stays the same

(2) decreases

(3) increases

(4) increases and then decreases

5   An archer shoots an arrow toward a target. In what direction does Earth's gravitational force act on the arrow?

(1) It pushes it backward.

(2) It pulls it forward.

(3) It pushes it upward.

(4) It pulls it downward.

6   A coil of wire is part of a closed circuit. An electric current will be induced in the wire if

(1) it is wrapped around an iron nail

(2) it is wrapped around a magnet

(3) it has an iron nail moving through it

(4) it has a magnet moving through it

7   The needle of a compass lines up with a magnetic field.

Which will cause a compass needle to move?

(1) Take out the battery.

(2) Remove the bulb.

(3) Cover the wires.

(4) Close the switch.

Directions (8–9): Record your answers on the lines provided below each question.

8 What is an electromagnet? [1]

_____

_____

9 What might cause the gravitational force between two objects to increase? [2]

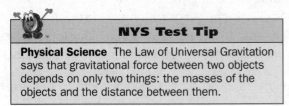

NYS Test Tip

Physical Science The Law of Universal Gravitation says that gravitational force between two objects depends on only two things: the masses of the objects and the distance between them.

_____

_____

Focus on the NYS Learning Standards

Lesson 56 Simple and Complex Machines

PS 5.2f Machines can change the direction or amount of force, or the distance or speed of force required to do work.

PS 5.2g Simple machines include a lever, a pulley, a wheel and axle, and an inclined plane. A complex machine uses a combination of interacting simple machines, e.g., a bicycle.

PS 5.2c PS 5.2e

Describe the relationship between force, work, and motion in simple machines.

Work is the transfer of mechanical energy to an object when a force on the object causes the object to move in the direction of the force. Work is calculated by multiplying force by distance (*Work = force × distance*).

A **machine** is a device that can make work easier by changing the magnitude or the direction of an applied force. A machine does not reduce the amount of work to be done. A **simple machine** is a machine with few moving parts. Each simple machine converts an *effort force*—the force exerted by the person on the machine into a *resistance force*—the force exerted by the machine on another object. A **complex machine** uses a combination of simple machines.

The **mechanical advantage** of a machine is the ratio of the resistance force to the effort force. Mechanical advantage (MA) $= \frac{force_{resistance}}{force_{effort}}$. The efficiency of a machine can be increased by reducing friction. The table explains some simple machines.

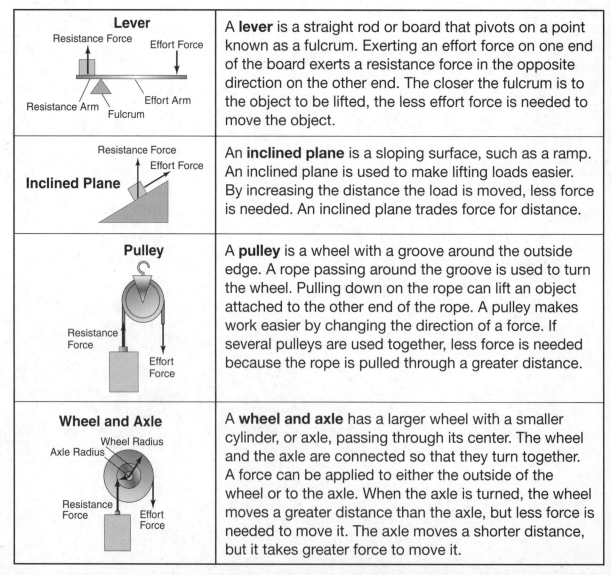

Lever Resistance Force Effort Force Resistance Arm Effort Arm Fulcrum	A **lever** is a straight rod or board that pivots on a point known as a fulcrum. Exerting an effort force on one end of the board exerts a resistance force in the opposite direction on the other end. The closer the fulcrum is to the object to be lifted, the less effort force is needed to move the object.
Inclined Plane Resistance Force Effort Force	An **inclined plane** is a sloping surface, such as a ramp. An inclined plane is used to make lifting loads easier. By increasing the distance the load is moved, less force is needed. An inclined plane trades force for distance.
Pulley Resistance Force Effort Force	A **pulley** is a wheel with a groove around the outside edge. A rope passing around the groove is used to turn the wheel. Pulling down on the rope can lift an object attached to the other end of the rope. A pulley makes work easier by changing the direction of a force. If several pulleys are used together, less force is needed because the rope is pulled through a greater distance.
Wheel and Axle Wheel Radius Axle Radius Resistance Force Effort Force	A **wheel and axle** has a larger wheel with a smaller cylinder, or axle, passing through its center. The wheel and the axle are connected so that they turn together. A force can be applied to either the outside of the wheel or to the axle. When the axle is turned, the wheel moves a greater distance than the axle, but less force is needed to move it. The axle moves a shorter distance, but it takes greater force to move it.

NYS Test Practice

Directions (1–7): Decide which choice is the best answer. Circle the number of the answer you have chosen.

1   How many simple machines are shown in the picture?

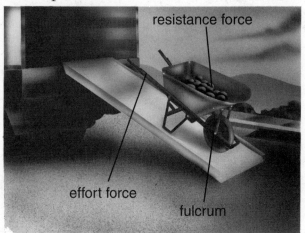

resistance force

effort force

fulcrum

(1) one

(2) two

(3) three

(4) four

2   A person exerts an effort force of 65 N on a machine, and the machine exerts a resistance force of 260 N on an object. What is the mechanical advantage of the machine?

NYS Test Tip

Physical Science Simple machines do not decrease the amount of work, but change how the work is done to make it easier.

(1) 0.25 N

(2) 4.0 N

(3) 195 N

(4) 325 N

3   If the fulcrum in a lever is halfway between the resistance force and the effort force, what function does the machine serve?

(1) It changes both the direction of the force and the amount of force needed to lift the object.

(2) It changes only the direction of the force needed to lift the object.

(3) It changes only the amount of force needed to lift the object.

(4) It changes neither the direction of the force nor the amount of force needed to lift the object.

4   A student wants to move a heavy box to a high table by pulling rather than by pushing or lifting the box. Which simple machine should the student use?

(1) a wheel and axle

(2) an inclined plane

(3) a lever

(4) a pulley

5   A person must lift a stack of books with a mass of 80 N up to a shelf that is 1.5 m high. The person slides the books up an inclined plane that is 6 m long to reach the 1.5 m height. Use a proportion to find how much force the person will need to apply to do the work.

(1) 20 N

(2) 40 N

(3) 75 N

(4) 80 N

6   A student adds oil to a wheel and axle. How does this make the simple machine more efficient?

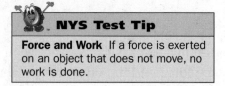

NYS Test Tip

Force and Work If a force is exerted on an object that does not move, no work is done.

(1) The oil changes the distance of the force.

(2) The oil reduces the total work done.

(3) The oil reduces friction.

(4) The oil adds to the net force.

7   The bed of a moving truck is higher than the sidewalk in front of a house. Which of these items results in the least amount of effort force to move items from the truck to the sidewalk?

(1) a set of two steps

(2) a set of four steps

(3) a short ramp

(4) a long ramp

Directions (8–9): Record your answers on the lines provided below each question.

8   How is energy involved in the use of a simple machine?   [1]

_____

9   How are complex machines related to simple machines?   [1]

_____

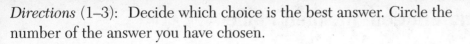

Directions (1–3): Decide which choice is the best answer. Circle the number of the answer you have chosen.

1   The graph below shows the motion of a 0.76 kg ball as a person takes it up 25 meters in an elevator, walks it across a roof, and drops it from the top of the building.

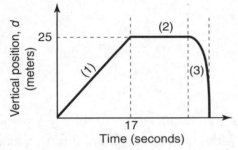

If the acceleration due to gravity on the ball is 9.8 m/s², what is the weight of the ball?

(1) 2.2 N   (3) 7.4 N

(2) 1.5 N   (4) 9.0 N

2   Three forces are acting on an object: a 30N force due north, a 40N force due west, and a 30N force pushing due south. In what direction will the objet accelerate?

(1) northeast   (3) west

(2) southwest   (4) east

3   The table describes two pairs of objects.

	First object's mass (kg)	Second object's mass (kg)	Distance between objects (m)
Pair A	5	7	2
Pair B	15	6	3

How does the gravitational force between the pairs of objects compare?

(1) The gravitational force is the same between both pairs of objects.

(2) The gravitational force is weaker between the objects in pair B.

(3) The gravitational force is greater between the objects in pair C.

(4) The gravitational force is greater between the objects in pair B.

Directions (4):   Record your answer on the lines provided below the question.

4   The farmer to the right is trying to pry a rock out of the dirt.

Describe the type of simple machine he is using and how it affects the work he is doing. Then tell how the position of the block affects his work. [2]

_____

_____

_____

_____

Higher-Order Performance Task
Work, Friction, Inclined Plane

Task:

You will study how using an inclined plane affects the amount of work needed to lift an object.

Materials:

- large book
- spring scale
- long wooden board
- bricks or books to support the ramp
- meterstick
- string three times as long as the book's height

Directions:

1. Open the book to one of the middle pages and lay the string in the center of the book parallel to the spine. Close the book. Tie the ends of the string together across the spine to form a loop.

2. Hook the spring scale on the string and lift the book. How much force is needed to lift the book?

_____

   Record this force as the output force in Data Table 1.

3. Use the board and the bricks to build a ramp that is approximately 10 cm high at its highest point.

4. Measure the height of the ramp and record it in Data Table 1.

5. Lay the book on the ramp and pull the book up the ramp using the string and the spring scale. Keep the spring scale parallel to the ramp as you pull steadily. The force needed to pull the book up the ramp is the input force. Record the input force in Data Table 1.

6. Use another brick to increase the height of the ramp by about 10 cm.

7. Repeat steps 4–6 until you have made measurements for five different ramp heights.

Data Table 1

Trial	Output force (N)	Ramp height (cm)	Ramp length (cm)	Input force (N)
1				
2				
3				
4				
5				

8. Work is calculated using the following equation: $work = force \times distance$

The ideal work is the work that would be done if there were no friction. To calculate the ideal work for this investigation, use the output force and the vertical distance (the height of the ramp) in the equation above. Calculate the ideal work for each of your trials and record your answers in Data Table 2.

To calculate the real work done, use the input force and the distance traveled (the length of the ramp) in the equation above. Calculate the real work for each of your trials, and record your answers in Data Table 2.

Data Table 2

Trial	Ideal Work (J)	Real Work (J)
1		
2		
3		
4		
5		

9. How do the real work and the ideal work compare for each trial?

_____

10. What causes the difference between the real work and the ideal work?

_____

_____

11. What is a benefit and disadvantage of using an inclined plane?

_____

_____

12. The mechanical advantage of a simple machine can be calculated with the following equation:

$$mechanical\ advantage = \frac{output\ force}{input\ force}$$

In which trial was the mechanical advantage the greatest?

_____

13. When you are finished, put all your materials back the way you found them.

Scoring Rubric

Performance Levels

Level	Score Range	Description of Student Performance
4	85–100	**Meeting the Standards with Distinction** • Student demonstrates superior understanding of the intermediate-level science content and concepts for each of the learning standards and key ideas assessed. • Student demonstrates superior intermediate-level science skills related to each of the learning standards and key ideas assessed. • Student demonstrates superior understanding of the intermediate-level science content, concepts, and skills required for a secondary academic environment.
3	65–84	**Meeting the Standards** • Student demonstrates understanding of the intermediate-level science content and concepts for each of the learning standards and key ideas assessed. • Student demonstrates the science skills required for intermediate-level achievement in each of the learning standards and key ideas assessed. • Student demonstrates understanding of the intermediate-level science content, concepts, and skills required for a secondary academic environment.
2	44–64	**Not Fully Meeting the Standards** • Student demonstrates only minimal proficiency in intermediate-level science content and concepts in most of learning standards and key ideas assessed. • Student demonstrates only minimal proficiency in the skills required for intermediate-level achievement in most of the learning standards and key ideas assessed. • Student demonstrates marginal understanding of the science content, concepts, and skills required for a secondary academic environment.
1	0–43	**Not Meeting the Standards** • Student is *unable* to demonstrate understanding of the intermediate-level science content and concepts in most of the learning standards and key ideas assessed. • Student is *unable* to demonstrate the science skills required for intermediate-level achievement in most of the learning standards and key ideas assessed. • Student is *unable* to demonstrate evidence of the basic science knowledge and skills required for a secondary academic environment.

Commonly Used Units

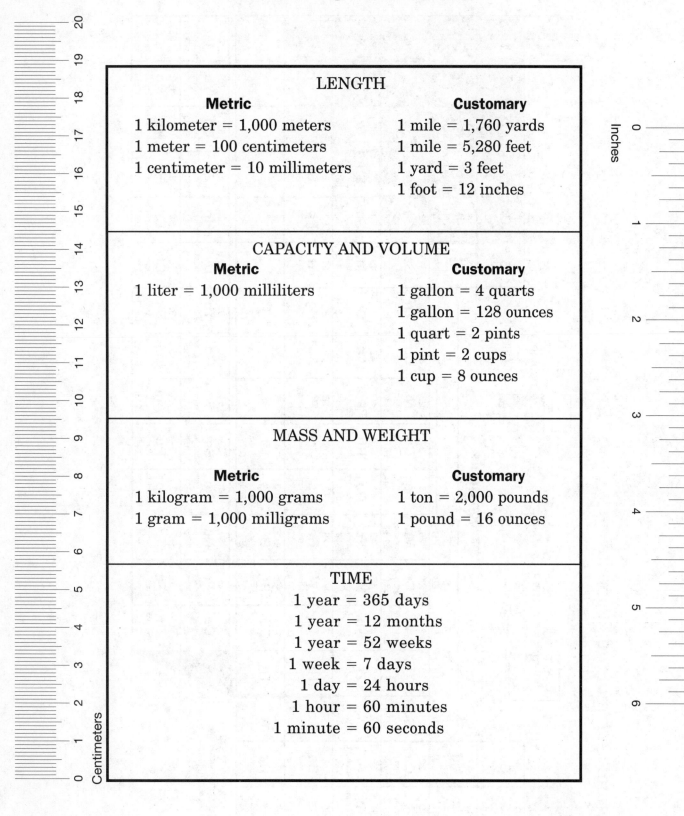

LENGTH

Metric	**Customary**
1 kilometer = 1,000 meters	1 mile = 1,760 yards
1 meter = 100 centimeters	1 mile = 5,280 feet
1 centimeter = 10 millimeters	1 yard = 3 feet
	1 foot = 12 inches

CAPACITY AND VOLUME

Metric	**Customary**
1 liter = 1,000 milliliters	1 gallon = 4 quarts
	1 gallon = 128 ounces
	1 quart = 2 pints
	1 pint = 2 cups
	1 cup = 8 ounces

MASS AND WEIGHT

Metric	**Customary**
1 kilogram = 1,000 grams	1 ton = 2,000 pounds
1 gram = 1,000 milligrams	1 pound = 16 ounces

TIME

1 year = 365 days
1 year = 12 months
1 year = 52 weeks
1 week = 7 days
1 day = 24 hours
1 hour = 60 minutes
1 minute = 60 seconds

Inches

Centimeters

Periodic Table of the Elements

Key

```
 11
 Na     ── Atomic number
Sodium  ── Element symbol
22.99   ── Element name
        ── Average atomic mass*
```

metals
nonmetals
semimetals

Transition Metals

1A (1)	2A (2)	3B (3)	4B (4)	5B (5)	6B (6)	7B (7)	8B (8)	8B (9)	8B (10)	1B (11)	2B (12)	3A (13)	4A (14)	5A (15)	6A (16)	7A (17)	8A (18)
1 H Hydrogen 1.01																	2 He Helium 4.00
3 Li Lithium 6.94	4 Be Beryllium 9.01											5 B Boron 10.81	6 C Carbon 12.01	7 N Nitrogen 14.01	8 O Oxygen 16.00	9 F Fluorine 19.00	10 Ne Neon 20.18
11 Na Sodium 22.99	12 Mg Magnesium 24.31											13 Al Aluminum 26.98	14 Si Silicon 28.09	15 P Phosphorus 30.97	16 S Sulfur 32.07	17 Cl Chlorine 35.45	18 Ar Argon 39.95
19 K Potassium 39.10	20 Ca Calcium 40.08	21 Sc Scandium 44.96	22 Ti Titanium 47.87	23 V Vanadium 50.94	24 Cr Chromium 52.00	25 Mn Manganese 54.94	26 Fe Iron 55.85	27 Co Cobalt 58.93	28 Ni Nickel 58.69	29 Cu Copper 63.55	30 Zn Zinc 65.39	31 Ga Gallium 69.72	32 Ge Germanium 72.61	33 As Arsenic 74.92	34 Se Selenium 78.96	35 Br Bromine 79.90	36 Kr Krypton 83.80
37 Rb Rubidium 85.47	38 Sr Strontium 87.62	39 Y Yttrium 88.91	40 Zr Zirconium 91.22	41 Nb Niobium 92.91	42 Mo Molybdenum 95.94	43 Tc Technetium (98)	44 Ru Ruthenium 101.07	45 Rh Rhodium 102.91	46 Pd Palladium 106.42	47 Ag Silver 107.87	48 Cd Cadmium 112.41	49 In Indium 114.82	50 Sn Tin 118.71	51 Sb Antimony 121.76	52 Te Tellurium 127.60	53 I Iodine 126.90	54 Xe Xenon 131.29
55 Cs Cesium 132.91	56 Ba Barium 137.33	57 La Lanthanum 138.91	72 Hf Hafnium 178.49	73 Ta Tantalum 180.95	74 W Tungsten 183.84	75 Re Rhenium 186.21	76 Os Osmium 190.23	77 Ir Iridium 192.22	78 Pt Platinum 195.08	79 Au Gold 196.97	80 Hg Mercury 200.59	81 Tl Thallium 204.38	82 Pb Lead 207.2	83 Bi Bismuth 208.98	84 Po Polonium (209)	85 At Astatine (210)	86 Rn Radon (222)
87 Fr Francium (223)	88 Ra Radium (226)	89 Ac Actinium (227)	104 Rf Rutherfordium (261)	105 Db Dubnium (262)	106 Sg Seaborgium (266)	107 Bh Bohrium (264)	108 Hs Hassium (269)	109 Mt Meitnerium (268)									

58 Ce Cerium 140.12	59 Pr Praseodymium 140.91	60 Nd Neodymium 144.24	61 Pm Promethium (145)	62 Sm Samarium 150.36	63 Eu Europium 151.96	64 Gd Gadolinium 157.25	65 Tb Terbium 158.93	66 Dy Dysprosium 162.50	67 Ho Holmium 164.93	68 Er Erbium 167.26	69 Tm Thulium 168.93	70 Yb Ytterbium 173.04	71 Lu Lutetium 174.97
90 Th Thorium 232.04	91 Pa Protactinium 231.04	92 U Uranium 238.03	93 Np Neptunium (237)	94 Pu Plutonium (244)	95 Am Americium (243)	96 Cm Curium (247)	97 Bk Berkelium (247)	98 Cf Californium (251)	99 Es Einsteinium (252)	100 Fm Fermium (257)	101 Md Mendelevium (258)	102 No Nobelium (259)	103 Lr Lawrencium (262)

* Parentheses means the atomic mass is the most stable isotope.

Properties of Common Minerals

LUSTER	HARD-NESS	CLEAVAGE	FRACTURE	COMMON COLORS	DISTINGUISHING CHARACTERISTICS	USE(S)	MINERAL NAME	COMPOSITION*
Metallic Luster	1–2	✔		silver to gray	black streak, greasy feel	pencil lead, lubricants	**Graphite**	C
	2.5	✔		metallic silver	very dense (7.6 g/cm^3), gray-black streak	ore of lead	**Galena**	PbS
	5.5–6.5		✔	black to silver	attracted by magnet, black streak	ore of iron	**Magnetite**	Fe_3O_4
	6.5		✔	brassy yellow	green-black streak, cubic crystals	ore of sulfur	**Pyrite**	FeS_2
Either	1–6.5		✔	metallic silver or earthy red	red-brown streak	ore of iron	**Hematite**	Fe_2O_3
Nonmetallic Luster	1	✔		white to green	greasy feel	talcum powder, soapstone	**Talc**	$Mg_3Si_4O_{10}(OH)_2$
	2		✔	yellow to amber	easily melted, may smell	vulcanize rubber, sulfuric acid	**Sulfur**	S
	2	✔		white to pink or gray	easily scratched by fingernail	plaster of paris and drywall	**Gypsum** (Selenite)	$CaSO_4 \cdot 2H_2O$
	2–2.5	✔		colorless to yellow	flexible in thin sheets	electrical insulator	**Muscovite Mica**	$KAl_3Si_3O_{10}(OH)_2$
	2.5	✔		colorless to white	cubic cleavage, salty taste	food additive, melts ice	**Halite**	NaCl
	2.5–3	✔		black to dark brown	flexible in thin sheets	electrical insulator	**Biotite Mica**	$K(Mg,Fe)_3$ $AlSi_3O_{10}(OH)_2$
	3	✔		colorless or variable	bubbles with acid	cement, polarizing prisms	**Calcite**	$CaCO_3$
	3.5	✔		colorless or variable	bubbles with acid when powdered	source of magnesium	**Dolomite**	$CaMg(CO_3)_2$
	4	✔		colorless or variable	cleaves in 4 directions	hydrofluoric acid	**Fluorite**	CaF_2
	5–6	✔		black to dark green	cleaves in 2 directions at 90°	mineral collections	**Pyroxene** (commonly Augite)	$(Ca,Na)(Mg,Fe,Al)$ $(Si,Al)_2O_6$
	5.5	✔		black to dark green	cleaves at 56° and 124°	mineral collections	**Amphiboles** (commonly Hornblende)	$CaNa(Mg,Fe)_4 (Al,Fe,Ti)_3$ $Si_6O_{22}(O,OH)_2$
	6	✔		white to pink	cleaves in 2 directions at 90°	ceramics and glass	**Potassium Feldspar** (Orthoclase)	$KAlSi_3O_8$
	6	✔		white to gray	cleaves in 2 directions, striations visible	ceramics and glass	**Plagioclase Feldspar** (Na-Ca Feldspar)	$(Na,Ca)AlSi_3O_8$
	6.5		✔	green to gray or brown	commonly light green and granular	furnace bricks and jewelry	**Olivine**	$(Fe,Mg)_2SiO_4$
	7		✔	colorless or variable	glassy luster, may form hexagonal crystals	glass, jewelry, and electronics	**Quartz**	SiO_2
	7		✔	dark red to green	glassy luster, often seen as red grains in NYS metamorphic rocks	jewelry and abrasives	**Garnet** (commonly Almandine)	$Fe_3Al_2Si_3O_{12}$

*Chemical Symbols:
Al = aluminum   Cl = chlorine   H = hydrogen   Na = sodium   S = sulfur
C = carbon   F = fluorine   K = potassium   O = oxygen   Si = silicon
Ca = calcium   Fe = iron   Mg = magnesium   Pb = lead   Ti = titanium

✔ = dominant form of breakage

Science Reference Sheet

Equations

| Acceleration (a) | $=$ | $\dfrac{\text{change in velocity (m/s)}}{\text{time taken for this change (s)}}$ | a | $=$ | $\dfrac{v_f - v_i}{t_f - t_i}$ |

| Average speed (v) | $=$ | $\dfrac{\text{distance}}{\text{time}}$ | v | $=$ | $\dfrac{d}{t}$ |

| Density (D) | $=$ | $\dfrac{\text{mass (g)}}{\text{Volume (cm}^3)}$ | D | $=$ | $\dfrac{m}{V}$ |

| Percent Efficiency (e) | $=$ | $\dfrac{\text{Work out (J)}}{\text{Work in (J)}} \times 100$ | $\%e$ | $=$ | $\dfrac{W_{out}}{W_{in}} \times 100$ |

| Force (F) | $=$ | mass (kg) $\times$ acceleration (m/s^2) | F | $=$ | ma |

| Frequency (f) | $=$ | $\dfrac{\text{number of events (waves)}}{\text{time (s)}}$ | f | $=$ | $\dfrac{n \text{ of events}}{t}$ |

| Momentum (p) | $=$ | mass (kg) $\times$ velocity (m/s) | p | $=$ | mv |

| Wavelength (λ) | $=$ | $\dfrac{\text{velocity (m/s)}}{\text{frequency (Hz)}}$ | λ | $=$ | $\dfrac{v}{f}$ |

| Work (W) | $=$ | Force (N) $\times$ distance (m) | W | $=$ | Fd |

Units of Measure

m = meter	g = gram	s = second
cm = centimeter	kg = kilogram	Hz = hertz (waves per second)
J = joule (newton-meter)		
N = newton (kilogram-meter per second squared)		

CYCLES ON EARTH

Nitrogen Cycle

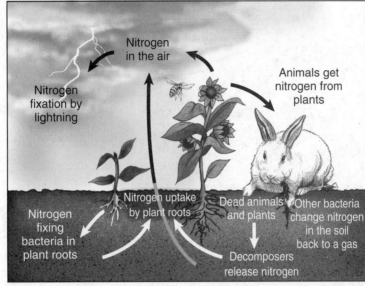

Water Cycle

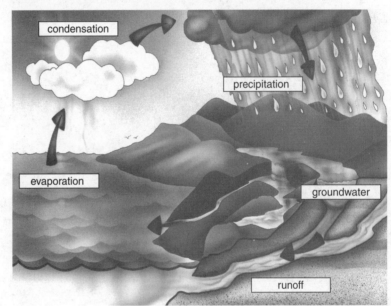

Carbon Cycle

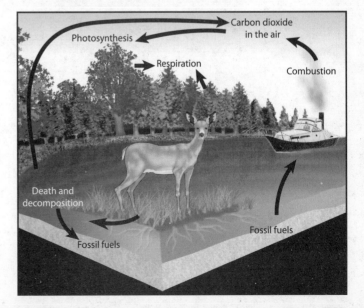

Graphic Organizer
Venn Diagram

Science • Level H   Copying is permitted.   Measuring Up Express™ for the New York State Test